*Views of Japan from
The Washington Post Newsroom*

装幀 ● 菊地信義
装画 ● 野村俊夫

翻訳協力 ● 中山俊宏
カット写真・イラスト ● ワシントン・ポスト

The copyright for the articles and illustrations in this book is held by *The Washington Post*.

Published by Kodansha International Ltd.,
17-14 Otowa 1-chome, Bunkyo-ku, Tokyo 112
No part of this publication may be reproduced
in any form or by any means without permission
in writing from the publisher.
Copyright © 1996 Kodansha International Ltd.
All rights reserved. Printed in Japan.

First Edition 1996

ISBN4-7700-2023-6
96 97 98 99 10 9 8 7 6 5 4 3 2 1

ワシントン・ポストが書いた「日本」
「Japan」クリッピング
*Views of Japan from
The Washington Post Newsroom*

東郷茂彦

Preface

Both the Japanese and the English languages set out to express the same kind of things.

Is what gets over really the same, though?

Take, for example, the English "I love you" and the Japanese "ai-shite iru." Both in theory express the same human feeling, yet if one examines cultural differences, the respective backgrounds that lie behind the two, one's head reels at the extent of the gap.

A top member of the U.S. Congress recently declared on the trade question, "The Japanese are cheating!" He repeated it vehemently three times, waving his fist all the while. This was translated, in the Japanese TV subtitle, as "日本人はうそつきだ" (the Japanese are liars). Since the original meaning was something like "the Japanese are not obeying the rules and are not playing fair," the subtitle was good enough, perhaps. Even so, it cannot convey the strength of indignation conveyed by the word "cheating" in a culture where "fair play" is one of the popular ideals and cheating— from a primary school student's cheating in a test to cheating on an international scale—is considered, in theory at least, unacceptable.

I am sure there are many people, too, who have had the experience in discussing Americans, or American society and culture, of finding that translations into Japanese of concepts about the U.S., and individual words are, naturally enough, not adequate. It is not enough, for example, to be acquainted with terms such as "civil rights movement," "affirmative action," or "pro life and pro choice" only through the Japanese "公民権運動," "人種差別撤廃のための積極的な措置," and "堕胎反対と選択の自由." One must go back and re-study the original English.

In the course of close to twenty years spent in the business of sending news about Japan to the U.S. in English, during which I have also had experience, via interpreting, translating and other such work, in turning English into Japanese, I have come to be bothered by a sense of how much is lost or wasted in converting one language into another.

From junior high school onward, the Japanese spend a great deal of time on English. With the trend to internationalization in

前書き

英語と日本語で、同じ内容を表現する。

そこで、はたして、本当に同じ内容が伝えられるのだろうか。

「I love you」と「愛してる」。同じ人間の感情を表現はしているが、文化の違い、それぞれが背負っている背景に目を注げば、あまりの違いに息もつまる思いがする。

米議会トップが最近、貿易問題に関連し「The Japanese are cheating」と言明した。拳を振り上げながら、激しい口調で3度も繰り返した。その言葉は、日本のテレビの字幕では「日本人はうそつきだ」と訳されていた。

元来の意味は「日本人は規則に従わないし、公正に行動しない」というようなことだから、字幕としては悪くないだろう。しかし、それでは「cheating」ということばが持つ憤りの強さを伝えることはできない。アメリカでは、「公正な行動」とは誰もが求める理想の1つであり、小学生がテストでカンニングをすることから国際問題にいたるまで、「cheating」とは少なくとも言葉の上では、受け入れがたいからである。

それに、アメリカ人とアメリカの社会や文化を語るとき、あまりにも当たり前のことだが、日本語に翻訳されたアメリカについての概念や言葉では語れない、という経験をされた方もおられるのではないだろうか。たとえば、civil rights movement、affirmative action、pro life and pro choice を日本語で「公民権運動」「人種差別撤廃のための積極的な措置」「堕胎反対と選択の自由」として知っていても駄目。あらためて、英語の表現を学び直さなければいけないのだ。

20年近く、日本のニュースを英語でアメリカに送る作業に携わる一方で、通訳や翻訳など、英語を日本語に訳す仕事も経験するうち、言語を代えることによって失われるものや無駄が、いつか気になり始めた。

日本人は、中学以来、英語にはずいぶんと時間をかけている。昨今の国際化のなかで、英語をとにもかくにも使いこなす人達も激増した。ならば、全体の流れは日本語で表現するとしても、もともと英語で表

recent years, there has been a sharp increase in the number of people who can at least manage in English. That being so, might it not be better, even where the general drift is expressed in Japanese, to leave in English, as they stand, what were essentially English concepts, so that the reader can understand them and absorb them directly? The time has come, in short, for the reader to chew on and digest such essentially English concepts as they stand.

Reading the novel *Shi-shosetsu from left to right* by Mizumura Minae published in September 1995, which provoked much comment by presenting English and Japanese in coexistence, I felt no sense of incongruity; what I felt, if anything, was that the amount of English used was less than I had expected.

It was soon after this that Kodansha International approached me about its projected bilingual books. The question of how the American media are reporting on Japan has a great bearing on the realities of Japan-U.S. relations. Thus the idea of these bilingual books would be to convey the impact of the original directly, in English, to the reader, to construct a new type of prose in which Japanese and English would coexist.

I was impressed: a truly challenging concept, I felt.

In the course of working out details of the project, we decided:
(1) That we should restrict ourselves to material from *The Washington Post*, since attempting to cover the whole of the American media would only dilute the effect.
(2) For the reader's sake, some of the texts should adopt the conventional format with Japanese and English on facing pages, and that passages combining both languages should be restricted to around one-quarter of the whole. The commentaries accompanying each article would be in bilingual style.
(3) The choice of articles and the content of the comments would be "objective," while taking advantage of the "personal" views derived from my own direct experience.

As a result, I selected a total of about 200 articles in the fields of politics, economics and social affairs from the 400–500 articles a year on Japan that have appeared in recent years in the pages of The *Washington Post*. The oldest among them, pieces concerning the Showa emperor, date from the 1920s and 1930s. The rest begin in 1976, when I started work at the Post's Tokyo bureau; most of them are from the

現されたこと、とくに key になる部分は、そのまま英語で表現し、読者も直接英語で理解し、吸収してしまったほうがいいのではないか。つまるところ、英語で表現されたものは、そのまま嚙み砕き、飲み込んでしまう時代が来ているのではないか、という思いである。

昨年9月に出版され、日本語と英語の共存で話題を呼んだ水村美苗氏の小説『私小説 from left to right』を読んでも、少しの違和感もなかったし、むしろ、予想したより、英語の使用量が少ないというのが実感だった。

そんなおり、講談社インターナショナルから、bilingual books の企画の話があった。

アメリカのメディアが、日本をどう報じたか。その内容は、日米関係の現実に大きく関わってくる。そのインパクトの源泉を、読者に、生のまま英語で伝えたいという。しかも、bilingual books はこれまでの対訳物とは違って、基本的に、日本語と英語が共存する新しい文章を構築してほしいという。

実に challenging な構想と、感動した。

企画を詰めていく段階で、
(1) アメリカの全メディアでは、かえって散漫になりかねないので、対象は *The Washington Post*（以下 WP）にしぼる。
(2) 読者の便宜を考え、従来の対訳方式も取り入れ、日本語と英語の共存する文は全体の4分の1程度とする。各記事に添える解説は、bilingual style にする。
(3) 記事の選択や解説の内容には「客観性」とともに、私の直接の経験に基づく「独断と偏見」を活かす。

などが定まった。

こうして、最近では、1年に400から500本の日本関連の記事が載る WP の紙面から、政治、経済、社会の3分野約200本の記事を選んだ。古いものでは、昭和天皇関連が1920、30年代から。それ以外は、私が WP Tokyo Bureau で働くようになった1976年以降。大半は、最近の5年間の記事となった。当然のことながら、東京発の原稿に片寄ら

past five years. They include, of course, pieces originating in Washington, so as to avoid over-emphasis on stories with Tokyo datelines.

Long ago, in the Nara and Heian periods, the Buddhist culture of the Asian continent was introduced into Japan. More recently, in the Meiji period, Japan embraced western civilization. It passed both of these through the Japanese melting pot to form its own individual culture. The important role here was played by the Japanese language; it was by passing these other cultures through the filter of Japanese that it was possible to give them a uniquely Japanese coloring. The same approach must, I believe, be maintained in the future too.

However, the taking over and Japanization of cultures via the medium of Nihongo—precisely, in part, because the Japanese do it so well—can go too far. There is a danger that while the broad essentials are conveyed, the crucial subtleties that cannot be expressed in another language, may be neglected.

Suppose, for example, there is a scene in a movie in which a lively discussion takes place among American, British, German and French actors who use English as the shared medium but inject words from their own languages from time to time. When the conversation is heard "straight," as it were, one gets vivid, immediate impression of the difference between the various cultures and of the weight of history. Translated into Japanese for, say, TV, how dull and insipid it becomes!

What I would call "bilingual Japanese" has nothing whatsoever to do with the destruction of Japan's own culture. It means that, amidst today's increasing internationalization, we should actively try to accept English as it stands, wherever that seems desirable. The aim, in a sense, is to bring together within the Japanese both a Japanese culture and a western culture that is closer to the essence.

In this book, *Washington Post* articles, statements made by Americans, American place names and a number of expletives have been left in English, while the basic text is in Japanese.

My hope is that in the future this kind of bilingual style will be seen not as an experiment, but as a common form of communication.

ないよう、Washington の本社発の原稿も新たに収集し、掲載した。

　日本はこれまで、奈良平安の昔に大陸から仏教文化を受容し、明治維新では西洋文明を受け入れ、それらを、日本という鋳型の中で一度溶かして、独自の文化を形成してきた。その際、重要な役割を果たしたのが日本語であり、一度、日本語というフィルターを通すことによって、海外の文化は日本固有の色彩を帯びることができたのだった。その姿勢は、今後とも堅持されなければならないと考える。
　しかしながら、日本語を媒介とした海外文化の受容、日本化が、優秀な国民性もあいまって、あまりにも見事に成し遂げられた場合、おおまかな受容は可能であっても、別の言語では伝達不可能な微妙な部分、微妙であるが故に、きわめて重要な部分が置き去りにされてしまったということはなかったろうか。
　たとえば、アメリカ、イギリス、ドイツ、フランスの俳優が、英語を共通の言葉としながら、時に、自国語も交え、活発な会話を繰り広げる映画のシーンがある。そこでは、生の言葉であるがゆえに、様々な文化の違い、長い歴史の重みのようなものが手に取るように伝わってくる。テレビなどで日本語に訳されてしまった場合、なんと味気なくなってしまうことか。
　bilingual な日本語とは、決して、日本固有の文化の破壊にはつながらない。これだけ国際化した中で、英語によるメッセージをそのまま取り入れた方が良い場合は、積極的にそうしようということである。いってみれば、日本人の中に、日本語文化と、より本質に近い英語文化の共存をねらうのである。

　本書の場合は、WP の記事、アメリカ人の発言、アメリカの地名、若干の感嘆詞などを英語で表現し、全体の流れは日本語とした。
　今後、このような bilingual style が、実験としてではなく、互いに共通したコミュニケーションの形として定着することを願うものである。

To Read *The Washington Post*

　WPの紙面を見る。日本の新聞と一番重要な違いは、すべての記事に署名がある—Bylineがある—ことだ。Byline。見出しの下に、筆者名を「By Xxxx. Yyyy」と記す。WPだけでなく、現在のアメリカの新聞ジャーナリズムの興隆とパワーは、筆者の個性を十二分に発揮させ、読者との密接なつながりを育てるこの制度なしには語れない。

　WPは(*The New York Times* = 以下NYT = も同サイズ)、日本の新聞に比べ、細長い。縦60cm×横35cm。日本のは、縦54cm×横40.5cmだ。厚さは2、3倍もあろうか。特に日曜版は計数百頁、ひと抱えもある。日本の新聞は、政治、経済、社会、文化、地方版など各部の記事がせいぜい2、3頁で、全体が1つ折り。WPは、主要ニュースを集めたA sectionをはじめ、Business、Metro、Style、Sportsなど各sectionが、それぞれ1つ折りになっているからだ。

　さらに、圧倒的に広告の割合が高い(紙面で7割、収入ベースでは8割。日本は、5割程度)のも、紙面を分厚くする一因となっている。

[A section—Front Page]

　重要なニュースの集まっているA section。30頁から40頁程度。その第1面、Front Pageは、WPのその日の顔だ。全sectionの中から、最重要で、読者に一番アッピールする記事が激しい競争の末に選ばれ、6、7本、掲載される。各記事の全文ではなく、最初の数paragraphだけで、残りは、それぞれ、後ろの頁に回される。日本関連であれば、Front pageの記事の末尾に「See Japan, A22, Col. 1」というふうに。A section第22頁の関連記事冒頭で、「Japan, From A1」と、受ける。

　各sectionのfront pageも、同様な作り方だ。最初からsectionの内側に掲載された場合、日本の記事のように1ヵ所にまとめられる場合も多い。

　WP取材陣の主要チームの1つが[National Desk]。約90人。日本で言えば、「政治部」だが、教育や事件など、社会部的な仕事も担当する「全米内政部」だ。自身のsectionはなく、A sectionがホームグラウンド。米議会や政府の動きに焦点をあわせた記事には[The Federal Page]も用意されている。

　A section最終頁手前の見開きに通常、[OP-ED]欄がある。editorial, letter to the editor, opinionの3者によって構成される。日本の新聞もほぼ同じ形だが、WPはじめ、アメリカのquality paperのop-edは、内容がはるかに多彩で、社会的影響力も大きい。

[B, C, D, E, F, G.... の各section]

　その他のsectionは、上記のように名付けていくが、その日の紙面構成によってどこがB、C....となるかは一定していない。主なsectionを紹介する。

[WORLD NEWS] は、海外へ特派されている二十数人のForeign

Correspondent が送る外国のニュースを主に掲載する。AP 電など通信社の原稿を扱うこともある。A section の中に編集されることも。

[Style] 社交、文化、娯楽、ラジオ・テレビ欄といった日本の「文化家庭部」的な要素に加え、人間に焦点をあてた長文の読み物が特徴。紙面の扱いも凝っていて、WP の目玉の1つ。

[BUSINESS] Financial Desk 目下約50人。国際経済問題から米政府の経済政策、振興いちじるしい Washington D.C. 地区の業界など米国内経済まで。

[METRO]は、Metropolitan、即ち、「首都圏」の略で、地元 Washington D.C. 並びに周辺 County を統括する。社会部といってよいが、アメリカの最も sensitive な issue である人種、麻薬、暴力なども精力的に取材している。

[OUTLOOK] WP で人気の高い section で、「Commentary and Opinion」という副題のように、通常のニュース報道より、個人の見方を強く打ち出すことが許される。日曜日のみ掲載。

日本関連のニュースが登場するのは、頻度からみて、WORLD NEWS、BUSINESS、A section、Style、OUTLOOK といった順番か。同じ WP とはいっても、どこに記事が載るかによって、社のニュース判断が示されるわけで、日本の政治家の話が A section になるか、Style か、などは注目して良いポイントとなる。

以上、本書を読まれるに当たって、WP という新聞について最低限必要と思われる事項を記した。

凡例　Editorial Convention

・本書では下記のような頭字語・略語を用いた。

IHT	→	*The International Herald Tribune*
LAT	→	*The Los Angeles Times*
NYT	→	*The New York Times*
WP	→	*The Washington Post*
FCCJ	→	*Foreign Correspondents' Club of Japan* （日本外国特派員協会）
FPIJ	→	*The Foreign Press in Japan* （在日外国報道協会）

<u>Rep.</u> James R. Jones <u>(D–Okla)</u> → Representative （下院議員）
　　　　　　　　　　　　　　　　Democrat （民主党員）
　　　　　　　　　　　　　　　　Oklahoma （オクラホマ州）

・紙面の都合上、記事の原文を割愛したところには「……」を入れたが、文脈上「……」を抜いたところもある。

Due to layout considerations, certain deletions have been made in the articles. These are generally indicated by ellipses [...], but in certain cases, in order to improve readability, ellipses have not been used.

CONTENTS

Preface 4

To read *The Washington Post* 10

Contents 12

Part 1 POLITICAL NEWS 19

Japan: Searching for its International Role 20

Chapter 1 Japanese Politics

1. Investigative Reports in Japan and *The Washington Post* 24
2. What America Wants in Japanese Politicians 28
3. Will Japanese Politics Change? 34
4. A Bureaucracy-Bound Nation? 40

Chapter 2 The Security Treaty and Foreign Policy

1. Will Japan Go Nuclear? 46
2. The Legacy of the Gulf War 52
3. The Future of the U.S.–Japan Security Treaty 56
4. Japan and Its Neighbors (Russia, China, Korea) 64

Chapter 3 The Legacy of the Pacific War

1. The Scars of Pearl Harbor 68
2. The Rights and Wrongs of the Atomic Bombs 74
3. The Underside of War 80
4. A Parade of Apologies 86

目次

はじめに 5

ワシントン・ポストを読むために 10

目次 13

第1部　政治ニュース　19

国際的役割を模索する日本 21

第1章　日本の政治
1. 調査報道の華 24
2. アメリカが求める日本の政治家像 29
3. 日本の政治は変化するか 35
4. 官僚支配の国か 41

第2章　安保と外交
1. 日本は核武装する！？ 47
2. 湾岸戦争の遺したもの 53
3. 安保体制はどうなる 57
4. 周辺諸国（露中韓）と日本 64

第3章　太平洋戦争の遺産
1. 真珠湾攻撃の傷跡 69
2. 原爆は正しかったか 75
3. 戦争の様相 81
4. 謝罪のオンパレード 87

Part 2 FINANCIAL NEWS   91

Japan-Basking: New Pacific Era? 92

Chapter 1 The Japanese Domestic Economy

1. Economic Superpower Japan Through American Eyes 96
2. The Land and Housing Problem 100
3. The Keiretsu 102
4. The Rise and Fall of the Bubble Economy 104
5. The Future of Lifetime Employment 108

Chapter 2 Japan–U.S. Economic Friction

1. The Same Old Story 110
2. Spring 1992 116
3. Automobiles: Competition and Cooperation 122
4. Reporting It Fair and Square 128

Chapter 3 The Global Economy and Japan

1. Asia, Japan, and U.S. 132
2. Confusian Morality Wins the Day? 134

Part 3 SOCIAL NEWS   137

A New Aristocracy in the Land of the Rising Sun 138

Chapter 1 The Imperial Family

1. Emperor Showa 142
2. The Reigning Emperor and Empress 150
3. The Crown Prince and Princess Masako 156

Chapter 2 Daily Life

1. The Mass Media 160
2. Living Tradition 164

第2部　経済ニュース　　　　　　　　　　　　　　　　91

ジャパン・バースキング（日本を暖める）：新太平洋時代？　93

第1章　日本の国内経済社会

1. アメリカから見た経済大国日本　97
2. 土地・住宅問題　101
3. 系列　103
4. バブルとその崩壊　105
5. 終身雇用制は続くか　109

第2章　日米経済摩擦

1. 十年一日、20年戦争　110
2. 1992年春　117
3. 自動車：競争と協調　123
4. 公平に報道する　129

第3章　国際経済の中の日本

1. アジアと日米　132
2. 儒教社会の功績か　135

第3部　社会ニュース　　　　　　　　　　　　　　　　137

新貴族階級が日出ずる国に形成される　139

第1章　皇室

1. 昭和天皇　142
2. 今上陛下，美智子皇后　151
3. 皇太子殿下と雅子妃　157

第2章　生活

1. メディア　160
2. 伝統生活　165

3. Modern Life 168

4. Company Life 180

Chapter 3 Issues and Opinions

1. Education 186

2. Woman's Place 190

3. Population Growth 194

4. The Law 196

Chapter 4 Japan and America

1. The Land of Guns and Violence 202

2. African Americans 206

3. Japanese Americans 210

4. From America with Love: America's Place in Japan 212

Chapter 5 The Japanese Image

1. From Japan with Love: Japan's Place in America 216
   - Japan's Interpreter with Punch 222
   - Japan's Hero Barks From Beyond the Grave 224
   - Haruki Murakami's Homecoming 226
   - Japanese Writer Oe Wins Nobel 226
   - After 51 Years, a Temple Is Restored 228
   - The Ando Dynasty 228
   - A Monster Hit 230
   - Japan's Porno Preoccupation 230
   - Sumo Exports 232
   - Lennon's Widow Faces Mobs and Memories 232
   - The Modern, Misunderstood Geisha 234
   - "The Power of People, the Love of Baseball" 234

About The Washington Post   237

Postface 246

Byline Index 250

3. 現代人の生活　169
4. 会社生活　181

第3章　問題提起と批判

1. 教育問題　186
2. 女性問題　191
3. 人口問題　195
4. 司法問題　197

第4章　日本とアメリカ

1. 銃と暴力の国　203
2. 黒人問題　207
3. 日系人問題　211
4. アメリカ発日本へ、日本の中のアメリカ　212

第5章　日本人の顔

1. 日本発アメリカへ、アメリカの中の日本　216
   - パンチの効いた日本の通訳　223
   - 日本のヒーロー墓のかなたから吠える　225
   - 村上春樹の帰郷　227
   - 日本の作家大江、ノーベル賞を受賞　227
   - 51年かけてに復元された寺院　229
   - 安藤王朝　229
   - 怪獣大ヒット　231
   - ポルノにのめりこむ日本　231
   - 相撲の輸出　233
   - やじ馬と思い出に対面するレノンの未亡人　233
   - 誤解されている現代の芸者　235
   - 「みんなの力、野球への愛」　235

ワシントン・ポストについて　237

あとがき　247
筆者別索引　250

Ben Bradlee
WP 副社長　編集主幹としてウォーターゲート事件を指揮し、世界中に名を馳せる

"I tried very hard to encourage everybody to have a good time and to be absolutely free to criticize.…"

Part 1

Political News
第一部　政治ニュース

News Conference Room
フロントページの記事をどれにするか、議論される

President Ford から WP へ　"I got my job through *The Washington Post*"

Japan: Searching for its International Role

By Don Oberdorfer

June 17, 1991

TOKYO—Japan is in the early stages of a great shift in thought and action about its role in the world. It will take time, as major changes always do in this consensus-bound country, but the repercussions will be important for the United States, Asia, and the rest of the world.

The Japanese have realized for quite some time that while this small island chain casts a big shadow economically, it hardly counts politically or militarily. Being a "half country," as some here have called it, bothered only a few intellectuals until the Gulf War, which brought the Japanese face to face with their impotence and even irrelevance in non-economic fields as world-shaking events unfolded....

Never before had Japan been forced to come to grips so directly with the international consequences of the U.S.-imposed post-World War II pacifism that, until recently, was widely praised abroad. The day of reckoning came at a time when Japan was, in other respects, more self-assured than ever as the world's second largest economic power.

Unable to contribute more directly, Japan provided money—lots of it—on U.S. demand to pay for the U.S. war in the gulf and help poorer front-line states. The United States tapped Tokyo for $13 billion, more than $100 for every Japanese and more than the nation's yearly foreign aid budget for all countries. Japanese were hurt, but hardly surprised, when the act of providing yen instead of risking lives did not win much respect abroad....

In the political field, Japanese rethinking is taking the form of greater independence from U.S. policies, especially in Asia.

国際的役割を模索する日本

ドン・オーバードーファー

1991年6月17日

東京発──日本は、世界における自らの役割をどのように考え、どのように行動するかにつき、大いなる変化を遂げ始めた。万事に意見の一致を求めるこの国で、大きな変化はいつもそうなのだが、時間がかかる。しかし、影響するところは、合衆国やアジアをはじめ、世界中に大なるものがあるのだ。

日本人は、かなり前から、この小さな列島が、経済的には大きな影を投げかけているにせよ、政治的、軍事的にはものの数ではないことに気がついた。日本が、一部の国民の言うような「半国家」であることは、湾岸戦争以前は、わずかな知識人しか気にかけてはいなかった。しかし、世界を震撼させたこの出来事が進展するに従って、非経済的な領域では、己が、単に無力というだけではなく、無用な存在である事実に日本人は直面することになった。

……第2次大戦後、アメリカによって課され、最近まで諸外国で広く賞賛されていた平和主義のもたらす国際的な結果に対し、日本がこれほど直接に対決しなければならなくなったことはない。日本が世界第2の経済大国として、かつてないほど自信に満ちているまさにその時、こうした問題に決着をつけねばならない日がやってきたのだ。

日本は、より直接的な貢献が出来ないため、湾岸地域におけるアメリカの戦費を払い、前線の貧しい国々を助けてほしい、というアメリカの要求に従い、お金を提供した──それも多額の金を。合衆国は東京に130億ドルを求めた。日本国民1人当たり100ドルを超え、この国の1年当たりの対外援助の総額を上回った。生命を危険にさらす代償に円を提供するという行為が、海外ではあまり尊敬を受けなかったことに日本人は傷つきはしたが、さして驚きはし

At this early stage, the Japanese are careful not to stray very far from Washington, however. Despite all the problems and continuing confrontations, America remains the central factor in Japanese foreign policy....

The depth of Japanese involvement in its own region is among the most dramatic changes evident since my days as *Washington Post* correspondent here in the early 1970s. Asia comes up early in nearly every conversation. This year for the first time in decades, Japan will export more to Asian countries than to the United States. Japan is investing about twice as much in the region as the U.S. private sector and is the leading source of foreign aid....

As this economic powerhouse begins cautiously to test its long-neglected political and military muscles in the world of the 1990s, Asia will be the place to watch for the first signs of a historic change.

【解説】

経済大国となった日本が、国際社会の荒波の中に突然投げ出されたのが、湾岸戦争だろう。本論は、戦争終結後まもなく、政治軍事の分野でもそれなりの役割を果たさねばならなくなった場合の日本の進路を、長期的視野に立って論じたものだ。Don は、93年4月にWPを辞めてフリーになるまでの18年間、米ジャーナリズム最高の diplomatic correspondent（外交問題担当記者）として活躍、冷戦終結へと至る米ソの角逐を『The TUЯN』に描いた。とくに有数のアジア通。朝鮮戦争直後、韓国で兵役に就いたのを皮切りに、米地方紙の特派員としてヴェトナム戦争も経験。WP退社直前の Don

なかった……。

　政治の分野で日本人の再考が始まれば、とくにアジアで、アメリカの政策からの大幅な独立という形をとるのだろう。しかしながら、まだ初期の段階である現在、日本人は、ワシントンからあまり距離を置かないように、注意深く行動している。数多くの問題や対立が続いているにもかかわらず、日本の外交政策において、アメリカは依然として中心的な位置を占めている……。

　WPの特派員として私が当地で過ごした70年代初め以来、明らかになった最も劇的な変化の1つは、日本が、自らの属するアジア地域といかに深く関わるようになったか、という点である。ほとんど全ての会話で、最初の話題の中にアジアが登場した。過去数十年来で今年初めて、日本は、アジアへの輸出がアメリカへのそれを上回る。日本は、アメリカの民間企業のほぼ倍の投資をこの地域で行い、外国からの援助のトップを切っている……。

　1990年代の世界にあって、この経済大国が、長い間放っておいた政治的、軍事的力を慎重に使い始める時、その歴史的変化の最初の兆候は、アジアにおいて見いだされることになろう。

と本社近く、魚料理と pickles が美味なレストランで一夕を共にした。「The most important difference between American and Japanese politics, is that in Japan, there are no political "issues."」「In Japan, change is evolutional, not revolutional.」といった見方が出る中、自民党単独政権の崩壊や、その際、政治における官僚優位の社会構造が変わるかといった、現在に至る変化と混乱を予測するような議論が熱っぽく繰り広げられたことだった(『THIS IS 読売』93年8月号拙論「ワシントン・ポスト外交記者を辞めるに当たって」参照)。

CHAPTER 1 JAPANESE POLITICS

1. Investigative Reports in Japan and *The Washington Post*
調査報道の華

「Are there any investigative reports (調査報道) in Japanese journalism?」とアメリカ人に聞かれると、「Oh yes, you have kicked out one president but we have nailed down three prime ministers.」と答えることにしている。アメリカのは、いうまでもなく WP の若手記者 Bob Woodward と Carl Bernstein の活躍を全社で支え、President Nixon 辞任に至った Watergate 事件だが、日本の3件にも直接間接、WPが関わっている。

第1は、田中角栄首相の場合。1974年秋、文藝春秋誌に立花隆の田中金脈研究が載ってから2週間後、東京日比谷の The Foreign Correspondents' Club of Japan(日本外国特派員協会)で首相昼食会見が開かれた。朝鮮戦争などで世界的に名を馳せたカメラマン Max Desfor 協会会長の「If you want to know his personal well-being or financial affairs, you can find probably more than enough in the latest issue of *Bungei Shunju*.」という with punch and potency なコメント(会場は爆笑)で会見は始まり、9つの質問中5つが金脈関連となった。米議会の対 Rockefeller 調査を引き合いに口火を切った *Los Angeles Times* の Sam Jameson に続き、WP の Don Oberdorfer は「Would you consider a report to the Japanese people on your assets?」と質した。

それまで日本の大手新聞やテレビがこの件に関し沈黙を守っていたため、WP の関連記事はこう始まっている (76/10/23)。「Today's meeting with foreign correspondents produced Tanaka's first public comment on a much-discussed recent magazine account of his wealth and

第1章 日本の政治

financial dealings.」。この件に対する田中首相の対応といえば、「"I came from the world of business and so far as they do not impair my political activities…" the prime minister said. He did not argue with the facts of the lengthy article in *Bungei Shunju* … but charged that the reports have generated "some confusion" between his public and private activities (「私はビジネスの世界出身だ。しかし、それがこれまで政治活動の妨げになったことはない」と、首相は述べた。彼は、『文芸春秋』に掲載された長文の記事の事実関係には言及しなかったが、この記事は、自らの公的ならびに私的活動の間に「いくらかの混乱」を生じさせたと批判した)。質問のきっかけになった Rockefeller については、「"In Japan there is no Rockefeller. There is no such billionaire here," he said.」と軽くいなそうとしたものの、金脈問題を取り上げ続ける外国メディアの態度に不快の念を顕わにし、予定時間前に会見を打ち切り、もっと別の問題を話したかったとの不満をあからさまにした。「The prime minister appeared to be irritated by foreign correspondents' persistent questions about the magazine's disclosures. He cut off the question-and-answer session about five minutes before its scheduled close, and remarked brusquely that he had hoped to have time to address a number of other subjects in today's encounter.」。

この日を境に、日本の主要メディアの態度は一変し、翌朝から筆をそろえたキャンペーンを展開、1月後の田中退陣につながるのだ。「Until today, Tanaka and his aides had waved aside all press requests for comment. Tanaka's comments under questioning at the Foreign Correspondents' Club luncheon were given heavy coverage in Wednesday morning early editions of some mass-circulation Tokyo dailies.」。ただし、この会見に関するWPの記事は、retired Adm. G. R. La Roque 証言などで沸

いた日本への核兵器持ち込み問題が中心で、見出しも「Tanaka: Japan Still Free of Nuclear Arms」、金脈関連は最後にまとめられただけだった。

　日本の調査報道にWPが結びつき、総理の失脚につながったもう1つの例は、宇野宗佑首相の場合だ。宇野首相の誕生直後、サンデー毎日誌がその女性問題を報道。当人の女性が告発の姿勢をとり、政治家の女性問題が正面きって論じられたのは日本では珍しかったことなどから、WPは外国メディアではほぼ最初に報じた (89/6/7, Sex Scandal Hits New Leader, By Fred Hiatt)。記事はこう始まる。「A respected Japanese magazine has broken an age-old Japanese taboo by reporting that newly installed Prime Minister Sosuke Uno engaged in a "scandalous" affair with a geisha more than three years ago.... Until now, a politician's private life has not been seen as fair game for journalists.」。掲載欄は、A section でも World News でもなく、Style だった。

　この問題が日本の政局にどのような影響があるかは、「It was unclear what impact the article, ...would have on Uno's administration.」だったが、WPの報道自体が日本のメディアに載り、国会でこの件が初めて取り上げられた時に社会党女性議員がサンデー毎日には触れず、「あのWPに載った」と質問したことなどもあって、政治の表舞台に登場、2ヵ月後の参議院選挙での自民党大敗──宇野退陣──の一因となったのだ。

　政治家の女性問題をどこまで報じるかは国によって違う。フランスでは法律でも厳しく制限されているが、アメリカでは当時、「The magazine drew a parallel to the sex scandal that forced former senator Gary Hart of Colorado to withdraw from the U.S. presidential race last year.」というような状況にあった。大統領たるべき人物には、特に role model as an ideal family man を求めるのがアメリカの常で、President Clinton の場合も相当な攻撃に晒された。現在はこうしたメディアのあり方はいきすぎとの声もあり、家族や当の女性の対応などによって社会やメディアの受容度も違ってくるのだろう。

日本の政界を揺るがしたリクルート事件は、盤石に見えた竹下政権を崩壊させたが、朝日新聞横浜支局による調査報道なしには事件そのものが存在しなかった。その軌跡は『追跡リクルート疑惑』に詳しく、Watergate 事件の『*All the Presidents Men*』のような迫力に、山本博同支局デスク（事件当時）へのインタビューをもとに「Uncovering A Scandal: Persistent Reporters Break Biggest Story in Japan」(89/2/20 By Fred Hiatt) という記事をまとめた。「The Police had decided not to arrest the deputy mayor for taking a bribe from Recruit Cosmos Co., and the young reporters in the local bureau of the *Asahi Shimbun* newspaper were despondent (落胆する). No arrest meant no story.... Then their deputy bureau chief, a soft-spoken, hard-eyed veteran, took a risk (危険を引き受ける). "What Recruit did is not a good thing," said Hiroshi Yamamoto. "I would like to pursue it a little further through our own efforts." And so what might have become a yellowing file folder in an outlying bureau blossomed instead into a scandal that threatened to topple (転覆させる) the government of Prime Minister Noboru Takeshita.... Yamamoto—"Yama-chan" to his friends, "The Piranha" to his enemies—can claim much of the credit (栄誉の大半を担える).」。

　この記事は、Investigative Reporters & Editors Inc. の機関誌に「Veteran leads cub reporters to light of scandal in Japan」(Summer 1989) と題して転載され、Hiroshi Yamamoto and his colleagues in Asahi Shimbun は同 Inc. の Special Award of Professional Excellence を受賞した。日本では、日本ジャーナリスト会議正賞は受けたものの、日本新聞協会賞は、この年に朝日新聞社のおこした「珊瑚事件」などのために見送りとなった。その話を聞いた Fred Hiatt は、「If a journalist like Yamamoto didn't get it, who else could have gotten the Pulitzer (prize)?」と驚いたものだった。

2. What America Wants in Japanese Politicians

Nakasone: A New Style For Japan

By Tracy Dahldy

November 25, 1982

Nakasone, an urbane politician with a dramatic and straight-forward approach that contrasts sharply with the traditional, unobtrusive style of politics here....

It could, they said, mean more dynamic leadership and facilitate a clearer statement of the direction of Japanese policy. U.S. officials have complained in the past that the lack of clear signals from Tokyo has complicated efforts to reach accord on key issues....

His charismatic qualities, which may fit more the mold of American politicians, have left him open to charges here of showmanship. His style, however, may give the English-speaking Nakasone an advantage in dealing with foreign leaders, some of whom have complained that the Japanese tend to melt into the background when issues of substance are discussed.

中曽根康弘が総理になった時、在京の外国プレスに高まった「Finally, Japan has a "scrutable" prime minister」という期待感はいまだに鮮明だ。福田赳夫、大平正芳らそれなりの人格見識を備えたエース級の総理も、対外的には personality がなかなか理解されにくかった。中曽根首相は就任直後の83年1月にワシントンを訪問。前任の鈴木善幸首相の、日米同盟は「did not have any military implications」(81/5/13 WP) という発言以来ぎくしゃくしていた日米関係を、WP朝食会でのいわゆる不沈空母発言などで立て直し、レーガン大統領との信頼を築いた。米メディアの扱いは好意的で、the Liberal Democratic Party(自民党)は「Nakasone Party」(86/7/7 WP など)、日本の新しい海外援助計画は「How about calling it the

2. アメリカが求める日本の政治家像

日本政治に新スタイルを持ち込む中曽根

トレイシー・ダルビー

1982年11月25日

都会風の洗練された政治家である中曽根の、劇的かつ率直なアプローチは、日本の万事控えめな伝統的政治手法とは際立った対照を見せている……。

中曽根政権は、よりダイナミックなリーダーシップをもたらし、日本の政策の方向性をより明確に主張することになるかもしれないと政治評論家は語っている。米政府高官は、東京からはっきりしたサインが送られてこないため、重要問題で合意しようとする努力に支障が生じたとの不満を、これまで述べてきた……。

アメリカの政治家の型にもっとも良くあてはまるであろう彼のカリスマ的な資質は、パフォーマンスだとして非難を受けている。しかし、その政治的スタイルは、英語を話す中曽根にとって、諸外国の指導者たちと交渉する際の利点となるかもしれない。彼らの中には、日本人は、実質的な問題が討議される時になると、何を言いたいのかつかめなくなってしまうと苦情を述べる者もいる。

Nakasone Plan?」(86/11/2) となり、貿易問題で苦境に立つと「Will Ron help Yasu?」(87/4/29)。中曽根は、長年自宅に外国特派員を招き、アメリカ人との家族ぐるみの交際にも心を砕き、座禅、書道、和服などの日本的演出にも積極的だった。最終的には 「Nakasone has never been able to persuade citizens and companies to step up foreign purchases in the dramatic way the trading partners wanted.」(87/4/29 By John Burgess) との批判を受けるが、「Some speak as if he was the only friend they have in Japan.」(同) といった高い評価はアメリカに今も残っている。

Japan's Quiet New Leader

By Jim Hoagland

December 19, 1987

Afflicted by the pangs of Nakasone withdrawal, the American press is not paying much attention to the doings and sayings of the new Japanese prime minister, Noboru Takeshita. That is just as well from the standpoint of Takeshita, who likes to move quietly and methodically toward goals he can achieve. …Takeshita's conciliatory style and his attention to substance may just fit the moment. It is a moment in which Japan must exercise quietly the enormous financial power it has accumulated in the past two years.

Japanese Official Hints At a Trade Compromise

By Paul Blustein

February 23, 1994

Ichiro Ozawa, one of Japan's most influential politicians, signaled a possible compromise in the U.S.–Japan trade dispute today, asserting that Tokyo should set targets for purchases of foreign goods so long as they are not binding.…

As a former power broker in the long-dominant Liberal Democratic Party, he was often involved in settling U.S.–Japan trade disputes, sometimes forcing reluctant bureaucrats and interest groups to make concessions for the sake of good relations between Washington and Tokyo. Clinton administration negotiators have suggested they hope he will play such a role again.

日本の政治家に対するアメリカの評価は、1つには国内でのリーダーシップの有無によって定まってくる。アメリカの求める日本の市場開放が実現できるかどうか、というわけだ。竹下登が中曽根首相の後継に選ばれたとき、「a deft (巧みな) behind-the-scenes political operator who is particularly good at raising money」(87/10/20 By Margaret Shapiro) など、調整型政治家としての実力に着目する報道もあった。竹下内閣の官房副長官として、対米貿易折衝の要ともなったのが小沢一郎である。87、8年の construction market、89年の cellular phone（携帯電話）をめぐる telecommunication の両問題でその政治力が発揮され、counterpart の trade negotiators との関係も in a very good chemistry だったという。95年末の New Frontier

日本の静かなる新指導者

ジム・ホーグランド

1987年12月19日

中曽根退陣の衝撃に戸惑ったアメリカのメディアは、日本の新しい総理大臣、竹下登の行動と言動にあまり注意を払っていない。それは、達成可能な目的に向かって静かに、かつ整然と進むのを好む竹下にとって、都合のよいことである……。

何事においても妥協をはかりつつ、物事の実質を重くみる竹下の姿勢は、現在の状況にぴったりかもしれない。日本は過去2年間にわたって蓄積した、膨大な資金力を静かに使わなければならない時期なのだ。

日本の政治家、貿易交渉で妥協をほのめかす

ポール・ブルースティン

1994年2月23日

日本で最も影響力のある政治家の1人、小沢一郎が、日米貿易紛争における妥協の可能性を今日、ほのめかした。日本政府は、拘束力を持たないものであるかぎり、海外製品購入の目標値を定めるべし、というのだ……。

彼は、長い間政権の座にあった自民党の陰の実力者として、日米貿易紛争の解決にしばしばかかわってきた。時には、ワシントンと東京間を良好に保つために、躊躇する官僚や圧力団体に譲歩させてきた。クリントン政権の交渉担当者たちは、彼が、再びそのような役割を果たすのを期待していることを示唆した。

Party（新進党）選挙で新党首に選ばれた小沢に、アメリカの目は再び注がれている。「Ichiro Ozawa, for years the backroom kingmaker of Japanese politics, became a likely candidate for prime minister.」(95/12/28 By Kevin Sullivan)。小沢は「injecting new energy into a Japanese political world suffering from lack of direction and leadership」という期待感である。

来る総選挙で、新進党がどのように闘うか。小沢一郎の政治的命運をふくめ、アメリカの目も注がれている。

Japan's Tough Trade Official Likely Leader

By Kevin Sullivan and Mary Jordan

January 6, 1996

U.S. officials in Tokyo said they welcomed the announcement.

"It's always good to have a strong leader who can make things happen and deliver on things he agrees to," said one U.S. diplomat. He said Hashimoto might be a more effective ally for the United States than Murayama because the Japanese perceive him as a stronger leader.

Hashimoto, best known for his slicked-down hair and his cigarette holder, is a flashy, flamboyant politician who once wore a bright green leather CHECK suit to a meeting with U.S. trade negotiators. He is brash and cocky: an American academic says Hashimoto once turned down an offer to speak at a conference at a prestigious American university because the conference was in a building where smoking was prohibited.

In an off-the-cuff remark that is almost impossible to imagine from any other Japanese politician, Hashimoto last summer described Kantor as "Scarier than my wife when I come home drunk."

アメリカ人にとって、政治家とは、何よりも力強くなければならない。主張は単純明快、最後まで妥協せずフェアに闘い抜けば、たとえ敵国の人間といえども尊敬するにやぶさかではない。橋本龍太郎についてアメリカは、そうしたプラス・イメージも含めて評価し、早くから日本の総理候補と見ていたようだ。

Time 誌は、95/9/25 号の Cover（表紙）に橋本を使い、「STRONG ARM: Assertive, arrogant and individualistic, Ryutaro Hashimoto is poised to be the next Prime Minister of Japan」と報じた。激烈を極めた日米自動車交渉中のタフな姿勢も、アメリカ側を「infuriated」(95/8/29 By Kevin Sullivan) ではあっても「impressed」(同) したとの評価である。しかし、総理就任後の橋本が住専問題で苦境に立つと、「Japanese Leaders In Logjam: Premier Hamstrung by Financial

日本政府の通商強硬派、指導者に

ケヴィン・サリバン ＆ メアリー・ジョーダン

1996年1月6日

東京駐在の米高官たちは、この発表に歓迎を表明した。

「物事を動かし、自ら信ずるところを遂行する強い指導者は、常に好ましい」とある外交官は述べた。橋本は日本側が強力な指導者とみなしているが故に、村山よりアメリカにとって確かな同盟相手になるかもしれないというのだ……。

橋本といえば滑らかに後ろへとなでつけられた髪と煙草のパイプで知られている。アメリカの通商交渉担当者との会合に、明るい緑色の皮製スーツを着てきたという華やかで、人目をひく政治家だ。傲慢かつ生意気でもある。あるアメリカの学者によれば、格式高いアメリカの大学での講演を、会議が禁煙の建物で行われるという理由で断ったという。

他の日本の政治家からはちょっと想像できない、即席のコメントの中で、橋本は去年の夏、カンターは「酔って帰った時の家内より恐ろしい」と述べた。

Crisis」(96/3/13 By Kevin Sullivan)。日本経済の根幹を脅かす不良債権、重なる大蔵スキャンダルと、薬害エイズ問題で露呈された厚生行政の犯罪的行為。Kevin は、アメリカが Watergate 事件で味わった苦悩を日本が今体験しつつあり、日本でこれほどの「a deep distrust of the government」が広がったことはないとし、「And Hashimoto is paying the price.」と記事を結んでいる。

3. Will Japanese Politics Change?

Japan's Ruling Monopoly Faces Vigorous Challenge

By T. R. Reid

April 13, 1993

Lackluster leadership and corruption within the party, together with an almost palpable hunger for change among the Japanese people, raise the possibility that the long-dominant party could finally lose its governing majority. Some analysts says this could happen in the next national election, which must be held by February. There is even speculation that the LDP could lose a no-confidence vote sooner than that.

New political contribution laws, prompted by repeated scandals, could undermine the pork-barrel-based support system that has sustained the ruling party.

With all of that, the citizens of this fast-changing country seem to be deciding that it is finally time for politics to change as well.

The most likely alternative to an LDP government would be a coalition, but some political experts here predict the emergence of a strong new opposition party, giving Japan a two-party system along liberal-conservative lines, such as in the United States....

1993年夏に起きた日本の政治改革を、Tom Reid はこの記事でおそらく最初に予測しただけでなく、変化を一貫して支持する。最初は、日本の政治腐敗に関する報道だった。「Japan's Culture of Corruption」(92/9/6)。後援会から地元の培養、冠婚葬祭などにいかに金がかかるかを、コミック誌の政治漫画をイラストに使って書いた。佐川・金丸の金権スキャンダルに対する国民の怒りの声が高まると「Japan's Anger Speaks Louder Than Money—a surprising new force is suddenly being felt: the will of the people.」(92/10/8)。自民党竹下派の分裂（新進党へと連なる）時の「Moves for Political Change Rise in Japan」(92/12/12) を経てこの記事となる。総選挙が近づくにつれ、「Japan's Political Crisis Sparked By Long-Ignored Average

3. 日本の政治は変化するか

日本の一党支配体制が直面する反対勢力

トム・リード

1993年4月13日

覇気を失った指導体制と党内の腐敗に加え、国民がほぼ明確に変化を乞い求め始めた結果、長期政権を担ってきた政党が、ついに政権与党の座を下りる可能性がでてきた。来年2月までに行われる総選挙でそうなる可能性があるという評論家もいる。それ以前に自民党は内閣不信任案を可決されてしまうという予測さえも出ている。

繰り返されるスキャンダルが引き金となって進められてきた政治資金法案は、与党を支えてきた地方と中央にまたがる利権政治の土台を崩す可能性がある。

あれやこれやで、この変化が急速に進んでいる国の市民は、ついに政治も変化する時が来たとの決断を下したかのようだ。

自民党政権に代わる可能性が最も高いのは、連立政権だろう。しかし政治のプロの中には、強力な新野党が出現し、日本もアメリカのように保守的な自由主義の流れに沿った2大政党制になると予測する者もいる……。

Voters」(93/6/20)、「Hunger for Change Stirs Japan」(7/5)、「Change Challenges Japan's Women」(7/17)と続いた。その見方は、Renaissance Party（新生党）結成時の記事の結びに明確だ。「But political "reform" is obviously the issue of the hour in Japan, and on this point the opposition parties have a unified message: To clean up politics, the voters must dump the scandal-plagued Liberal Democrats.」(6/24)。

Reformer Picked to Lead Japan

By T. R. Reid

July 30, 1993

Leaders of Japan's newly formed ruling coalition agreed today to elect Morihiro Hosokawa, an ingenious political tactician and an outspoken advocate of opening Japan's markets to imported goods, as the country's next prime minister.

Hosokawa won the right to head the first "realignment" government after four decades of conservative one-party rule largely because he guessed right about Japanese politics a year ago. He was the first major politician to recognize that voters were fed up with repeated corruption scandals plaguing the long-dominant Liberal Democratic Party....

In fact, the youthful prime-minister-to-be and the youthful U.S. president have a good deal in common. Both spent most of the 1980s as rural southern governors—Hosokawa in Kumamoto Prefecture—gaining reputations as strong campaigners and policy innovators....

The two men met when Clinton was in Tokyo earlier this month and they got along famously. "The president was extremely impressive," Hosokawa gushed to TV cameras afterward....

New Japan Party（日本新党）の結成直後、細川護熙へ Paul Blustein とインタビューしたとき、最後の問いは「When do you think you will be the Japanese prime minister?」だった。聞く方も答える方もほとんど冗談、ため息混じりの笑いに終わったのを覚えている。記事 (92/7/9) はこのエピソードには触れてもいない。政治は激動し、細川が首相になり、クリントン大統領の「Change」のメッセージとあいまって米メディアは日本の変化を大歓迎する。しかし、本当に大丈夫なのかとの懸念もあった。「Japan's politics became a bit more democratic on Sunday, but the old-line politicians could still have a great deal of say over what happens next」(93/7/22 WP editorial)。外務省で外国メディア担当の国際報道課長を務め

日本を指導するために選ばれた改革者

トム・リード

1993年7月30日

日本に新たに誕生した連立政権のリーダーたちは、細川護熙——巧みな政略家であり、日本市場を輸入製品に開放すべしと、高唱してきた——を、日本の次期総理に選ぶことに合意した。

　細川が40年に及ぶ保守政党の単独支配を再編する政権を率いる権利を手に入れたのは、1年前に彼が日本政治の動向を的確に予測したことが大きい。長期に亘り政権の座にいた自民党を侵食した度重なる政治腐敗スキャンダルに、有権者が嫌気をさしているのに気付いた最初の大物政治家こそ、彼であった……。

　事実、この若き次期総理と、若き合衆国大統領は、多くの共通点をもっている。共に、80年代の大部分、地方の南部で知事を務め、共に選挙運動に長け、政策改革の旗手としての評判を得た。

　今月はじめ、クリントンの東京滞在中に両者は会談し、大いに意気投合した。「大統領は、実に印象的だった」と細川は会談後、テレビカメラに向かいとうとう語った……。

た近藤誠一が『米国報道に見る日本』で、「日本の政治変革は、国民パワーではなく権力闘争との見方を終始とった」と書いた NYT の David Sanger は、「Japan's Promising New Leader Seems to Lose His Magic Touch」と細川政権への悲観的な見方を93/12/20付で早くも明らかにしている。

Socialist Elected Japanese Premier

By Paul Blustein

June 30, 1994

Socialist Party chairman Tomiichi Murayama was elected Japan's prime minister tonight with the support of the once-dominant Liberal Democratic Party, dealing a stinging setback to the country's political reform movement.

The election of a Socialist leader in business-oriented Japan was another twist in Japan's unfolding political drama, and questions swirled here about whether the new government's policies would create new conflicts with the United States over trade and security issues....

Change Likely to Further Stall Trade Talks

By Peter Behr and Clay Chandler

June 30, 1994

The laboring, year-old U.S.–Japanese trade talks appear likely to drop into an even lower gear after the selection of Socialist leader Tomiichi Murayama as the new head of a divided Japanese government, Clinton administration officials said yesterday....

Some analysts said Japan's revolving door political leadership had sapped hopes for progress. David Hale, an economist at Kemper Securities in Chicago, said Murayama's selection is "a disaster."

WPは最後まで村山政権と反りが合わなかったようだ。Tom Reid は、政権の発足時、選挙に負けた政党がなぜ政権をとるのかという視点で、「yet today, the people running Japan's government are the very people who decisively lost the last election」(7/18)、社会党が自衛隊や日の丸、君が代容認などの原理原則を変えたときは、「Ditches Socialist Platform」「cast aside the chief pillar of his own party's platform」といった調子で書いた (7/21)。それからまもなく、ワシントンに行った時、社内の誰からも、「What's going on in Japanese politics?」と聞かれ、「The new government is like a beefsteak. The whole meat is the LDP. The socialists are just pepper and salt. So don't worry too much.」と説明した

日本の首相に社会主義者が選出される

ポール・ブルースティン　　　　　　　　　　　1994年6月30日

日本社会党の村山富市委員長が、かつての支配勢力であった自民党の支持を受け、日本の首相に、今夜選ばれた。この国の政治改革にとって、手痛い後退となるであろう。

　経済に主導された日本での、社会党リーダーの選出は、この国で展開している政治劇のねじれ現象の1つである。そして、新政府の政策が、貿易と安全保障をめぐり合衆国との間に新たな対立をもたらすのではないかという疑念がここに沸き起こっている……。

政権の交代により貿易交渉は停滞しそう

ピーター・ベア ＆ クレイ・チャンドラー　　　1994年6月30日

分裂した日本の新政府の長に、社会党の指導者である村山富市が選ばれたことにより、この1年、骨を折りながらも進めてきた日米貿易交渉のペースは、より遅くなるだろうと、クリントン政権の高官たちが昨日述べた……。

　一部アナリストは、日本の回転ドア式の政権移譲は、改革への希望を消し去ってしまったと述べた。シカゴにあるケンパー・セキュリティーズのエコノミスト、デヴィッド・ヘイルは、村山の選択は「最悪の事態」と指摘している。

ものだった。その後の村山政権の安定で、「The Murayama Surprise: the government is actually working out surprisingly well」(94/10/24 NYT editorial) といった肯定的評価も米メディアには出たものの、退任時には「Still, Murayama and his fragile coalition government were criticized for showing little leadership on many issues.」(96/1/6 By Kevin Sullivan and Mary Jordan) とされたのだった。

4. A Bureaucracy-Bound Nation?

Taking On the Japanese Bureaucracy

By Clay Chandler

February 12, 1994

As President Clinton and Japanese Prime Minister Morihiro Hosokawa grimly announced the collapse of trade talks at the White House yesterday, five blocks away the men Clinton's aides say are largely to blame for the failure lounged at the Madison Hotel.

These men—and virtually all of them are men—are Japan's bureaucrats, members of a highly educated elite who enjoy vast authority over government policies. As trade negotiations bogged down in recent days, the White House has increasingly cast them as villains.

At a breakfast with U.S. reporters Thursday, Treasury Secretary Lloyd Bentsen marveled that he sees the same bureaucrats in the background, no matter which Japanese cabinet member he meets. And senior Clinton economic adviser W. Bowman Cutter recently derided Japan's officials as stubborn "mandarins" whose "attitudes change slowly."

"I am very much disturbed by the use of the term 'mandarin,'" said one Japanese official. "It's offensive.... We don't control things in Japan."

上記の記事が出た直後の2月17日、President Clinton は Imus Radio Talk Show に出演し、こう語った。「So there is a big fight going on in Japan right now. The permanent government agencies there that have dominated policy for years and years, for decades, the trade and finance agencies (通産と大蔵官僚のこと！) think the system they've had has worked. It's given them low unemployment and a high savings rate, big exports and no imports, and they want to keep it.」。それに対し、日本を「fully modern state with fair and open trade」にしようと闘っている改革者達がおり、「in a way we're helping the cause of the reformers」という図式である。米側のこうした見方は中曽根内閣の頃からあり、「But

4. 官僚支配の国か

日本の官僚制に挑戦する

クレイ・チャンドラー

1994年2月12日

クリントン大統領と細川護熙首相が昨日、ホワイトハウスで、貿易交渉の決裂を厳しい表情のうちに発表していたのとまさに同じ時、5ブロック離れたマディソン・ホテルでは、失敗の原因の大半を帰すことが出来るとクリントンの補佐官に言わしめた男たちがくつろいでいた。

この男たちは——そう、まさに全員男性なのだ——、日本の官僚であり、政府の政策につき、大きな権威を享受している、高水準の教育を受けたエリート達だ。貿易交渉が泥沼にはまるようになったここ数日、ホワイトハウスは、彼らをますます悪役と見なすようになった。

木曜日に行われたアメリカの報道陣との朝食会で、ロイド・ベンツェン財務長官は、日本の閣僚の誰と会談しようが、いつも同じ官僚達が背後に控えていることに驚きの念を表明した。クリントンの経済担当顧問W・ボウマン・カッターは先日、日本の官僚を、「ゆっくりとしか変化しない」、頑迷な「マンダリン」(訳注中国清朝官吏。反動的な高級官僚といったニュアンスあり)であると嘲笑した…。

「私は、『マンダリン』という表現が使われたことに大変不快感を持っています。まことに攻撃的な物言いです……。我々が、日本を動かしているわけではありません」とある日本の役人は述べた。

---

for all his western airs, Nakasone has been able to deliver only what his party and bureaucrats would permit」(87/4/29 By John Burgess) といった記述が見える。Clinton は93年春、ロシアの Boris Yeltsin 大統領との会談で「"Japanese negotiators tend to say 'yes' when they mean 'no'."」(93/4/13 WP など) と発言し、日本側の反発をかってもいる。

Bowing to Nobody

By Paul Blustein
October 31, 1993

Isayama, MITI's 52-year-old director-general for international trade policy, represents a new generation of top ministry bureaucrats who take a much harder line on autos and other trade disputes than Washington is accustomed to facing.

Mostly men in their forties and fifties and earned graduate degrees from Ivy League universities in the United States, these officials believe Japan should drop its age-old practice of yielding to American pressure. They prefer a new approach that might be summed up by the phrase: "See you in court"— the recently created World Trade Organization (WTO).

A Japanese Starts Talking Back

By Fread Hiatt
November 13, 1989

As a prospering and confident Japan searches for a new voice on the world stage, the rumbling tones of Taizo Watanabe are likely to be the voice the world hears first....

His approach reflects a new sense here that relations with the United States would improve if Japan spoke up with more confidence, even when saying something America does not want to hear....

Watanabe's unorthodox performance has provoked some resentment within the Foreign Ministry and the Japanese press corps.

通産省は毎春、『不公正貿易報告書』(*Report on Unfair Trade Policies 19XX*) を出している。U.S. Trade Representative（米通商代表部）の『*National Trade Estimate Report on Foreign Trade Barriers*』の日本版ともいえ、世界貿易の不公正慣行に対し、もの申す日本の理論的根拠として、米メディアも注目している。「Japanese Study Calls U.S. Trade Policies Unfair」(92/6/8 By Elaine Kurtenbach)、「Taking the Offense on Managed Trade: Japan Defends Policies」(93/5/21 By Paul Blustein)。この報告書が出るようになったのは92年から。上記最初の記事の通産省新人脈が表舞台に出始めた時期と一致する。ただし、新国際機構がもしアメリカを出し抜くために使われるなら、議会を中心に「real problem」が起きるだろうが、「MITI guys」

頭を下げない日本

ポール・ブルースティン 1993年10月31日

通産省の通商政策局長、52歳の伊佐山健志は、自動車その他の貿易問題に関し、ワシントンがこれまで慣れ親しんできたどんな応対ぶりより、はるかに強硬な姿勢をとる新世代の高級官僚を代表している。

そのほとんどは、40代から50代の男性で、米国のアイビーリーグの大学の学位を持ち、アメリカの圧力に屈するという時代遅れの行為をもはやとるべきではないと信じている。彼らは、「法廷で会いましょう」という句によって、一括できるであろう新しいアプローチを好む。法廷とは、創設されたばかりの世界貿易機構(WTO)である。

ある日本人、反論を始める

フレッド・ハイアット 1989年11月13日

成功し、自信に満ちた日本が、世界の檜舞台における新たな声を捜すなかで、世界は渡辺泰造の轟く声を、まず聞くことになるだろう……。

そのやり方は、日本がもっと自信をもって発言すれば、たとえアメリカの聞きたくない内容でも、日米関係は改善するだろうという新しい考え方を反映している……。

こうした渡辺の従来の流儀に必ずしも沿うとはいえないパフォーマンスは、外務省と日本の報道陣の間にいくらかの反感をよんでいる。

は、「don't care about or don't take seriously enough」と記事は警告している。なお、国際派とされる外務省で外国メディア担当の責任者が外務報道官。その中で、抜群に外国記者の人気が高かったのが渡辺泰造(1989–90)だった。その活動に焦点を当てた2番目の記事だが、アメリカからは、日本全体が発言を始めた具体例として見られていたことがわかる。

Kicking Daiwa Out

Editorial

November 4, 1995

Instead of notifying the American regulators, Daiwa Bank had gone to the Japanese Ministry of Finance—which told no one.

These revelations were followed by a wave of exculpatory hokum from Tokyo about the unique nature of Japanese culture and its admirable inclination toward cooperation and conciliation....

The Daiwa case demonstrates that international cooperation in financial regulation still isn't working well enough to be reliable. The indictment is a message not only to foreign bankers but to their governments, beginning with Japan's.

Prime Minister Joins Criticism of Ministry

By Mary Jordan and Kevin Sullivan

February 8, 1996

The agency credited with master-minding Japan's postwar economic miracle, the symbol of how Japan governs, may be at the end of its heyday.

Today, Prime Minister Ryutaro Hashimoto joined the growing chorus of leaders discussing the once unthinkable: the possible dismantling of the Finance Ministry....

Many believe that at least some cosmetic changes will be made to the Finance Ministry, but they question how meaningful any restructuring will be.

斎藤次郎大蔵次官（当時）を、Paul Blustein が「widely described as one of the nation's most powerful men—by some accounts, the most powerful」と描写したのが 95/6/26日付のことだった。それから1年余り、ほとんど信じられないほどの出来事が大蔵省に起きたが、米メディアにとっての最終的パンチは、事務方の個人的不祥事や、金融政策の誤りではなく、外国との信義違反であった。大和銀行ニューヨーク支店での巨額損失事件を、銀行幹部から聞かされながらも米当局への通報を期限内に行わなかった点について NYT 東京特派員 Sheryl WuDunn は、大蔵省が「did not act on the information nor did it inform American counterparts ...」(95/10/10)、*Newsweek* 誌 Wall Street editor の Allan Sloan も、米当局を激怒させ

大和銀行を追い出す

社説
1995年11月4日

米政府の取り締まり当局に報告する代わりに、大和銀行は、日本の大蔵省に駆け込んだ。そしてその大蔵省が完全に口をつぐんだのだ。事件が明るみに出た後、東京からは、日本文化のユニークさや、協力と和解を重視するまことに賞賛すべき傾向といった、でたらめな弁解の連続であった……。大和事件は、金融規制の国際的協力体制が、依然として信頼するに足るほど、しっかりと機能していないことを示した。今回の犯罪告発は、外国の銀行に対するメッセージであるばかりではない。該当する国の政府に対するものであり、日本は、その第1弾なのだ。

総理も大蔵批判に加わる

メアリー・ジョーダン ＆ ケヴィン・サリヴァン
1996年2月8日

戦後の日本が成し遂げた経済の奇跡を演出、実行してきた功績を有し、日本の類まれな統治を象徴するとされてきた省庁が、その全盛期の終わりを迎えたのかも知れない。

今日、橋本龍太郎総理が、かつては考えられなかった多くの指導者達の間で起きている議論に加わった。即ち、大蔵省解体の可能性について、である……。多くの人々は、大蔵省を多少は変える措置が取られるだろうが、それがどのくらい意味のある改革であるかは疑問としている。

たのは「Daiwa and Japanese regulators disrespected it by withholding the bad news for weeks.」(95/11/7 WPのコラム) などと驚きを込めて書いた。事態の背景として文化の違いに言及した同省高官発言も「has further eroded international confidence in Japan's ailing banking system and the regulators' ability to straighten it out」(93/10/13 By Sandra Sugawara) と、火に油を注ぐ結果になったのだ。

CHAPTER 2 | THE SECURITY TREATY AND FOREIGN POLICY

1. Will Japan Go Nuclear?

A Yen for the Bomb?

By Selig S. Harrison

October 31, 1993

For the first time since the bombing of Hiroshima in 1945, Japan no longer rules out the possibility of producing its own nuclear weapons. Fears of a nuclear armed, unified Korea, together with growing Chinese military power and a new mood of national assertiveness, have provoked a growing debate between hawks and doves over post-Cold War Japanese security policy.

American policymakers react with dismay to the prospect of a nuclear Japan....

The Japanese plutonium program is primarily motivated by the national desire for energy independence. But it also reflects sentiment in favor of keeping the nuclear weapons option open. The soon-to-be-tested H-2 rocket will have a thrust comparable to the most advanced U.S. intercontinental missiles....

Tokyo, Seoul, and Pyongyang are closely eyeing each move made by the other in what has become a three-cornered nuclear drama in Northeast Asia....

日本人にとっては考えられないようなシナリオが、アメリカでは常識のように論じられたのが、北朝鮮(朝鮮民主主義人民共和国)の「核疑惑」に揺れた1993年秋のことだ。巨大な原子雲のイラストつきでStyle欄に掲載された本論は、その代表格だ。Selig Harrisonは、Carnegie Endowment の Senior Associate で、元WP東京支局長を務めた極東問題専門家。北朝鮮の Yongbyon (寧辺)の原子力発電所で、核爆弾が製造されているのではという疑惑が、有事へ備えるのは国家戦略として当然とするアメリカで、日本の核武装論に直結した。論拠として、プルトニウムやH-2ロケット製造のほか、冷戦の終結後、日本はアメリカの核の傘への信頼感を失い、専守防衛論や非核三原則等に疑念が生じたなどを挙げている。被爆国としての核アレルギー

第2章 安保と外交

1. 日本は核武装する!?

¥で核爆弾を?

セリグ・ハリソン　　　　　　　　　　　　　　1993年10月31日

1945年の広島への原爆投下以来、初めて日本は、自前の核兵器製造の可能性を否定しなくなった。核武装し、統一された南北朝鮮に対する恐怖心と合わせ、増大する中国の軍事力、新たに登場した自己主張の雰囲気は、この国のタカ派とハト派の間で、冷戦後の自国の安全保障政策をめぐる論争を引き起こしている。

米国の政策立案者は、日本の核武装の可能性を危惧の念をもって眺めている……。

日本のプルトニウム計画は、主として、エネルギー面における自立という関心によって動機づけられている。しかし、それは同時に、核武装のオプションを残しておきたいという心情をも反映している。まもなく試されるH-2ロケットは、米国の最新型大陸間弾道ミサイルにも引けをとらないだけの推進力を持っている……。

東京、ソウル、ピョンヤンは、北東アジアで展開されようとする三極核ドラマの中で、相手の一挙一動を注意深く見守っている……。

は薄れ、核武装論が最早タブーではなくなったというのだ。

「yen for」は「激しく求める」の意味だが、この見出しは、お金の「円」とのかけ言葉になっている。

Japan's Nuclear Stance

By Seiichi Kondo

November 14, 1993

Counselor for Public Affairs
Embassy of Japan, Washington

Mr. Harrison's allusion to the convertibility of Japan's rocket programs to intercontinental ballistic missiles also was grossly misleading. Japan's space development programs are limited by law to peaceful purposes only.

Japan, which is dependent on foreign sources, has a nuclear power development program supplying more than one-fourth of Japan's electrical needs since 1985. Japan maintains a firm policy of not accumulating excess stocks of plutonium.

North Korea's Coming Bomb

By Charles Krauthammer

November 5, 1993

North Korea has already tested a missile with enough range to hit Japan. A nuclear North Korea would set off a deadly arms race in the North Pacific. Japan would go nuclear very quickly. South Korea would follow. This would not sit well with China and Russia.

The president's task is clear. Lead. Stop talking to the North Koreans—it is time for an economic blockade—and start talking to the American people.

「日本核武装論」は、93年秋、米議会やメディアや学会などで相次いだ。W.P. Writers Group の人気コラムニスト Charles Krauthammer は、新聞紙面だけでなく、ABCテレビの看板番組 Night Line で「Japan will go nuclear if Korea does」と断言 (11/16)。The House Committee on Foreign Affairs Subcommittee on Asia and the Pacific (下院外交委員会アジア太平洋小委員会) や American Enterprise Institute のフォーラムでも、政府関連や学会のそうそうたる論客が日本核武装の可能性を論じた (11/3)。これに対し、米メディアに現れた日本側の反論は、上記のワシントン日本大使館近藤誠一参事官によるWPへの Letter to the Editor 程度で Harrison は、直ちに日本側で核容認ともとれる発言をした政治家や官僚

日本の核に対する姿勢

近藤　誠一

1993年11月14日

ワシントン日本大使館
参事官

ハリソン氏は、日本のロケット計画が大陸間弾道ミサイルへ転換可能であると暗に指摘しているが、これは、全くの誤だ。日本の宇宙開発は、法律によって、平和目的にのみ限定されている。

　海外の資源に依存している日本は、電力需要の4分の1以上を供給する原子力発電推進計画を、1985年以来採用している。そして、過剰なプルトニウムのストックを蓄積しないという強固な方針をかたく守り続けている……。

北朝鮮の来たるべき爆弾

チャールズ・クラウトハマー

1993年11月5日

北朝鮮は、日本を射程距離内におさめるミサイルのテストをすでに成功させている。核武装した北朝鮮は、北太平洋において、激烈な軍拡競争を引き起こしてしまう。日本は急速に核武装するだろう。そして、韓国もそれに続くことになる。中国や、ロシアにとっては、まことに好ましからぬ事態だ。大統領の務めは明らかだ。リーダーシップをとれ。北朝鮮相手にではなく——彼らに対しては、経済封鎖を断行せよ——アメリカ国民に、語りかける時が来たのだ。

の名前をあげた再反論を投書した。米政府自体は、「I think it's fair to say that Japan does not wish to become a nuclear power.」(President Clinton 会見 11/23) とまずは冷静だったが、豪州の世論調査では、4割が日本は核兵器を持っていると答える (朝日新聞 94/5/22) など、日本の反核の決意が世界でどのように見られているかはよく知る必要があるだろう。

North Korea and the Specter of War

By Lally Weymouth

April 6, 1994

As for Japan, if sanctions were imposed by the United Nations, the Japanese government would be required to cut off the substantial flow of funds provided by North Koreans living in Japan to their relatives in Korea. Would the Japanese government comply? Such action would expose Japan to North Korean terrorism, Japanese officials believe.

There's a second key question concerning Japan: Has the United States secured from Tokyo its consent to let America use Japanese airfields in case of war? The Japanese Defense Agency believes North Korea would target U.S. bases in Japan for missile attack. Given this threat, it's possible Prime Minister Morihiro Hosokawa will prove too weak politically to allow the United States access to the bases. Needless to say, it's essential that America secure its supply lines, but so far Clinton administration officials, when asked about the matter, have merely responded that the question of the bases is sensitive and that U.S. relations with Japan are good.

朝鮮半島有事の際、日本はどんな行動をとるか。アメリカのこの重大な関心事を端的に書いたのが、保守派コラムニストで Katharine Graham の娘の Lally Weymouth である。その時こそ、同盟国の真価が問われるというのだ。北朝鮮の現金収入の大部分は、「originates in Osaka's noisy, bustling pachinko parlors」(93/11/1 NYT By David Sanger) であり、核問題が経済制裁につながった場合、在日朝鮮人による母国への送金──送る側にとっては「a form of ransom」(前同)とも言える金の流れを止められるのか。さらには、日米安全保障条約に基づき、日本はどこまで米軍の行動に協力するのか。集団的自衛権は認めないという憲法解釈の枠の中で、十分な協力が出来るのか、といった点である。北朝鮮の核問題は、94年7月の Kim Il Sung 主

北朝鮮と戦争の亡霊

ラリー・ウェイモス

1994年4月6日

日本に関して言えば、もし国連による制裁が発動されるなら、日本政府は、在日北朝鮮人が母国の親戚へ供給している、莫大な資金の流れを止めるよう要求される。日本政府は、これに応じるだろうか。このような処置をすれば、北朝鮮によるテロリズムに晒されることになると、日本の当局側は信じている。

　日本について、第2の重要な問題がある。戦争が起きた場合、米軍がこの国の飛行場を使うという同意を、合衆国は東京から取りつけたのであろうか。日本の防衛庁は、北朝鮮が日本国内の米軍基地を、ミサイル攻撃の標的にしていると考えている。このような脅威の下で、合衆国に対し基地使用を許すには、細川護煕首相の政治力は弱すぎるかもしれない。いうまでもなく、アメリカにとって補給路の確保が、何にもまして重要である。しかし、いまのところ、クリントン政権の高官は、この件に関する質問に対し、基地問題は微妙であるが、日米関係は良好である、としか答えていない。

席の死を経て95年3月、米日韓による同国の核管理機構 Korean Peninsula Energy Development Organization (KEDO) が発足、とりあえずは平和裡に進行している。しかし、沖縄問題で揺れる95年秋、来日した Defence Secretary William Perry は、日本記者クラブの会見で、「When we had a crisis last summer with the North Korea …」(11/1) と、朝鮮半島情勢が、いかに極東の安定とそれを支える在日米軍の展開に密接につながっているかを語っている。

2. The Legacy of the Gulf War

The Japan Problem

By Robert J. Samuelson

April 10, 1991

I once naively thought that someday there might be a "solution" to the U.S.–Japan "problem." Wrong. There's no single "problem" capable of a "solution." There is instead a permanent state of anxiety, reflecting different cultures and world views.

The Japanese are correct when they say we're jealous of their success and, at times, try to punish them for it. But Americans are equally correct when we sense that Japan's spirit is to take more from the world than it gives. There's a touch of selfishness and amorality. This, and not the precise amount of Japan's financial contribution, is the basic American discontent crystallized by the gulf crisis....

What we learned from the gulf crisis is much simpler: We can't rely on Japan in the clutch. The Japanese aren't yet dependable allies.

イラクのクウェイト侵攻により、湾岸危機が発生。日本の政府・民間の対応にアメリカの不満はつのった。外務省北米局審議官の職にあった丹波實はワシントンより「The decisions made in Tokyo about the gulf crisis will determine the next 10 to 20 years of the U.S.–Japan relationship." "The gap between what the Americans want and what the Japanese are willing to do is simply enormous.」との危機感に満ちた電報を送った。1月前には、米下院が対日非難の決議を行い、「to begin withdrawing 5,000 American troops a year from Japan unless that country pays the full cost of the U.S. military presence in Japan」(90/9/13 By Dan Morgan) と報じられる情勢にあった。計13億ドルの拠出金を出すことになっても日本の

2. 湾岸戦争の遺したもの

日本問題

ロバート・J・サミュエルソン

1991年4月10日

　私はかつて、米日（編注：WPは米国の新聞で、記者も米人だから米日とする）両国間に横たわる「問題」に、何らかの解決策があるかもしれないとナイーブにも思っていた。しかし、間違いだった。「解決」できるような単一の「問題」は、存在しない。両国間にあるのは、異なる文化と世界観を反映している、恒常的な懸念である。

　アメリカ人は日本人の成功に嫉妬し、時としてそれを罰しようとしている、と日本人が主張するのは正しい。しかし、同様に、日本人の精神とは世界に与えるより、多くを取ろうとするものだ、と感じているアメリカ人も正しい。そこには、身勝手さと道徳観念の欠如がうかがえる。この点こそまさに、湾岸危機によって、はっきりと見えてきたアメリカ側の基本的な不満なのだ。財政的な貢献が正確にはいくらであったのかが問題なのではない……。

　我々が湾岸危機から学んだのは、もっと単純なことだ。我々は、危機に際しての日本は信用できない。日本人は、まだ、信頼に足る同盟相手ではない。

評価にはつながらず、海部首相は「it just makes me gnash my teeth (歯ぎしり) that the kinds of things we've done have not been properly valued」(91/3/17 By Tom Reid) と無念の思いをもらす。上記第2の記事は、WPと *Newsweek* 共通のコラムニスト Robert J. Samuelson がそうした状況を総括し、日米経済摩擦の key word の1つ「The Japan Problem」を題に書いたものである。

Japanese Minesweepers Set Sail for Persian Gulf

By T. R. Reid

April 27, 1991

YOKOSUKA—Hoisting the red-and-white Rising Sun banner that was once the scourge of the Pacific, a small squadron of Japanese navy warships churned out to sea today, launching this nation's first overseas military mission since the last desperate days of World War II....

In the 46 years since this country suffered total devastation in World War II, the Japanese have held resolutely to a pacifist, isolationist stance in geopolitical affairs. Now, due to external pressures and its own emergence as an economic superpower, Japan is in the throes of a probing and sometimes painful reevaluation of its place in the world.

Japan Debates Price of Peace Keeping

By Paul Blustein

May 6, 1991

In any nation, the killing of a countryman serving with United Nations peace-keeping forces would elicit some attention and sorrow.

But in Japan the news that a Japanese policeman was slain in Cambodia has hit like a thunderbolt and stirred impassioned debate about whether the government should pull Japanese personnel back to safe areas of the country—or perhaps all the way back to Japan.

旭日旗がはためき、軍艦マーチが奏でられる中、海上自衛隊の掃海艦群は横須賀基地を出航していった。その光景に、Tom Reidと「This is history. Something is changing now.」と言い合ったものだ。この様子を報じるWPは、いみじくも「NEW ROLES FOR OLD ALLIES」の総合見出しの下、ドイツがNATO域外へ初の出兵をしたというニュースと組んで横須賀発の原稿を掲載した。宮沢内閣下での国連平和維持活動 (PKO) 協力法成立の経過は逐一報道され、カンボジアへの部隊派遣となる。だが、民間ボランティアと文民警察官の死亡という事態に、日本の反応を外国メディアは注目する。「Japan: Is Cambodia Too Costly?」(5/8 By Paul Blustein) の中で、派遣隊員の人命を危機にさらすのに反対する「a maverick member

日本の掃海艇、ペルシア湾に向けて出航

トム・リード

1991年4月27日

横須賀発——かつては太平洋における戦乱の象徴だった赤と白の旭日旗を掲げ、第2次大戦末期の絶望の日々以来初の海外軍事作戦を展開すべく、日本海軍の小艦隊が、今日、海に繰り出していった……。

第2次大戦において、完全な荒廃に直面して以来46年間、日本人は、地政学的な事柄に関し、一貫して平和主義かつ孤立主義に立脚した姿勢を保ってきた。それが今、自ら経済超大国になったこと、並びに外圧によって、日本は、世界における己の位置を必死に捜し求め、時として痛みを伴った再評価を行っている。

平和維持活動の代償について議論する日本

ポール・ブルースティン

1991年5月6日

どんな国でも、国連の平和維持軍の任務についているその国の人間が殺されれば、ある程度の関心と悲しみを呼ぶだろう。

しかし、日本人の警察官が、カンボジアで殺害されたというニュースは、落雷のような衝撃をこの国に与え、政府は日本人隊員を、安全な場所まで——場合によっては、はるばる祖国まで——後退させるべきかどうかをめぐって、激しい議論が展開された。

of the cabinet」の発言が紹介される。そして、明石康・国連事務総長特別代表との間で、日本隊の安全に配慮する取り決めがなされると、日本側は国連に「pleading」した結果、「Tonight, Japanese officials were heaving sighs of relief over an agreement that allayed some of their fears—but that could spark charges of favoritism.」(5/11 By Paul Blustein)

と皮肉混じりに批判するのだ。

3. The Future of the U.S.–Japan Security Treaty

The Rearming of Japan—and the Rest of Asia

By Henry Kissinger

June 29, 1987

As for Japan, American leaders seem to believe that growing military strength will ease America's defense burdens. They hold, too, that a larger Japanese defense effort will dull Japan's commercial competitive edge.

But, Japan, with a history of self-government nearly as long as China's, will rearm for its own purposes....

Japan's increased military contribution is largely unnecessary to maintaining global equilibrium....

Japan could make a more significant contribution to global peace by increasing aid to developing nations than with a large military program. Japanese rearmament will therefore inevitably be driven by considerations of Japan's role in Asia....

It will make a huge difference whether Japan increases its defense effort gradually or suddenly, whether it stresses defense as an outpouring of a new nationalism—political and mercantilistic—or as a contribution to a cooperative world order. Thus, a key objective of American foreign policy should be to draw Japan into larger political relationships *before* its military might develop its own momentum.

本論の背景には冷戦の激化がある。80年代の大半、WP東京支局の重要な年中行事は、日本の防衛費の伸び率を追うことにあった。「U.S. Will Urge Japan to Raise Military Spending」(80/1/14 By William Chapman)、「Japan Raises Defense Spending Goal」(85/9/19 By John Burgess)、「Japanese Agency Asks Immediate Defense Buildup」(87/8/29 By Margaret Shapiro) などである。そうした中で、Kissinger は、日本の防衛力増強の意味を世界的な観点から問い、「It cannot be in America's interest to have one Asian power or group of powers so strong that it can dominate the rest.」と論じた。平和憲法下の日本の軍事防衛問題は、各特派員共通のテーマで、それからまもなく、Margaret Shapiro は「Japan

3. 安保体制どうなる

日本の再軍備とアジア諸国

ヘンリー・キッシンジャー　　　　　　　　　1987年6月29日

日本に関して言えば、アメリカの指導者たちは、日本の軍事力が増強すれば、アメリカの防衛負担は軽減すると信じているようだ。彼らは、日本の防衛努力が増えれば、経済面での競争力が鈍化するだろうとも考えている。

しかし、中国とほぼ同じ長さの自己統治の歴史を持つ日本は、独自の目標のもとに再軍備するだろう……。

日本による軍事的貢献の増大は、地球規模での均衡を達成するには、ほとんど必要ない……。

日本は、大規模な軍備計画よりも、発展途上国への援助を増やすことによって、世界平和にもっと有意義な貢献ができるだろう。従って、日本の再軍備は、アジアにおける日本の役割を考えることによって必然的に方向が定まるであろう……。

日本が、軍事力増強を、漸進的、あるいは急激に行うか、また、政治的及び商業的な新ナショナリズムの発露として行うか、あるいは協力的な世界秩序のために行うかは、大きな違いをもたらす。従って、アメリカの外交政策の鍵は、日本の軍事力が勢いをつける前に、日本をより大きな政治的枠組みの中に引き入れることである。

Tries to Balance No-War Ethics, Arms Buildup」(88/5/1) と書いた。そして、阪神大震災の被災地で当初、石を投げられた自衛隊が、撤退するときには拍手で送られたというエピソードを書き出しにした長文の分析記事 (95/11/15 By Mary Jordan) は、在日米軍のある将校の「Japan is planning to stand on its own two feet, and anyone who doesn't believe that is naive.」で終わっている。

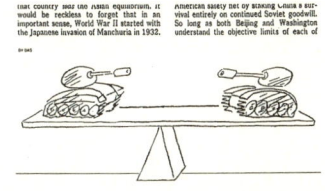

Marine General: U.S. Troops Must Stay in Japan

By Fred Hiatt

March 27, 1990

CAMP BUTLER, Okinawa, Japan—U.S. troops must remain in Japan at least for the next decade in large part to prevent Japan from remilitarizing, the top Marine general here said in a recent interview.

Maj. Gen. Henry C. Stackpole III, commander of Marine Corps Bases in Japan, said Japan will beef up "what is already a very, very potent military" if U.S. forces withdraw.

"No one wants a rearmed, resurgent Japan," the general said. "So we are a cap in the bottle, if you will."…

"The Japanese consider themselves racially superior," he said. "They feel they have a handle on the truth, and their economic growth has proved that.

"They have achieved the Greater Asia Co-Prosperity Sphere economically, without guns," he added, referring to the Asian empire that Japan lost when it was defeated in World War II by the United States.

米海兵隊最大の海外基地沖縄の第7艦隊航空母艦の母港である横須賀は、常に東京支局の取材対象だ。この記事は、沖縄の海兵隊司令官との現地インタビューによるもので、「ビンの蓋」論は、日本の安全保障論の key words の1つにもなった。中国や韓国など過去のいきさつから対日不信がいまだ根強い周辺アジア諸国の中で、日本が信頼を得、軍事的に突出しないためには、日米の軍事的つながりが緊要であるという論理である。93年秋、沖縄の少女暴行事件で、日米安保体制そのものも議論の対象となった。中にはアメリカに対する日本の「dependency」、即ち「ビンの蓋」が、「creates an unhealthy situation in which the United States is sometimes made to look more concerned for Japan's security than the Japanese」(95/11/6

海兵隊の将軍「米軍は日本に駐留しなければならない」

フレッド・ハイアット

1990年3月27日

キャンプ・バトラー・沖縄発──少なくとも今後10年間、米軍の部隊は、主に日本の再軍備を防ぐために、この国に留まらねばならない、と最近のインタビューで当地海兵隊を司る将軍が述べた。

在日海兵隊司令官ヘンリー・C・スタックポール将補は、もし米軍が引き上げれば、日本は、「すでに大変な能力をもつ軍隊」を、さらに増強するだろうと述べた。

「再起し、軍備を再び備えた日本など誰も望まない。だから、こんな言い方はどうかね、我々はビンの蓋なんだ」と将軍は言った……。

「日本人は、自らを人種的に優った民族と見做している。自分たちこそ、真実の手がかりを掴んでおり、経済成長がそれを証明したと考えている」とつけ加え、さらに、「彼らは銃を用いずに、経済的に大東亜共栄圏を作り上げた」と第2次大戦で米国に敗れた際に日本が失ったアジア帝国にも言及した。

editorial) という主張も見られた。なお、この事件でWPは米メディアとしては最初に沖縄入りし、「Over the years, the Okinawa people have been angered by rapes and murders committed by U.S. servicemen stationed here …」(95/9/20 By Mary Jordan) との記事を掲載、米政府に事態の深刻さを早く知らせるのに役だったという (Ezra Vogel 談)。

ower' to New Home Port in Japan

Rebuilding Military Ties to Tokyo

By Daniel Williams

February 19, 1995

The Clinton administration has embarked on a quiet, intense, year-long round of talks with Japan to rejuvenate U.S. military links with Tokyo, in part to repair hard feelings over President Clinton's heavy focus on trade during the first half of his term in office.

As the administration hammered Japan to open its markets to U.S. goods, intelligence and defense officials became alarmed that the military relationship was left to languish and Japan would drift on its own. That process, if allowed to continue, would raise fears in Asia of Japanese remilitarization, and in Washington of a loss of key U.S. military bases on the Japanese islands....

The talks, dubbed the "Nye initiative," are designed to address with Japan the same kind of post-Cold War identity crisis as that facing NATO: Why maintain tight defense links if there is no enemy to worry about? ....

Nye, in a memo to Secretary of Defense William J. Perry, proposed talks on bilateral, regional, and global cooperation to clear up doubts.

Joseph Samuel Nye, Jr.。Harvard 大学教授。government studies educator, administrator。59歳。見るからのegghead だ。クリントン政権有数の安全保障政策の専門家で、94年秋から95年末まで Assistant Secretary of Defense for International Affairs を務めた。その基本戦略は『*United States Security Strategy for the East Asia-Pacific Region*』(February 95, Departmetn of Defense) にまとめられた。「Foreign Affairs」誌の July/August 95号にも「East Asian Security: The Case for Deep Engagement」を執筆。「In the long term, the U.S. and Japan have a balanced, interdependent security relationship.... Japan provides forward bases (前方展開基地) for the American presence and serves as the

東京との軍事的なつながりを再構築する

ダニエル・ウィリアムズ

1995年2月19日

日本との軍事的なつながりを再活性化するため、クリントン政権は、静かにではあるが、強い意志のもとに、1年に及ぶ東京との話し合いに乗り出した。目的の1つは、クリントン大統領が任期の前半、貿易問題に重点を置いたがために生じた悪感情を修復することにあった。

クリントン政権が、アメリカ製品に市場を開放するよう、日本をがんがん叩いているうちに、情報や国防関係の高官達は、日本との軍事関係が弱まるのではないか、この国は1人歩きを始めるのではないかという、危惧の念を抱き始めた。もし、このような事態が進み続けるなら、アジアには、日本が再び軍国主義化するのではないかという恐怖が生まれ、ワシントンは、日本列島上の重要な米軍の基地を失うことになる……。

「ナイ・イニシアティブ」と呼ばれる一連の話し合いは、ポスト冷戦期のNATOが直面しているのと同様の問題を、日本へも話しかけるのを目的にしていた。即ち、組織の存在理由が問われる危機、心配すべき敵がいないのに、なぜ、緊密な軍事的関係を維持しなければならないのか、という点である……。

こうした疑念を払拭するため、ナイは、ウィリアム・ペリー国防長官に、2国間、地域的、世界的という3段階の協力関係について話し合う覚え書きを提出した。

---

cornerstone of our security strategy for the entire region.」と、冷戦後の日米安保の意義を明確に論じた。同誌には、Chalmers Johnson (President of Japan Policy Research Institute) ら、安保条約解消論者の意見も載っているが、彼らは「forget that our engagement is not a "favor" we're doing for anyone else, but rather reflects our own interests in the region」と、東京のFCCJで力強く訴えた。その当日9月4日の夜、沖縄であの忌まわしい事件が起きるなど、誰が予想しただろう。

For Clinton in Japan: Accord and Smiles

By Mary Jordan & Kevin Sullivan

April 19, 1996

Japan's agreement to reexamine its military responsibilities to the United State represents the biggest shift in Japanese military policy since the U.S.–Japanese alliance was forged after World War II.... There words are taken here to mean that U.S. and Japanese defense officials soon will meet to draw up plans about the kind of immediate backup Washington can rely on if war were to break out, say, on the Korean Peninsula....

Some critics in the United States protest that the agreement is nothing more than a bag of air, a foreign policy bonbon in an election year....

Ignorance Isn't Bliss: What We Don't Know About Japan

By Kevin Sullivan

April 14, 1996

Especially for students, China is more hip than Japan. It's the East's Wild West, unpredictable, romantic and dangerous. Japan is Dad's blue suit: dependable but dull.

Japan may be an economic giant and one of America's most vital trading partners, but it is losing its grip on the American imagination. "Japan bashing" has given way to what many call "Japan passing."....

96年4月の President Clinton の訪日は、湾岸戦争以来、アメリカ側にあった「いざという時に日本は頼りに出来るのか」という不信感を、一応は払うことが出来た。極東有事の際の日本の対米協力の研究、平時やPKO における役務の提供などを約し、日米安保条約の意義を「アジア太平洋の平和と安定に資する」と明言したからだ。だからこそ、沖縄・普天間基地の返還も可能となったのだろう。だが、日本にとっては大変な決断であっても、一般のアメリカ人にとっては、So What ではないか、という点に答えようとして書かれたのが初めの記事だ。その結論は、平和時の役務提供について「Once two armies have joint maneuvers in peacetime, it is inconceivable they would not work together at time of

日本でのクリントン：合意と笑顔

メアリー・ジョーダン ＆ ケヴィン・サリヴァン

1996年4月19日

アメリカに対する軍事的な責任を再考するという日本の合意は、第2次大戦後、日米間で同盟が構築されて以来、最大の軍事政策上の変化である……。(橋本総理の)こうした言葉は、当地では、アメリカと日本の防衛当局者がまもなく話し合い、もしも、朝鮮半島で戦端が開かれた場合、ワシントンが即座に頼りにできるような計画を策定するととらえている。

アメリカにおける評論家の一部は、この合意には膨らんだ風船のように中身はなく、大統領選挙の年にあたっての、外交上の点稼ぎに過ぎないと批判する……。

知らぬが仏とはまいらない：日本について知らないこと

ケヴィン・サリヴァン

1996年4月14日

とくにアメリカの学生にとって、中国のほうが日本よりもかっこいいのだ。東のワイルドウエスト、西部の荒野だ。何が起きるのか予測できない。ロマンチックで危険に満ちている。日本は、親父のダークスーツ。頼りになるけれど、退屈だ。

日本は、経済の巨人で、アメリカの最重要な貿易相手国の一つかも知れない。しかし、アメリカ人の想像力をかきたてる力を失った。「ジャパン・バッシング」が、多くの人の呼び方によれば「ジャパン・パッシング」にとって代わられたのだ……。

crisis.」と述べる元外交官で安全保障問題の専門家岡崎久彦の言葉で終えている。

次の記事は、マスコミがとかく注目しない、環境や犯罪対策など、いわゆる common agenda に着目。とくに、アメリカ人の学生をもっと日本で学ばそうという計画を掘り下げ、日米間のcredibility gap の原因にまで踏み込み、本社でもかなりの反響があった。

4. Japan and Its Neighbors (Russia, China, Korea)
周辺諸国(露中韓)と日本

WPのAssistant Managing Editor for Foreign News(外報担当編集局次長)のJackson Diehlに、WPにおける日本のニュース価値について聞いた。「Japan is very important as compared to any other countries except Russia. Russia is permanent, constant. Others are more situational.」。たしかに、本社と直通の電話回線があるのはモスクワ支局だけだし、特派員の数も多かった。だからであろうか、東京へ赴任する記者達も、日ソ、現在は日露関係に常に大きな興味を示してきた。

Eduard Shevardnadze, Mikhail and Raisa Gorbachev, Boris Yeltsinら90年代に入ってからは要人の来日は詳細にカバーする。アメリカにとっての重要な関心事は北方領土問題と日本の対露援助の2点だ。もちろん、両者は密接にからんでいる。

寒風が頬を刺す早春の納沙布岬を訪れ、北方4島の元島民を取材した。「And yet, to a visiting American, this frigid peninsula arching out from Hokkaido, Japan's northern island, is most reminiscent (思い出させる) of south Florida. It's not the weather, obviously, that brings Miami to mind. It's the politics.」(91/3/18 By Tom Reid)。元島民達は、マイアミにいるキューバ難民に似ているというのだ。彼らはともに、「were driven from their island homes by Communists and who have made their plight (苦境) a burning public issue that dominates political discourse (論議)」。そして、「We feel the same way the Kuwaitis did when their home was taken. We feel we have a right to get our land back, just like they did.」という元島民の言葉が大きくうたわれている。

ただし、記事の流れは、4島返還を主張する日本の立場に全面的に共感するというわけではない。「but the dispute over the islands threatens to doom progress in those areas.」と

いう表現や Yeltsin 訪日時の「World War II Territorial Dispute May Block Progress in Talks」(93/10/12 By Tom Reid) といった見出しにも、それは現れている。「Are these islands really worth sacrificing relations with Russia?」「But after all, didn't Japan lose the war?」といった議論が、前から支局で交わされたものだ。

　国際社会が対露支援に乗り出す中、日本はどうするか。島をとるのか国際協調をとるのか。「Japan Clears Way For Aid to Russia, Tokyo Drops Link to Dispute Over Islands」(93/3/25 By Paul Blustein) の中で明快にこう書いている。国際的な圧力を受けた日本は「is relaxing—though not abandoning—its long-standing policy of withholding large-scale assistance for Moscow unless progress is made toward the return of disputed islands held by Russia.」。

　日本の周辺諸国の中で、中韓両国は、過去の戦争の傷痕を一番強く残している。いわゆる日本の戦争責任や謝罪問題は次の章で触れるとして、現在の日本と両国との関係をWPはどのようにとらえてきたか。

　経済成長を続ける中国市場は、アメリカにとってあらためて重要な意味をもってきた。対中貿易赤字が増え、日本に替わる貿易摩擦が起きるという声も出る一方、時代は「Japan Bashing」から「Japan Passing」へと変わったと懸念する向きもある。大陸の市場——特に中国、やがてロシア——をめぐり、日米両国は健全な競争と協調の途を今から確立しなければならない。それこそが太平洋戦争の最大の教訓だというのはかねがね思ってきた所だが、その意味で、天安門事件直後の興味深い記事がある「For Some Japanese, It's Business as Usual in China」(89/6/16 By Fred Hiatt)。アメリカが人権にこだわり、対中関係に厳しい態度をとっているうちに、日本は漁夫の利を占めるのではないかという懸念と怒りが見え隠れする。「Japanese businessmen who evacuated China last week are streaming back to Beijing, pleasing the Chinese government but creating concern here that

Japan may open itself to international criticism for returning too quickly to business as usual.」。

　米メディアの東京特派員は、すべて朝鮮半島の特派員をかねている。この数十年、日本以上に激動を続ける韓国へ、何度緊急取材に飛び出していったかわからない。韓国と日本との現在の関わりにも、やはり「過去」が濃く色をおとしている。

　たとえば、「S. Koreans Almost Sink Sea of Japan Plan」(94/9/24 By Tom Reid) という記事。日本人が「日本海」と呼ぶ両国間の海は、断固、「東海」と呼ぶべきだと韓国が主張、国際会議が危うく失敗しそうになったという内容だ。日本海の汚染の問題を討議する日中韓露による国連主催の会議が、突然韓国の抗議で中断する。理由は、汚染問題とは関係ない。「Rather, the outrage was directed at three words at the top of the document: "Sea of Japan." Around the world, virtually all maps and all international geographic organizations agree that the body of water between Japan and the Asian mainland is the Sea of Japan. But in Korea, those words evoke angry memories of Japan's brutal 40-year occupation of Korea in the first half of this century.」。結局、韓国内ではすべての政府機関の地図は、外国語も含め、「East Sea」または「Tonghae」とせよという命令が改めて出され、国連の書類は、海に名前をつけず、緯度と経度で表現することで事態は決着した。

　また、在日朝鮮人の問題は、人権擁護の観点を含め、何度も記事になっている。「Koreans in Japan Excluded From Growing Prosperity」(84/9/4 By John Burgess) では、President Chun Doo Hwanの来日を控え、「Chun to Seek Better Treatment」と、この件が外交問題となっていることを伝える。「Japan's Koreans Still Struggling, Opposing Factions Seem to Share Common Enemy: Discrimination」(90/5/20 By Fred Hiatt) では、祖国が分断されているように、日本国内でも在日朝鮮人は2つに分かれているが、差別にあっている点は同じだとし、「Still, resistance to assimilation (同化。この場合は、日本に帰化すること)

remains widespread among Koreans here. They resist, in part, because they believe they will face the same prejudice（偏見）anyway—from Japanese companies as well as from prospective in-laws（これから結婚する相手の家族のこと）, who often hire detectives to search out any hint of non-Japanese ancestry.」と書いている。

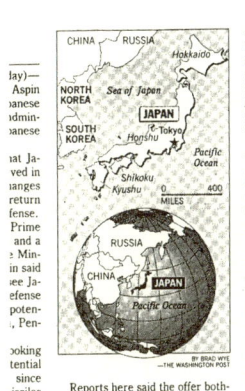

CHAPTER 3: THE LEGACY OF THE PACIFIC WAR

1. The Scars of Pearl Harbor

In Japan, No Regrets on WW II

By John Saar

December 7, 1976

Although President Franklin Roosevelt called it "a date which will live in infamy," December 7, 1941, is not a date Japanese schoolchildren are encouraged to remember....

Koei Honda, 43, is one of many teachers troubled that the majority of children in Japan grow up ignorant of World War II or learn a version of it that most Americans would agree is incorrect. "We have many children who think Japan did no wrong in the Pacific war." Honda said.

For Americans, Pearl Harbor is synonymous with duplicity and treachery. Japanese history books convey no contrition for the surprise attack.

The deepest discrepancies lie in the interpretation of events that led up to Pearl Harbor. In the Western view, Japan fell into the hands of blindly aggressive militarists and expansionists who wanted to colonize China and other Asian countries to get markets and raw materials. While conceding that the war was a mistake, almost every current Japanese textbook says the war was forced on Japan the oil and economic sanctions applied by the United States and other nations.

ほぼ20年前に書かれた記事ではあるが、真珠湾をめぐる日米間の問題点が入っている。まず、戦争の根本原因について。アメリカは「an expansionist war involving surprise attack, cruel mistreatment and every kind of evil thing」と見るのに対し、日本は、「after mistakenly invading China, Japan surrounded by hostile powers, was going to be choked and made a war for survival.」（衛藤瀋吉東大教授の言葉など）とする。日本では終戦後、連合軍により、「biased version laying exclusive emphasis on Japanese culpability (罪過)」のみが教えられたが、バランスを取り戻したのが今の姿だというのだ。次に、日本では戦争を十分に教えていないという点。日本人の大半は、戦争は悪いと思いつつも「prefers to ... buried in the

第3章 太平洋戦争の遺産

1. 真珠湾攻撃の傷跡

日本では、第2次世界大戦の反省なし

ジョン・サール　　　　　　　　　　　1976年12月7日

フランクリン・ルーズヴェルト大統領が、「最も恥ずべき行いの日として、永久に記憶の中に生きる日」と呼んだにもかかわらず、1941年12月7日は、日本の子供たちにとって、覚えておくように奨励される日付けではない……。本多公栄(43)は、日本の子供の大半が、第2次大戦について無知なまま大人になるか、ほとんどのアメリカ人が同意するような見解は間違っているとする解釈を学ぶことに問題を感じている多くの教師の1人だ。「太平洋戦争で、日本は間違ったことを何もしていないと思っているたくさんの子供たちがいる」と本多は語る。アメリカ人にとって、真珠湾とは、二枚舌と裏切りの同義語だ……。日本の歴史書には、奇襲に対する深い悔悟の色は見られない……。もっとも深刻な不一致は、真珠湾攻撃を引き起こすに至った事態をめぐる解釈にある。西側の見解では、日本は、市場と原材料を獲得するために中国や他のアジア諸国の植民地化を目論む盲目的に侵略を企てる軍国主義者と拡張主義者の手に落ちたのだ。それに対して、現在の日本のほとんどの教科書は、戦争は失敗だったと認めるものの、それは、合衆国や他の国々による石油と経済の制裁によって強いられたとする。

---

distant past」。中、韓両国といわゆる教科書問題が起きるのは1982年半ばのことである。第3が、事前通告の遅れ。1994年秋、外務省が初めて通告遅延の関係書類を公表した時、Tom Reidは、この問題は「not widely known among Americans」(11/22)で、通告の有無に関わりなく「it was morally wrong for Japan to start a war no matter what the circum-stances」という立場があると書いている。

The Day Washington Found Its Future

By Haynes Johnson

December 7, 1991

Everything that went before represented the old America, an America that would never be the same. Everything that came after stood for a new America emerging reluctantly, painfully out of self-imposed and smug isolation to center stage on the world scene....

America was taken by surprise, but war came as no surprise to Washington. For months the capital had been on an intense war footing.... By Pearl Harbor Day, the capital had been transformed into the greatest boomtown in the world.

The Day The War Hit Home

By Katharine Graham

December 7, 1991

It was the sort of news you hear, but don't believe, can't believe.

I was 24, recently married and working on *The Post*'s editorial page. That Sunday I was attending a luncheon party given by my mother.... She had quite a lot of people that day, the usual mix—government, press, business, and others.

It's funny, but I can't remember how the news came....

The strongest memory I have is the reaction—how stunned we felt, how horrified. Everybody was in pieces.

1991年12月7日付のWPは、真珠湾関係の記事で溢れた。政治記者のなかで、David Broder と並ぶ双璧 Haynes Johnson が1面の特集「50 Years After Pearl Harbor」で書いたのが上記第1の記事だ。興味深いのは、一般大衆の無関心とは裏腹に、41年12月7日のWP 朝刊も、戦争の切迫を伝える記事が溢れていたという下りだ。1面では、UP 通信東京7日発が「Japan indicated early today that she stands on the verge of abandoning efforts to achieve settlement of the Pacific crisis by diplomatic negotiation at Washington」、日本政府のスポークスマンは「Japan's patience may be tried only a little longer」と言い、op-ed 欄には「We Face a World War」の大見出しが躍った。真珠湾奇襲の知らせに、ある政府職員は、誰も

ワシントンが未来を見つけた日

ヘインズ・ジョンソン　　　　　　　　　　1991年12月7日

それ以前に起きたことは、すべて古き良きアメリカ、二度と同じ姿を見せることはないアメリカを体現していた。それ以降に起きたことは、すべて新しいアメリカの大義に立っていた。自ら課していた独善的な孤立主義から、ためらい、苦しみつつも、世界の桧舞台へと登場するアメリカである……。アメリカ自体は、不意をつかれたが、ワシントンにとって、戦争は驚きではなかった。もう何ヵ月もの間、合衆国の首都は厳しい臨戦体制下にあった……。真珠湾の日までに、世界で最も活気のある都市に変容していたのだ。

戦争が故郷を直撃した日

キャサリン・グレアム　　　　　　　　　　1991年12月7日

それは、たとえ耳にしても、信じようともしなければ、信じることもできない類のニュースでした。私はまだ結婚したばかりの24歳で、ポストの論説担当のセクションで働いていました。その日曜日、私は、母の主催する昼食会に出席していました……。その日、母はたくさんの人を招待し、いつも通り、政府、報道、財界その他各方面の方達が来ていました。奇妙なことですが、私は、そのニュースがどのようにして伝わったのか覚えていません……。鮮明な記憶は、みんなの反応でした。どれほど驚き、どれほど恐れおののいたことか。私たちはみんな、ばらばらになってしまったのでした。

がそう考えたように「なすべきことはただ1つ。Get in there and beat the living hell out of them now. They've got it coming.」と考える。第2の記事の筆者は、アメリカで最も影響力のある女性の五指に常に入る Katharine Graham WP 会長だ。「The Day the War Hit Home」という特集に寄稿したものである。

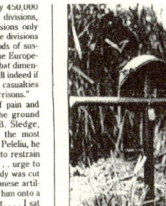

Japanese Dove: My Grandfather Tried to Prevent Pearl Harbor

By Shigehiko Togo

December 5, 1993

As negotiations got underway, Togo's real opponent was not the United States but the Japanese military. For two weeks, at the "Liaison Conference" between the government and the military high command, he sought a compromise....

Many generals and officers in the Japanese high command called the Hull note a "help from heaven."

For Togo and the Japanese government, it was "an ultimatum without time limit." Acceptance, Togo recalled, would kill "the honor and the prestige of the nation." ....

When Roosevelt read only the first parts of the intercepted message on the evening of December 6, he said, "This means war." ....

But because of executive and clerical hitches in the embassy, its delivery was carried out only after the attack on Peal Harbor took place. The delay was inexcusable, but not intentional. Yet the anger of the American people was further aroused by the "stab in the back."

私事になるが、93年秋から半年間、本社で勤務した。その時の真珠湾記念日にあわせ、Outlook に書いた記事である。10年がかりで祖父の伝記を出版した直後のことで、その経験を書いたらという話だった。アメリカ人にも理解しうる形で、開戦時の外相、即ち、日本政府の公式の和平努力を、短い紙面に凝縮するのに苦心した。陸軍と対立しながら大陸からの撤兵をどう図ろうとしたか。アメリカはすでに「lost trust and patience with Japan's aggression on the Asian continent」という状態で、President Roosevelt は「was eager to join the war in Europe, to help Britain and put an end to Nazism」だったこと。Hull noteがいかに和平派に打撃を与えたか。交渉打ち切りの通告は、戦争布告の意図が充分に相手方に伝わるもので、遅

日本の鳩派、祖父は真珠湾攻撃を阻止しようとした

東郷茂彦　　　　　　　　　　　　　　　　　　　　1993年12月5日

日米交渉が進むにつれ、東郷の真の敵は、アメリカではなく、日本の軍部であることが明らかになっていった。2週間にわたる大本営と政府の連絡会議で、彼は、妥協案を模索した……。

　統帥部の将軍や将校達は、ハル・ノートを「天佑なり」と呼んだ。
　東郷と日本政府にとって、それは、「タイム・リミットなき最後通牒」であった。受け入れることは「国家の誇りと威信」を葬り去ることになる、と東郷は回想している……。
　12月6日に傍受された電文の冒頭だけを読んだルーズヴェルト大統領は、こう言った。「これは戦争を意味する」……。
　しかし、ワシントンの日本大使館幹部ならびにスタッフによる事務上の不手際のため、電報が届けられたのは、真珠湾が攻撃された後になったのだ。遅延は、許されざる行為ではあったが、意図したものではなかった。だが、「卑怯きわまりない背後からの一撃」により、アメリカ国民の怒りが、一気に燃え上がったのだ。

延は決して意図的ではなかったこと。さらに米側に交渉で事態を打開するつもりはなく、「its attitude cannot be described as truly peaceful. Negotiation implies give and take」という祖父の言葉を記した。掲載後、電話や手紙、直接のメッセージなどが二十数件寄せられたが批判的なものはなく、「I didn't know about it」「such a moving story」といった類だけだった。

2. The Rights and Wrongs of the Atomic Bombs

Doves Fill Sky over Hiroshima

By T. R. Reid

August 7, 1992

HIROSHIMA—A hard rain fell near the end of today's memorial exercise, but there were no hard words. There was no mention of Pearl Harbor. There was barely a word of criticism of the Japanese leaders who took their people into World War II in the first place, or of the American leaders who sought to end it—and did, in a matter of days—by dropping their new weapon on a largely civilian target.

Rather, the A-bomb was treated, as it always is here, as some tragic truth of the world that floats in the memory free of history, free of cause and blame, free of politics and power.

This tendency to focus on the disaster itself rather than its causes reflects the approach of Japanese society as a whole toward World War II. It is an attitude that has made Japan somewhat less candid than its Axis ally, Germany, in facing up to responsibility for the war.

At the same time, that keen awareness of past agonies has given the people of Japan in general and Hiroshima in particular a sense of personal obligation to act as a collective conscience of the world in an effort to make sure that nuclear weapons are never used again.

原爆はなぜ落とされたのか。太平洋の戦いの終結を早めるため、というのがアメリカの大方の見方である。94年の暮れ、第2次大戦の米製記念切手に、キノコ雲と「Atomic bomb hasten war's end, August 1945」の caption 付の原爆切手が、さも当然のように登場したのは、そうした国民感情があるからだ。日本人が原爆体験を「人類への警鐘」として受け止め、平和運動の原点とする生き方は、アメリカからは戦争の正当化につながるように見られかねないのだ。

94年6月、広島の原爆資料館に東館が加わった。戦争への道筋と経過を展示した新館は、従ってアメリカのメディアからは日本の好ましい変化の象徴として受けとめられる。NYT の David Sanger は、それまでは「they could easily be forgiven for thinking

2. 原爆は正しかったか

広島の空に満ちる鳩の群れ

トム・リード　　　　　　　　　　　　　　　　1992年8月7日

広島発——今日の記念式典が終わりを迎える頃強い雨が降り出した。しかし、強い言葉を聞くことはできなかった。真珠湾への言及もなかった。第一義的に第2次大戦へと自国民を引っ張っていった日本の指導者、あるいは、大部分は民間施設であった標的に新兵器を落とすことにより戦争を終わらせようとした—事実、数日のうちに終わった——アメリカの指導者に対する批判はほんの少しはあった。

だが何よりも、原爆は、この国ではいつもそうであるように、歴史、因果、責任、さらには政治と権力から隔絶した記憶の中に自由に漂う、世界の悲劇的真実として扱われた。

原爆投下の原因より、原爆の惨事そのものに関心を集中するこうした傾向は、第2次大戦に対する日本社会全体の態度を表している。このような態度のおかげで、戦争責任を問われた時、日本は、枢軸側の同盟国ドイツよりもどこか素直さに欠けるようになってしまった。

同時に、この過去の苦しみに対する鋭い自覚は、核兵器が二度と用いられないようにするために、世界の良心をまとめて行動に移す1人ひとりの義務感を、日本人、特に広島の人々に対して植えつけた。

---

that World War II started on Aug. 6 1945」(94/8/5 IHT) だったが、ようやく「Hiroshima Takes Fresh Look at Why Bomb Fell」(IHT 見出し) と書いた。Tom Reid は「this display depicts Japan's brutal effort to conquer and colonize East Asian countries, and shows how Japan's aggression in Asia and at Pearl Harbor led directly to the mighty bomb」(95/8/6) と報じ、戦争について、教科書や受験でも扱うようになったとしている。

Kurosawa's 'August' Fallout

By T. R. Reid

March 27, 1991

In the crucial scene between the strong Japanese heroine and a somewhat wimpy Gere, Kurosawa quite clearly forgives America for dropping history's only A-bombs on his country.

For Japanese audiences, this act of forgiveness is an interesting and perhaps touching development. But in the West, it will provoke obvious questions: Is it really America that needs to be forgiven for the tragedies of World War II? Why doesn't this movie ever point out that Japan started the war? Why focus on Nagasaki and ignore what Japan did at Nanking, Pearl Harbor, Bataan?

Japan Ignites A firestorm Over Atom Bombings

By Paul Blustein

March 16, 1995

Japan's long-simmering anger over the U.S. atomic bombings of Hiroshima and Nagasaki burst to the surface today as the mayors of those two cities condemned the United States for the nuclear attack, with Nagasaki's mayor likening the 1945 bombings to Hitler's genocidal killing of Jews.

"I think that the atomic bombings were one of the two greatest crimes against humanity in the twentieth century, along with the Holocaust," said Hitoshi Motoshima, Nagasaki's mayor, in a speech to the Foreign Correspondents' Club here.

多くの、とくに一定の年齢以上のアメリカ人にとって、第2次大戦は完全なる正義の戦いであった。それに、少しでも抵触するような物言いがあると、針ネズミが全身を逆立てるように反発する。黒沢明監督の「八月の狂詩曲」で、長崎の老婆がアメリカを「許す」という筋立てに対する反応も、そうした心情を元にしている。ワシントンの Smithsonian's National Air and Space Museum での、広島へ原爆を投下したEnola Gay機の展示計画が紛糾した根も同じだろう。WP の editorial (95/2/1) は、原爆の悲惨さと人類の未来への脅威をも展示に加えようとした当初の案は、「Narrow-minded representatives of a special-interest and revisionist point of view」によるもので、当時の大多数のアメリカ人が「witnessed and

黒沢が「8月」に落とした死の灰

トム・リード

1991年3月27日

力強い日本人のヒロインとどこか弱虫のようなギアが展開する最も大事なシーンにおいて、黒沢はきわめて明確に歴史上唯一彼の国に対して落とされた原爆に関し、アメリカを許している。日本の観客にとって、この許しの行為は、興味深く、おそらくは感動的な場面なのだろう。しかし、西側においては次のような明白な疑問を引き起こす。果たして、第2次大戦の悲劇を許されるべきは、本当にアメリカだろうか。なぜ、この映画は、日本人が戦争を始めたという事実を一切指摘しないのか。なぜ、長崎だけに注目し、南京、真珠湾、バターンにおける日本の行為を無視するのであろうか。

原爆投下論争に火をつける日本

ポール・ブルースティン

1995年3月16日

長きにわたってぐつぐつと煮え続けてきた広島、長崎への原爆投下に対する日本の怒りは、この水曜日、両市の市長が米国の核攻撃を糾弾したことにより、一気に表面化した。なかでも長崎市長は、1945年の爆撃をヒットラーによるユダヤ人の大量虐殺に結びつけた。

「原爆投下はホロコーストと並び、20世紀における人類への最も大きな2つの犯罪のうちの1つと考える」と本島長崎市長は、当地の外人記者クラブにおけるスピーチで述べた。

---

understood」していた「historical event」を「hollow out (空洞化)」すると非難した。FCCJ での広島、長崎両市長の会見で最も印象的だったのは 「How can you compare the Holocaust to Hiroshima and Nagasaki? All Jews who had been killed did nothing wrong. But the A-bombs were a war action and at least brought an undeniable end to the war.」という、普段は冷静なPaulの涙を流さんばかりの怒りだった。

Apologies for Hiroshima?

Editorial

April 15, 1995

Mr. Clinton is right on both points and need not have added that cautious qualification. Japanese politicians are unwise to keep pressing this point, since it only recalls the questions about who started the war and how the aggressors conducted it....

Against that claim you have to set, among other things, the reality of the battle for Okinawa,...

The chances of an early and voluntary surrender in the homeland were poor.

The nuclear bombs were a success in the crucial sense that they were followed by an immediate end to the fighting with no further American deaths. The immense casualties in the bombings were largely civilian, but that is true of any bombing of large cities, whether nuclear or conventional.

By John F. Harris

April 8, 1995

Additionally, Clinton was asked whether the United States owes Japan an apology for using two atomic bombs to end World War II and whether President Harry S. Truman had made the right decision. Clinton replied: "No, and based on the facts he had before him, yes."

President Clinton が、テキサス州ダラスで開かれた新聞人の会議で、原爆投下の是非について言及した上記第2の記事は、大統領と議会の政治闘争関連ニュースの最後に添えられただけだった。まもなく、東京から日本国内の反応について出稿される。「Clinton Comment Stirs Demands for A-Bomb Apology」(4/14 By Tom Reid)。村山首相の日本人記者団に対する「日本人の気持ちに少しは思いやりをもって欲しかった」、江藤隆美衆議院議員のWPによるインタビューでの「原爆は indiscriminate slaughter of civilians」であり、大統領は「Using the bomb was a mistake」と言って欲しい、さもなければ「the logic of his position will be that anything is justifiable if you win, and that is a completely unethical stance」という2つの発言が伝えられた。この

広島へ謝罪するのか？

社説
                                1995年4月15日

クリントン氏は、両方の点で正しく、注意深い但し書きを付け加える必要などありはしない。日本の政治家が、この点[謝罪]を要求し続けるのは賢いことではない。なぜなら、それは、誰が戦争を始め、どのようにして侵略戦へ導かれたのかという質問を喚起するにすぎないからだ……。

このような主張に対しては、何よりも沖縄戦の現実に目を据えなければならない……。

[日本]本土決戦で、早期かつ自発的な降伏の可能性は、極めて低かった。

核爆弾の投下に引き続き、日本は即座に降伏し、さらなるアメリカ兵の犠牲者をもたらさなかったという重要な点で、原爆は成功であったといえる。大量の犠牲者の多くは民間人だったが、大都市への空襲は、核兵器であろうが通常兵器だろうが、同じような結果をもたらすのだ。

ジョン・F・ハリス
                                1995年4月8日

さらに、クリントンは、第2次大戦を終結させるために2つの原爆を用いたことについて、日本に謝らねばならないかどうか、そしてハリー・トルーマン大統領が、正しい決定を下したかどうか尋ねられた。「まず最初は、ノー。次に、トルーマンが直面した事実から判断すれば、イエス」とクリントンは答えた。

問題については、この年の8月6日に広島を訪れた米平和運動家の言葉もこう伝えている。「A key reason we wanted to make this apology to Hiroshima was that President Clinton earlier this year said that no apology was necessary. Well, it may be that the government is not in a position to apologize, but some of us Americans can act on our own.」(8/7 By Tom Reid)。

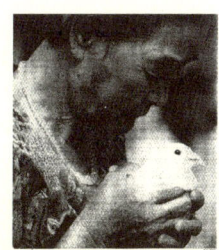

3. The Underside of War

WW II Germ Deaths Laid to Japan

By John Saar

November 19, 1976

Japanese scientists killed at least 3,000 Chinese prisoners during World War II through bacteriological warfare experiments and escaped prosecution by sharing their findings with American occupation forces, a Japanese television documentary has alleged.

They were not prosecuted, according to a journalist who has investigated the death unit for three years, and some now hold eminent positions in government and leading universities.

Five former members of the unit told television reporter Haruko Yoshinaga they were promised complete protection in return for cooperation with U.S. authorities. [Press officers at the U.S. Defense and Justice Departments said they had no information on the charges but would investigate.]

By Tracy Dahlby

May 26, 1983

HARBIN, China—In contrast to the Nazi death camps in Europe in World War II, Harbin's holocaust left no surviving victims to tell the tale. Han Xiao and his team of investigators have pieced together their picture of atrocities by methodically sifting through human bones and other debris left among the ruins of the 731st's camp. They have also interviewed many of the 500 villagers still alive who were forced to serve as laborers at the germ factory.

WP東京支局で勤務し始めてまだ1ヵ月もたたない11月初め、なにげなくつけたテレビのドキュメンタリー番組で、731部隊に触れた時の衝撃はいまだに忘れられない。この記事がきっかけになり、オランダやイギリスのメディアが取材に動いたという。森村誠一の『悪魔の飽食』のちょうど5年前の話である。日本軍の残虐行為については、戦後50年を機に、欧米では多くの出版がなされている。中でも話題の書が『Prisoners of the Japanese: POWs of World War II in the Pacific』だった。オーストラリアの歴史家・運動家である著者 Gavan Daws へのインタビューを元にした「The Prisoners A World Forgot … Calling Japan on War Crimes」(95/3/16 By Ken Ringle) は、処刑直前の連合軍捕虜の写真などを大きく扱い、Style に掲載

3. 戦争の様相

第2次大戦の細菌兵器による死者、日本に突きつけられる

ジョン・サー

1976年11月19日

日本の科学者たちが第2次大戦中、細菌兵器の実験で少なくとも3000人の中国人捕虜を殺害し、米占領軍に実験結果を渡すのと引き換えに訴追を免れた、と日本のテレビドキュメンタリーが報じた。この殺人部隊について3年間調査してきたジャーナリストによれば、(訳注:細菌兵器の実験をした)科学者たちは訴追されず、なかには、政府や有名大学で重要な職についている者さえいる。

この部隊のメンバーであった5人は、テレビの放送記者吉永春子に対し、米国側と協力するかわりに完全な保護を約束されたと述べた……。[米国の国防、司法両省の報道担当官は、このような告発に関する情報はないが、調査をすると返答した]。

トレーシー・ダルビー

1983年5月26日

中国, ハルビン発──第2次大戦中のヨーロッパにおけるナチスの死の収容所とは対照的に、ハルビンのホロコーストには、犠牲者のなかに事実を伝える生存者がいない。(地方政府の役人の)ハン・シャオとその同僚による調査団は、731部隊の駐屯地の廃虚に残された人骨や残骸を組織的に選り分けることによって、残虐行為について調査団としての全体像を描き出した。彼らは、細菌工場で強制労働させられた500人の村民のうち、存命中の多くにインタビューもした。

された。長文の記事の最後は、著者の「with judicious ... good, measured, morally sound pressure from Western nations」によってのみ、「Japan can bite the bullet on this issue and start looking honestly at its past」となり、「until it does, no one, not even the Japanese, can be certain it won't happen again」で終わる。

81

Japan Pursues Debate on 'Rape of Nanking'

By John Burgess

January 25, 1985

The 1937 "Rape of Nanking," a symbol of Japanese brutality during World War II, is under increasing attack from revisionist historians and veterans' groups here as a myth fabricated by the victorious allies.

In articles and books published here in recent months, they concede that some atrocities occurred. But they contend the death toll was nowhere near the 200,000 figure cited during war crimes trials after Japan's surrender in 1945.

"It was absolutely necessary for the trials to have a crime against humanity," said Masaaki Tanaka, author of a new book entitled *The Fiction of the Nanking Massacre*. "In Japan there was no Auschwitz… Therefore they needed Nanking."….

In 1982, Peking reacted angrily when the Japanese Ministry of Education proposed softening school textbook accounts of Japanese brutality in Nanking and other chapters in Japan's long war in China.

A relatively small group of people and organizations is publicly arguing the case. Still, their actions and the publicity they have received offer new evidence that the Japanese are gradually dropping taboos against questioning the victors' account of Japan's conduct in the war.

「Millions of Chinese civilians were gratuitously (いわれなく) slaughtered, 300,000 in a single massacre at Nanjing」(95/8/16 NYT editorial)。南京事件の内容は、欧米では確定したものとして扱われ、数字は一人歩きしている。それに比べると、この記事は日本の実状を正確に伝えようと努めたものだ。「I don't think our mission is to judge. That's not possible. Let's just write objectively two side's views.」といった議論が支局内で交わされた。旧陸軍将校のクラブ偕行社の調査など、「南京事件は東京裁判で初めて世界的な問題となり、犠牲者の数が大幅に改竄拡大された」と主張する「Revisionists」達の見方と、中国へ調査団を送り、従来の説が正しいとする学者らの動きをともに書き込んでいる。一方的な正義感や単純な分類にと

「南京事件」について、日本で異論が起きる

ジョン・バージェス

1985年1月25日

1937年に発生した「南京事件」は、第2次大戦中の日本の蛮行の象徴だが、当地では、修正主義的な歴史家や旧軍人達による批判が強まっている。勝利をおさめた連合国側によって捏造された神話だというのだ。

ここ数ヵ月に出版された本や記事によると、彼らはある程度の残虐行為が行われたのは認めている。しかし、死者の数については、1945年日本の降伏後に行われた東京裁判で言及された20万人とはほど遠いものと主張している。

「裁判上、人道に対する罪が絶対に必要だった」と、出版されたばかりの『「南京虐殺」の虚構』の著者田中正明は述べた。「日本には、アウシュヴィッツがなかった。だから、彼らは、南京を必要としたのだ」……。

1982年、南京での日本の残虐行為や、長期にわたる中国での日本の戦争による行為について記した日本の学校の教科書の内容を、文部省が和らげようとした時、北京は怒りの反応を示した。

この件で、公に議論を展開しているのは、比較的少人数の人達と組織だ。にもかかわらず、彼らの行動、それが世間で注目されたという事実は、日本人が、戦争中の日本の行動に対する勝利者側の説に、異を唱えることについてのタブーを、少しずつ破り始めたことを意味する。

らわれず、戦争を公平かつ客観的に見るのは難しいようだが、WPは「アメリカの強硬姿勢が日本の孤立を誘い、三国同盟に走らせたのではないか。In fact, the U.S.–Japan problem of the 1930s could be encapsulated in a phrase: "The American sentimentalization of China and China policy."」という論文も掲載している (91/11/30 By Edwin M. Yoder Jr.)。

A Long Road Home

By Richard L. Harwood

July 26, 1995

In a memoir of his days as a 19-year-old mortarman with the 5th Marines at Peleliu in the Palau Islands, E.B. Sledge had no remembrance of "wondrous beauty." He remembered dead comrades: "One man had been decapitated. His head lay on his chest; his hands had been severed from his wrists.... [They] had cut off his penis and stuffed it in his mouth....

At Iwo Jima one day, we came across a Japanese soldier, charbroiled by a flame thrower. He wanted water. He got, instead, the lighted end of a cigarette in his mouth, courtesy of a boy from Brooklyn....

E.B. Sledge, who got a doctoral degree and became a teacher of biology in Alabama and a specialist in ornithology, heard the news on Okinawa....

"We received the news with quiet disbelief coupled with an indescribable sense of relief.... Sitting in stunned silence we remembered our dead. So many dead. So many bright futures consigned to the ashes of the past. So many dreams lost in the madness that had engulfed us. The survivors of the abyss sat hollow-eyed, trying to comprehend a world without war."

We cannot comprehend such a world even now. And that is worth remembering as this historic anniversary of victory in the Pacific approaches.

対日戦勝利の記念日をアメリカでは「V-J Day」という。Victory against Japan の略だ。上記の記事は、50回目のV-J Dayを記念したWPのSpecial supplement『Remembering World War II, A Long Road Home』(95/7/26 広告無しの16頁) 冒頭を飾っている。WPの reporter, editor, and ombudsman などを長く務めたRichard Harwood は、自ら太平洋で戦った海兵隊員で、戦争の熱気と虚しさを見事に描いている。ところで、戦後50年にあたり、米政府は日本に気を遣って V-J Day という言葉を使わないことにした。「V-J Day Passé in P.C. Era」(95/3/5 By Tom Reid)。日本が降伏文書に調印した当日の9月2日、米政府の記念式典は、ハワイとワシントンで行われた。「5,000 Attend Ceremony in Arlington to Commemorate

家路への長き道のり

リチャード・ハワード　　　　　　　　　　　　1995年7月26日

海兵隊第5連隊の迫撃砲手として、パラウ諸島ペリリュー島で過ごした19歳の日々の記憶に「驚くような美しさ」はまったくなかった、と E. B. スレッジは回想する。覚えているのは、死んだ仲間のことだ。「1人は、首を切られ、頭が胸の上に乗せられていた。手は、手首の所で切断されていた……。奴らは、ペニスを切り、それを口の中に差し込んでいた」……。硫黄島でのある日、私達は、火炎放射器で黒こげになった日本兵に行き会った。彼は、水をほしがったが、かわりに、ブルックリン出身の若い兵士のお情けで、煙草の火のついた端を口に入れられた……。E. B. スレッジは、やがて、鳥類学の専門家となり、アラバマ州で生物学を教え、博士号を取るのだが、(日本降伏の)ニュースを、沖縄で聞いた……。「そんなことはとても信じられないという冷めた気持ちと、言い表わせないほどの安堵感とのない交ぜになった状態で、その知らせを聞いた……。深い衝撃を受け、沈黙の中に座りこんだ我々は、死んだ仲間のことを考えていた。なんと多くが死んだことか。なんと多くの輝かしい未来が、過去の灰塵に帰したことか。なんと多くの夢が、我々を飲み込んだ狂気の中に散ったことか……。地獄からの生還者達は、呆然と座り、戦争のない世界というものを理解しようと努めた」。今日においても、私達は、このような世界を理解することが出来ない。だからこそ、太平洋における勝利の歴史的な記念日が近づくに当たり、この事実を記憶にとどめなければならないのだ。

V-J Day」(95/9/3 by Peter Finn)。マスコミでは「V-J Day」は禁句ではない。ワシントンでの式典には、戦争中、情報部隊に応召した日系の Yukio Kawamoto と Sayo 夫人もいた。記事はこう結ばれている。「Sayo Kawamoto was in Japan during the war and survived the Tokyo firebombing. "I was the enemy before, but today we are together," she said. "It is an honor."」

4. A Parade of Apologies
   謝罪のオンパレード

アメリカのメディアにとっては、50年前に、自国が、日本を完膚なきまでに武力で叩きのめし、戦犯を処刑するだけでは不十分なようだ。国際正義が実現するために、また、日本が一人前となるためには、自らの犯した行為は非道な侵略であり、誤りであったことを認め、apology（謝罪）することが必要と考え、執拗に追及するかのごとくだ。手元にあるWPの見出しを中心にみていく。まず、日本と周辺アジア諸国との関わりから。

「Finally, Japan Regrets」(90/5/27 Editorial)と書いたのは、韓国の Roh Tae Woo 大統領訪日時である。天皇陛下が、何十年にわたる日本の「stiffness and arrogance」を破り、「offered his country's first explicit apology for its imperial past」というのだ。この時、陛下は、「deepest regret」、お言葉では「痛惜の念」を使われている。戦争に対する対応では、日本とドイツがほとんど必ず単純に比較される。「Japan's Asian neighbors have often criticized this island nation and compared it unfavorably with Germany for its refusal to admit and apologize for its wartime conquests and atrocities (残虐行為).」(5/25 By Fred Hiatt)のように。

その翌年、海部俊樹首相が、東南アジアを歴訪する。「Japan Issues Apology for War Actions, Kaifu Statement Bespeaks (示す) New Japanese World Role」(91/5/4 By Paul Blustein)。シンガポールで「I express sincere contrition (悔悟、演説では「厳しく反省」) at Japanese past actions that inflicted unbearable suffering and sorrow upon a great many people of the Asia–Pacific region」と述べた時だ。

日本が最大の被害をもたらした中国との関わりでは、92年に天皇陛下が訪中された時、「Japanese Emperor to Visit China, Possible Apology of Wartime Actions Generate's

Controversy」(92/8/26 By Tom Reid)、「Emperor Regrets War Act In China, Japan's Akihito Stops Short of an Apology」(92/10/24 By Lena H. Sun)と報じる。この時、陛下は「deep sorrow」、お言葉では「深く悲しみとするところ」を使われた。95年には日本の首相として初めて村山首相が盧溝橋を訪れた。「Japanese Leader Makes Near Apology For World War II Aggression in China」(5/5 By Steven Mufson)。村山は「came as close as any Japanese leader ever has to apologizing for his country's role in the war」という。

　日本の過去の行為の中で、政治問題化した従軍慰安婦について、「'Comfort Women': A Barbaric Act」(92/1/18 Editorial)。この中で「Acts of inhumanity can and do occur when governments go to war」ではあるが、従軍慰安婦は「it was the Imperial Army itself that encouraged and supported that purpose」であり、さらに過去半世紀にわたり、日本政府がこの「notorious degradation（卑しめる行為）of women all over the Pacific theater was the work of private merchants」としてきたことが理解できないと論じている。その後の展開は、「Japan Apologized to Sex Slaves, Premier Cites WWII Abuse of Captive Women」(93/8/5 By Tom Reid)、「Japan to Apologize to "Comfort Women," Prime Minister Plans Letter to WWII Victims」(95/7/13 同)となる。

　アメリカにとっては、日本が真珠湾攻撃について、どのように発言するかが、このところ、極めて強い関心事になる。「Official Voices Japan's "Remorse" Over War」(91/12/4 By Tom Reid)。真珠湾50年のこの時、渡辺美智雄外務大臣がWPとの単独インタビューで、日本としては初めてアメリカに深い悔恨の念を表明したというので、1面最上段を左右にぶち抜く異例の大見出しのトップ記事となった。「we feel a deep remorse about the unbearable suffering and sorrow Japan inflicted on the American people and the peoples of Asia and the Pacific」であり、戦争に突入したのは「because of the reckless decision of our military」なのだと述べている。

1994年6月の天皇陛下訪米の時、真珠湾を御訪問されるかどうかが日米で問題となった。WPは、「訪問し謝罪するのが当然」との論調である。「If Akihito visits Hawaii, he will likely offer new apologies for the Japanese raid.」(94/1/7 同)、「this summer, Japan's Emperor Akihito is scheduled to visit the Pearl Harbor memorial in Honolulu and apologize to Americans for the sneak attack there.」(5/5 同)。結局、真珠湾御訪問は行われなかった。

太平洋戦争全体に対する日本の態度は変化しているのか。

日本の政治家の、いわゆる問題発言も、その度に必ず取り上げられる。「Minister Forced Out Over Defense of Japan's War Role」(88/5/14 By Margaret Shapiro) では、奥野誠亮国土庁長官が「after he refused to apologize or take back his controversial remarks」に、罷免されたと報じた。

ここ数年では、総じて日本には「Some still argue that Japan's conquest of East Asia was a benevolent (善意の) act. Others say Japan was a brutal aggressor.」(95/4/14 By Tom Reid) のように2つの流れがある、と単純化してはいるものの、全体として戦争責任を認める方向に向かっている、と肯定的だ。

細川連立政権下での終戦記念日の記事は「Openly Apologetic, Japan Recalls War's End」(93/8/16 同)。これまで「deep remorse」「self-reflection」としか述べず、学校でも十分に教えて来なかったが、「Times are changing, however」であり、今回は、「willing and evidently eager to face up to the nation's war guilt」というのだ。戦後50年の国会決議は「Japan Expresses 'Remorse' for WWII 'Acts of Aggression'」(95/6/7 同)。この年の終戦記念日の村山総理談話については、「A pacifist and longtime critic of his country's colonial war, Murayama apologized directly to Japan's wartime enemies today in an important speech that goes further, in some ways, than any previous official statement on the war.」(8/16同)。しかしながらアジア諸国の反応はいまだに複雑だ。「But the reaction around Asia was less clear, and it seemed obvious that the 50-year-old question of what kind of Japanese apology would be adequate is still a burning political issue.」。見出しは「Asia Underwhelmed by Japan's Apology」である。

なおNYTも、前北京特派員だったNicholas D. Kristof東京支局長が日本の謝罪問題を幅広く取り上げている。戦後50年国会決議に関連し、「Japan Expresses Regret of a Sort for the War」(6/7)。「THE CHOSEN WORD 反省—Reflections, remorse」「Two WORDS NOT CHOSEN 後悔—remorse, regret 謝罪—Apology」と漢字のイラスト付きだ。その背景に切り込もうとしたが、「Why a Nation of Apologizers Makes One Large Exception」(6/12)、「Why Japan Hasn't Said That Word」(7/5)である。8月15日の村山総理談話を受けては、「Japan Apologizes」(8/16 Editorial)の中で、日本の首相が「finally offered the apology for his nation's World War II conduct that generations of Asians have waited so long to hear.」としている。

Dropped from the exhibit is this picture of Japanese prisoners of war in a Allied camp listening to their emperor's surrender speech.

Len Downie 編集主幹（右）と Bob Kaiser 編集局長（左）
2人で News Conference を主催

Part 2

Financial News
第二部　経済ニュース

WP 外報部

Japan-Basking: New Pacific Era?

By T. R. Reid

June 16, 1991

At a time when the Japan-bashers in the Bos-Wash corridor are matched in fervor by the America-bashers in the Tokaido corridor, when the Tokyo bookstores have set up whole sections just for volumes on the "U.S.–Japan Crisis," when some Democrats are hoping to cast Japan in the Willie Horton role for the next campaign, it is easy to overlook one salient fact about relations between the two richest countries on Earth.

In almost every substantive area, U.S.–Japan relations right now are in excellent shape—considerably healthier, in fact, than America's relations with many other allies.

On security matters, international politics, foreign aid, global environmental problems, you name it, the United States and Japan are in close accord all over the world. Culturally, the Japanese love affair with Mickey Mouse, McDonald's, and M.C. Hammer is matched by Americans' devotion to Super Mario and the Mazda Miata. Even on trade, a recurring source of friction, the statistics are much better now than a few years back....

Why, then, do we keep reading these headlines about "trade war" and "treachery"? The answer may have less to do with facts and more to do with fads in academic and publishing circles.

There are a thousand points of heat in U.S.–Japan trade. But the dynamic of these disputes is as familiar now and as predictable as a TV western or a samurai movie....

While the revisionists focus on the trade arguments, less attention is paid to the settlements. The most striking thing

ジャパン・バースキング(日本を暖める):
新太平洋時代?

T.R. リード

1991年6月16日

かたやボストンからワシントンへと至るアメリカ東海岸のジャパン・バッシャー達。かたや日本の東海道に広がるアメリカ・バッシャー達。両者白熱の取り組みを展開し、東京の書店には「日米危機」関連だけを扱った特別コーナーが設けられ、一部の民主党員は、次の大統領選挙で、日本を(訳注:ブッシュ対デュカキスの大統領選挙で悪の権化として宣伝された)ウイリー・ホートンに仕立て上げたいと願っているまさにその時、この地上で最も豊かな2国間の、ある明白な関わり方を見過ごしてしまうのはたやすいことだ。

日米関係は現在のところ、重要な分野のほとんどすべてにおいて、大変に良好な状態にある。事実、アメリカの他の同盟諸国より、はるかに健全なのだ。

安全保障、国際政治、対外援助、地球的環境問題などあらゆる分野で、日米は世界各地で極めて近い立場にいる。文化面では、ミッキーマウス、マクドナルド、MCハマーに対する日本人の熱烈な思いと、アメリカ人のスーパーマリオやマツダ・ミアータ(訳注:ユーノス・ロードスター)に傾倒するアメリカ人の気持ちが、ぴたり一致する。繰り返し摩擦の原因となってきた貿易面でも、統計は、数年前に比べ、現在の方がはるかに良くなっている……。

では、なぜ「貿易戦争」や「裏切り」といった見出しを、ずっと読むはめに陥っているのだろうか。その答えは、事実が何かということよりも、学会や出版界の流行り廃りによるのかもしれない。

日米間の通商貿易面には、確かに、燃え盛る対立点が無数にある。しかし、こうした紛争の力学は今や周知のものとなり、テレビの西部劇や日本の時代劇映画と同様、筋書きが予想できるようになった……。

about U.S.–Japan trade right now is not the number of disputes, but rather the number that have been resolved....

The force that drives this relentless peace-making is the same force that will make U.S.–Japan relations continue to improve, despite the bashers on both sides: The mutual awareness that the two economies, and the two countries, badly need one another.

The Japanese need our market, our work force, and the free-spirited creativity we bring to technology and marketing.

More important, the Japanese need our friendship....

The United States, in turn, needs Japanese capital to finance industrial investment and to cover the national debt that we aren't willing to pay off ourselves....

We need the products that Japan makes: without Japanese VCRs, our music companies couldn't sell anybody videos. We need Japanese technical skill....

We need the tourists; that's why you now see signs in Japanese at museums, hotels, and resorts. We need the jobs; since 1988, the number of Americans directly employed by Japanese-owned companies has increased 50 percent, to 300,000. Mostly, those are industrial jobs that pay a lot better than hamburger-flipping.

The political and economic connections are drawing the two countries closer, and the smart politicians on both side understand that.

【解説】

戦前の日米の対立が、軍事面に集約されていったとすれば、戦後は、日本の経済力の復興にともない、経済通商面に対立が集約されていった感がある。その原因を探るのと同様に重要なのは、日米双方それぞれ1割から3割を占める輸出入をはじめ、双方の政治、文化、社会、経済など各方面の膨大な繋がりと相互依存、何千万人という人々の営々たる努力の積み重ねの中で、真に摩擦や対立と言えるものがどのくらい有るのかという点である。私事になるが、日米関係について話す機会がある度に、まず「極論すれば両国の

修正主義者が貿易上の対立点に焦点を当てる時、合意にはあまり注意が払われない。現在の日米通商問題で、もっとも驚くべきことは、争いの数ではなく、解決した事項の数の多さである……。

日米間に間断なく平和を到来させようとしている勢力は、双方のバッシャー達の存在にもかかわらず、今後とも日米関係を改善し続けようとしている勢力なのだ。その力とは、この2つの経済、2つの国家が、是が非でも互いを必要としているという認識だ。

日本人は、我々の市場、労働力、そして技術や市場開発の分野に我々が導入している自由な創造性を必要としている。さらに重要なことは、日本人が我々の友情を必要としている点だ……。

これに対し、アメリカは、産業投資と、自らが支払うのをためらっている財政赤字を埋めるために、日本の資本を必要としている。我々は、日本が製造した商品を必要としている……。日本製のビデオ・デッキがなければ、アメリカの音楽会社はビデオを誰にも売ることが出来ない。我々には日本人の技術力が必要なのだ……。

観光客も必要だ。博物館、ホテル、リゾート地で日本語の標識を見かけるのもそのためだ。我々には、仕事も必要だ。1988年以来、日本人の所有する企業に直接雇われているアメリカ人は、50%増加し、30万人に達した。その多くは、工業部門の仕事で、ハンバーガーをひっくり返して焼く作業より、はるかに高給が払われている。

政治的、経済的つながりは両国間の距離をますます近づけ、両国の賢明な政治家は、その点をしっかりと理解している。

関係の95%は健康で良好。対立は5%。しかし、メディアには対立に焦点を当てる宿命があり、報道の実態はその逆。摩擦を論じるのは大事だが、日本の進路を誤らせないためには全体のバランスが大事」といったことを申し上げている。TomはWPに入る前の70年代初め、熊本で英語の教師をして以来の日本ファン。特派員としても日本語を活かし、日本人の中に飛び込む手法で生き生きとした日本報道を行ってきた。本論は、そうしたTomの代表的日米関係論。とかくメディアの表面に現れない日米関係の広さと深さを知るべきだ、というのが論旨で、そのうちの経済関係を主に紹介した。

CHAPTER 1 | THE JAPANESE DOMESTIC ECONOMY

1. Economic Superpower Japan Through American Eyes
アメリカから見た経済大国日本

Harvard University の Professor Ezra F. Vogel が、『*Japan As Number One: Lessons for America*』を書いたのが1979年だった。その「Part 1: The Japanese Challenge, Part 2: The Japanese Miracle」の末尾には、こうある。「The institutions that follow (同書で取り上げている日本の分析対象のこと) were chosen because they are crucial for understanding overall Japanese success and because they could be models that America would do well to emulate. (見習う)」。

それから15年。太平洋戦争終結50周年の95年8月15日、WPは、Tom Reid と Paul Blustein の co-byline による「*Japan's 50-Year Miracle: Rubble to Riches*」を掲載した。

「The Japan of August 15, 1945, was one of the poorest nations on Earth… There was devastation everywhere…」であった。それが「The Japan of August 15, 1995, in contrast is an economic superpower. In total gross national product, Japan ranks just behind the United States as the second-richest nation on Earth.」。日米経済摩擦、あるいは、日本経済に構造的に含まれる様々な問題点(本書でもこのPartで取り上げる)が指摘されるようになって久しい中で、日本に対してまことに暖かい見方といって良いだろう。

その Miracle の原因について、記事は以下のように分析する。まずは日本国民自体だ。「First, it did have some resources to draw on. Japan's miracle sprang largely from its most valuable resource—its people.」。勤勉さ、高い教育、工業製品の質へのこだわり。次が日本型の資本主義。

第1章 日本の国内経済社会

「Another key was the development of a uniquely Japanese system of capitalism, based on lifetime employment—at least for male employees at major companies—and "corporate families" that permit management to place top priority on long-term growth and jobs rather than on quarterly profits and dividents.」。

記事は、日本内部の要因の他に、もう1つ重要な外部的要因をあげる。すなわち、アメリカ合衆国——Tom の持論である。「One other precious resource that contributed greatly to the Japanese miracle was its best friend, biggest market, and military protector—the United States.」。こうして、アジアにも冠たる経済大国日本が誕生したというわけだ。「Postwar Japan also has established a commanding economic presence in Asia, thereby gaining through peaceful means at least part of what it had hoped to get through military conquest and colonial rule.」。

だが、日本経済の成功が、アメリカにとって脅威となる日がやってきた。ここ20年来の経済、貿易に関する米メディアの報道をみると、日本市場のあり方については、アメリカ的な価値観や経済システムを優位ととらえ、その枠で分析する傾向が目だつようになった。

その際の錦の御旗は、「市場のアンフェアな閉鎖性」と「その開放は、アメリカ製品が売れるだけでなく、日本の消費者にとってもプラス」という論理である。こうした変化を求めることは「いかにアメリカ式やり方に変えるか——日本のアメリカ化」ということにほかならない。

例えば、この国のどこにでもある個人経営中心の商店街。このまことに日本的な papa-mama store について、WP はどんな記事を書いてきたか。

「Why This Grasshopper Likes Japan: The Apples

May Cost $2, But None of Them Are Rotten」(89/2/5 By Fred Hiatt)。自分の住む東京六本木の、顔なじみのお店や日常の買い物の経験を踏まえ、古き良き時代へのある種の挽歌となっている。「It may be dangerous, in this trade-tension era, to admit to any sympathy for the Japanese point of view. So let me start by saying that … I have not become accustomed to paying $6 for a box of raisin-bran cereal. I do not believe the Japanese market is open … But living here has shown that there are surprising virtues to the system that also brings $6 raisin bran. And as the U.S. and Japan enter a new era of trade friction, in which Washington may move from product-by-product badgering to a comprehensive attack on the Japanese way of doing business, it is worth remembering what value judgments as well as economic calculations are involved.」。果物や野菜の高品質。丁寧な包装。献身的サービス。人と人とのつながり。そして「to breathe easily even when our three-year-old daughter temporarily walks out of sight in a crowded department store」という安全。高価格の見返りにこうしたものを得ているというのだ。

その半年後に書かれた「Cracking Japan's Small Shop Monopoly」(89/8/13 By Paul Blustein)では、アメリカの要求が直截に示される。「But to the United States, the domination of Japan's retail market by the papa-mama store is an anachronism that helps to keep American products and other foreign goods from reaching Japanese consumers. The U.S. government is pressing hard for changes in Japan's distribution system, arguing that both small retail shops and the layers of wholesalers that supply them constitute a major barrier to foreign firms trying to crack the Japanese market.」。

そして、町の商店街の対極にあるアメリカ式大規模商店街「モール」での、低価格販売こそ長引く不況から脱出するための鍵

という議論も。「If there is any light at the end of the tunnel for Japan's sickly, stagnant economy, it is the brilliant white light of the big neon sign atop the fancy new shopping mall here—the sign that says "OUTLET MALLRISM."」(94/1/1 By Tom Reid)。扱っている商品は、住宅からハンバーガーまで。日本経済の回復は「That matters to Americans in two ways.」。第1に、内需が拡大しなければ、購買力は上がらず、アメリカ製品を買う力がない。第2に、円高ドル安の御時世、アメリカ製品は安くて良いという評判が日本に定着し、アメリカの輸出増大には今が絶好の機会というわけだ。最近の言葉で言えば「価格破壊」。それが日本経済にとって重要なファクターなら、この記事も的を射ていることになる。

さて、日本経済の今後は——。冒頭の Tom と Paul による co-byline の記事の末尾はこうである。「With all these uncertainties looming, August 15 1995—a day when the Japanese might be expected to look back on the 50 years since the end of the war—will probably evoke more worries about the years to come.」

2. The Land and Housing Problem

Crowds Are Made in Japan, Too

By Margaret Shapiro

February 13, 1989

Sociologists and others agree that the crowded environment in which most Japanese grow up helps explain the Japanese tendency to be considerate of others, to work well in groups while sublimating one's own desires.

Many Japanese, accustomed to a densely packed lifestyle, seem to prefer it that way.

Yet, the intense crowding has also led to tragedy. Several years ago, in the heavily populated industrial city of Kawasaki, a woman threw a neighbor's dog out the window, saying she could no longer bear the constant barking. The neighbor responded by stabbing her to death.

Japan's Housing: Pricey and Chilly

By T. R. Reid

March 4, 1991

A nation shivering through winter in houses that lack modern heat and plumbing hardly fits the world's image of Japan as an economic superpower.

And yet, most Japanese routinely accept housing conditions that would spark rent strikes and lawsuits almost anywhere in America.

戦後日本の経済、社会、生活の中で、唯一最大の問題は、住もと土地の問題だろう。その深刻さ、巨大さを肺腑の底までえぐった外国メディアはない。「土地本位制」という世界でも類例のないシステムが産みだした悲喜劇を、現在の「不良債権問題」まで含め、実相から原因、根源的対策にまで言及した米メディアもない。一つには、特派員はじめ外国企業の東京駐在員は、概して恵まれた社宅に住み、不動産を所有せず、相続税の問題も自身の問題ではないからかもしれない。従って、報道は、現象面が中心となり、これなら、まさに花盛り。「Cramped Life in "Rabbit Hutches": Despite Economic Boom, Most Japanese Can't Afford Own Home」(82/3/14 By Tracy Dahlby)。「Tokyo's Land Madness」(87/9/20 By Margaret Shapiro)。

2. 土地・住宅問題

群衆もまた日本製

マーガレット・シャピロ　　　　　　　　　　1989年2月13日

社会学者をはじめ、多くの人々は、ほとんどの日本人が育ってきた混雑した環境の与える影響に同意している。即ち、他人を思いやる傾向、自分の欲求を抑え集団内で行動する傾向などである。

　人口密度の高い混み合った生活に慣れている多くの日本人は、むしろそれを好むようだ。

　だが、激しい混雑は悲劇をも生み出す。数年前、人口過密な工業都市川崎で、近所の犬を窓からほうり投げた女性がいる。一時もやまない犬の吠え声に耐えられなくなったというのだ。犬の飼い主は、お返しに、彼女を刺し殺してしまった。

日本の住宅事情：高値で寒い

T.R. リード　　　　　　　　　　　　　　　1991年3月4日

近代的な暖房設備と水洗トイレのない家で冬の間凍えている人々―そんな姿は、経済超大国としての日本の国際的イメージとは一致しない。しかし、多くの日本人は、アメリカなら、どんな所でも、家賃支払い拒否や裁判沙汰をただちに引き起こしてしまうような住宅事情を当たり前のことのように受け入れている。

「For Crowded Tokyo, The "Last Frontier" May Be Underfoot」(88/8/25 同)。「Down and Out in Asumigaoka: New Japanese Riches Can't Buy It All」(89/4/21 By Fred Hiatt)。「High-Rises Blanket (覆う) the Ancient City of Kyoto」(90/10/21 By T. R. Reid)。そして、バブル経済崩壊の引き金となった政府の総量規制により、土地の値段が下がり始めれば、当然、大きなニュースとなる。

3. The Keiretsu

Unbowed by Hard Times

By Paul Blustein

September 24, 1995

I began exploring the keiretsu system five years ago when I came to Tokyo, during the midst of Japan's spectacular boom. In a two-part series that appeared in 1991, I examined the role the system has played in shaping modern-day Japan Inc. The keiretsu, I wrote, had helped engender both Japan's phenomenal economic success and its maddening insularity.

Now, as my Japan assignment ends, I am struck by what has changed in the world of the keiretsu—and by what has stayed essentially the same.

The biggest change, of course, is that Japan's economic juggernaut has been stalled in recession for more than three years. This downturn has put the keiretsu system under great pressure as stagnant sales, slumping stock prices, and soaring costs strain the links that bind Japanese firms together....

But powerful forces and traditions are working to hold the system together....

For better or worse, when Japan emerges from its long recession, its economic model will almost surely continue to differ starkly from America's. The question is, will these differences continue to be so consequential as to make Japan's economy somehow "incompatible" with ours or threatening to it?

上記にある、系列をめぐる Paul の2部構成の記事の第1回 (91/10/6) には、米国旗のイラストの下に「Keiretsu is the bedrock of the way Japan competes internationally. A lot of the other issues have been corrected.... Now we're down to bedrock.」という J. Michael Farren, Under Secretary of Commerce の言葉が取り上げられている。この前後から、系列問題は、日米貿易の交渉の主要な争点となり、メディアの関心を呼び、Washington の本社でもその解明に力を注ぐよう支局に檄が飛ばされた。95年半ばの自動車協議も、詰まる所はこの問題に帰着する。日本独特の経済慣習では「談合」も又、対日非難の俎上に上がった。「Trustbusters Take On the *Dango*: Japan, U.S. Crack Down Though

3. 系列

苦境においても屈服せず

ポール・ブルースティン

1995年9月24日

今から5年前、日本の華々しい大好況の真只中、東京に来た私は、系列システムの探求を始めた。1991年に掲載された2部構成の記事の中で、今日の日本株式会社が形成されるにあたってこのシステムが果たした役割を検討した。そこで指摘したのは、系列が、日本の驚異的な経済成功とその実に腹立たしいまでの偏狭な島国性の双方を生みだしたということであった。

日本での駐在が終わりを迎えた今、系列の世界がいかに変わったか、と同時に、本質的には変わっていないことにただ驚くばかりである。最大の変化は、当然のことながら爆走を続けてきた日本経済が、3年以上にわたる不況で停滞したことだ。売上は減り、株価は暴落、高騰するコストが、日本企業を固く結んでいた絆を限界にまで張りつめさせているなか、系列システムは、大変な圧力にさらされている……。

しかし、強力な力と伝統が、このシステムを保つために機能している……。善かれ悪しかれ、日本が、この長期にわたる不況から立ち直る時、その経済モデルとなるものは、きっとアメリカのそれとは明確に違った形を取り続けるであろう。問題は、こうした差異がこれからも、決定的な要因となって、日本経済がどういう形であれ、アメリカの経済とは相容れないものとなったり、アメリカ経済にとって脅威となったりし続けるかどうかである。

Firms Deny Wrongdoing」(91/5/14 By Paul Blustein)。*dango* はもう立派な英語である。Paul とともに、こうした経済記事の取材に専念した石澤靖治記者は、「このような日本の既存の制度について報じる時、日本のエスタブリッシュメントが迷惑そうな対応をするのは当然としても、日本社会で受け入れられていないアウトサイダー的な人たちの私たち外国メディアへの期待が実に大きいのには驚いた」と話している。

4. The Rise and Fall of the Bubble Economy

Japan's 'Growth Recession'

By Jim Hoagland

April 16, 1992

The slump offers evidence that the Japanese are not the invincible, ten-foot-tall business monsters depicted in some current fiction (à la Michael Crichton's *Rising Sun*) or analysis (see the CIA-sponsored "Japan 2000" think piece). Japanese bankers and industrialists make bad loans and impulsive investments, too.

Wishful thinkers see a Japanese that would abandon successful work habits for the purpose of helping out America.

The Japanese are determined, resourceful competitors, able to think and act strategically to maintain their advantage. That is not cause for demonizing them, and even less for underestimating them. Americans can come to terms with that reality by working harder to understand the Japanese and to improve America's own economic performance.

日本経済がバブル期を迎えた87年暮れ、WPは1面で「Dolls and Dogs in Mink: Newly Affluent Japanese Bask in Luxury」(87/12/12 By Margaret Shapiro) と報じ、その絶頂期には「Japan's New Era: The Power and Problems of Wealth」という3回の連載を特集した。豊かさの中にすでに不安の影が感じとられ、第1回 (90/2/11 By Fred Hiatt and Margaret Shapiro) は、日本は成熟した民主主義への斬新的な歩を進めてはいるものの「I feel as if the ship of Japan were now leaving the harbor to face stormy, misty, uncharted seas」という朝日新聞の松山幸雄論説委員長の言葉で終えている。バブルが崩壊すると「When this Recession Is Over, Japan May Never Be the Same」(92/6/22 By Paul Blustein)。

4. バブルとその崩壊

日本の成長が鈍る

ジム・ホーグランド　　　　　　　　　　　　　　　1992年4月16日

日本経済の不振は、彼らが昨今の小説の一部(例えば、マイケル・クライトンの『ライジング・サン』)や研究分析(CIA主導で行われたレポート『日本2000年』参照)に描かれているような、無敵の身長10フィート(訳注：約3メートル)のビジネス・モンスターではないことの証しである。日本の銀行家や企業家も、不良貸し付けを抱えたり、軽率で衝動的な投資もする。

　希望的観測をする人は、アメリカにとって都合のいいように、日本が、これまで成功を勝ち得てきた勤労の習慣を捨て去ることを願っている。

　だが、日本人は、決断力があり、知識に富んだ競争相手である。自らの優位性を守るために戦略的に考え、行動できる人々だ。このような理由で、日本人を悪魔に仕立て上げることはできないし、過小評価するなんてもってのほかだ。アメリカ人は、日本人を理解するためにもっと努力し、アメリカ自身の経済状況の改善に励むことによって、日本人の真の姿を受け入れることができるであろう。

このスランプは、経済上昇の単なる一時的な休止ではなく、たとえ不況を脱出しても「The Japanese economy appears unlikely to expand at the furious pace that, over the past two decades, led to the devastation of American industries such as television manufacturing and certain type of computer chips.」。この分析は、おそらく当たっているのだろう。

Clouds Over the Rising Sun

Gangsters Aggravating Japanese Banking Crisis

By Sandra Sugawara

December 15, 1995

Japan is known as possibly the world's closest thing to a no-crime society. But operating in most any community of any size are the yakuza, organized into tight syndicates that profess to live by feudal codes of honor....

But when the economic bubble burst and land and stock prices plummeted, banks were left with yakuza borrowers who refused to repay their loans or relinquish their assets, according to Miyawaki....

Other delinquent borrowers turned to the yakuza for protection from financial institutions seeking to reclaim their loans, sometimes even putting the gangsters on their boards, said a researcher at a leading corporate research group....

Another twist on the yakuza connection is that some banks have used gangsters to collect loans, said the researcher....

Miyawaki said that the first needed step is more detailed disclosure of bad loans and other financial activities by banks. "The relationship between financial institutions and yakuza has been kept in a black box," he said. "This black box has to be broken. If all the Japanese public knows about this, then we can put a brake on the yakuza's freewheeling activities against financial institutions."

バブル経済とその処理に端を発する不良債権問題は、日本経済にかつてない深刻な影響を与えている。「An Ocean of Troubles: Sour Loans, Sagging Stocks, Shake Japan's Banking System to Its Roots」(95/7/9 By Paul Blustein) は、大波に洗われる「¥」が今にも砕けそうなイラストつきだ。「住専」が騒がれるなか、WPは、これは問題のほんの一部と見る。「The *jusen* represent only a fraction of the estimated $400 billion to $1 trillion in bad loans in Japan. Indeed, Japan's entire financial system is struggling to regain its balance as it fights to emerge from a structure designed for a different era.」(96/2/8 By Sandra Sugawara)。a different era——即ち、密室での決定、コネが幅をきかし、

日本の銀行の危機を悪化させるギャング

サンドラ・スガワラ　　　　　　　　　　　　　　　1995年12月15日

　日本は、犯罪のない社会に、考えられる限り最も近いと、世界に知られている。しかし、大小を問わず、ほとんど全ての地域でヤクザが活動している。ヤクザとは、堅い結束のもとに組織された犯罪シンジケートで、封建的な掟を誇りに生きることを公にした集団だ……。

　バブルがはじけ、地価と株価が急落すると共に、銀行は、借金の返済を拒むか、資産を譲渡してしまうヤクザの債務者を抱え込んでしまった、と宮脇（磊介）は語る……。

　借金を返さない債務不履行者の中には、貸した金を回収しようとする金融機関から身を守るため、ヤクザの助けを求める者もいる、とある大手企業の経済研究所員は話す。中には、ヤクザを役員の席に据える者もいるという……。このヤクザ・コネクションを複雑にねじれさせたもうひとつの理由は、一部の銀行が、債務の取り立てにギャングを用いたためだ、とこの研究所員は言う……。

　まず最初にしなければならないのは、銀行による不良債権ほか全ての金融取り引きを詳細に明らかにすることだと宮脇は述べる。「金融機関とヤクザの関係は、ブラックボックスの中にしまいこまれてきた。しかし、この箱は壊されなければならない。もし、日本の一般大衆が、みんな事実を知るようになれば、ヤクザの金融機関に対する、勝手な行動に歯止めをかけることができる」と彼は、述べた。

官民は癒着、天下りが強い影響力を発揮する時代だ。PaulやSandyとともに、重要課題の1つとして、不良債権問題を追い、暴力団関係の取材にも当たった柏木明子記者は、「国民の怒りの声を、これほど強く感じたのは初めて。外国の血生臭い事件とは違うかもしれないけれど、日本にとっては、すごく重要な出来事だと思う」と話す。

5. The Future of Lifetime Employment

Japan's "Lifetime Job" Tradition Trembles

By Paul Blustein

March 3, 1993

Few expect Japanese-style job security to collapse in the near future, but any significant modifications, were they to occur, could mark a revolutionary shift for the corporate system that generated this nation's postwar economic miracle.

The guarantee of lifetime employment has helped Japan Inc. keep wage costs from spiraling out of control, and it has helped instill Japanese workers with their legendary corporate loyalty.

In Japan, a Bow to Competitive Realities

By Sandra Sugawara

November 26, 1995

In the United States, during the last big rush of restructuring, change normally meant cutting costs to create a leaner and meaner fighting machine.

But in Japan, the primary goal often is described as something less visible than the next quarterly report. Many companies say their real objective is to create an environment that fosters leadership, a difficult task in a society where people are taught to submerge their identities into that of the group and to avoid conflicts with members of that group.

長引く不況は、日本的雇用形態に影響を与えるのか。上記 Paul の記事は「the lifetime employment system will ultimately be jettisoned (投げ捨てる) to sustain (維持する) corporate profitability」というエコノミストのコメントを結論としている。終身雇用制だけでなく、年功序列制も変わる。好況時の管理職は、the portable shrine (神輿)に乗っているようなものだったが、状況は変わったと Sandy は、上記で分析する。大手金属会社で、自分より年配の部下に敬語を使いながら指示をする管理職。しかし、若い人には実力を試すことができて、かえってよいという見方もある。「Japanese companies worry that abrupt (突然の) layoffs would be too destructive to the ties that bind their society together.」という見方

5. 終身雇用制は続くか

日本的終身雇用の伝統、震動す

ポール・ブルースティン

1993年3月3日

日本型の職業保障制度が、近いうちに崩壊すると予測する人はあまりいないが、もし重大な変化が起きるなら、戦後日本の奇蹟的な経済復興を生みだした企業システムの革命的変転を意味するかもしれない。

終身雇用の保障は、給与の無軌道な急上昇から日本株式会社を守り、日本人労働者の企業に対する伝説的忠誠心を植えつけるのに貢献した。

日本では、競争社会の現実に頭を下げる

サンドラ・スガワラ

1995年11月26日

アメリカにおける前回の大リストラの嵐の中で、改革とは通常、無駄のない効果的な戦闘マシーンを作り上げることを意味していた。

しかし、日本では、主要な目標は、次の4半期事業報告に直接顕れる類のものではない。多くの企業は、真の目的は、リーダーシップを育てるような環境を創ることだと言う。集団の中に自分を埋没させ、集団内の対立を回避するよう教えられる社会では、極めて困難な試みである。

もある中で、「If the system does not change ... the Japanese companies cannot survive.」というある出向社員の言葉でやはり、記事は終えている。

CHAPTER 2 | **JAPAN–U.S. ECONOMIC FRICTION**

1. The Same Old Story
十年一日、20年戦争

日米経済紛争をめぐっては、実に多くのことが起き、論じられ、書かれてきました。そこでクイズを出そうと思います。以下に、この20年間、WPが掲載した日米貿易、摩擦関連の記事13本の見出しがあります。これを、掲載された順に従って並べると、どうなるでしょう?

1. 「U.S. Trade Team Finds Japan Heedless of Crisis Warning」(危機の警告に日本は注意を払わない／米通商代表団筋表明)

2. 「Getting Tough with Japan」(日本には強硬な態度で)

3. 「Japan's Barriers Falling, but U.S. Still in Trouble」(日本の障壁は崩れるが、アメリカにとってはまだ問題あり)

4. 「Japan Plans Cutback in Trade Bars / Seeking to Open Markets to More Foreign Products」(日本、貿易の障害を減らそうと計画／外国製品を増やすため、市場開放を目指す)

5. 「Japan Shows Bitterness at U.S. Trade Tactics / Tokyo Also Said to Discuss Retaliation」(日本、通商問題での米の駆け引きに不快の念／東京は、報復の検討も表明)

6. 「Tokyo Panel Readies Major New Report / Study to Urge Striking Economic Changes」(東京の協議会、抜本的な新報告／大胆な経済の変化を促す)

第2章 日米経済摩擦

7.「Reluctance to Boost Domestic Demand Sours Trade Ties with U.S. / The perception in Washington: Japan only moves if it is slapped in the face with strong, unexpected action.」(内需拡大に力が入らないため、アメリカと通商関係が悪化/ワシントンの見方は「日本は、突然、頬を1発、強く張らないと動かない」)

8.「Japan Defends Business Ties / Tokyo Won't Yield to U.S. on Tradition」(日本は、仕事上の繋がりを守る/東京は、伝統については、対米屈服せず)

9.「Japan's Premier-Apparent Talks Tough on U.S. Trade Disputes」(日本の総理、対米通商問題で強硬策か)

10.「Japan Moves to Create Goodwill / As Its Trade Surplus Soars, Increased Imports Are Planned」(日本、友好創設のため行動す/貿易黒字の急増で、輸入促進を計画)

11.「Saying No to America / Japan Adopting Tough New Trade Position As U.S. Does Same Thing, Fueling Friction」(アメリカに「ノー」という日本/米の対日強硬策により、日本も同様な措置。摩擦激化)

12.「Japan Urged to Slash Trade Surplus / White House Presses Nation to Open Markets / Agree Soon on Goals」(日本、貿易黒字削減を求められる/米政府、市場開放の圧力/合意達成間近)

13.「Japanese Face Tough Trade Fight」(日本、厳しい通商戦争に直面)。

正解をお答えする前に、それぞれの byline や内容、背景

など、いわばヒントとなるような点について簡単に解説してみましょう。

1. By William Chapman。この年、米国の貿易赤字が300億ドル、対日がその3分の1近くなり、日本の国内市場の問題点が初めて深刻に指摘された。「日本は、自由貿易制度最大の受益者だ。That system is now in jeopardy and Japan could take some steps to reduce that threat.」と米通商代表団筋は語った。当時の顔触れは、Robert Strauss や Richard Rivers 等だ。

2. Editorial。「急増する対米貿易黒字（85億ドル）。高まる米国内の保護主義の声。だから日本は早急に対策をとれ。Doing more, however, requires not only government decisions to spur growth but also changes in entrenched habits among Japanese industries and consumers.」といった主張を展開。

3. By William Chapman。輸入規制枠や関税、政府系の独占企業による日本の貿易障壁は、劇的に減った、と Rep. James R. Jones (D-Okla.) 主宰の下院調査委員会が発表。ただし、日本にいるアメリカ人ビジネスマンのなかには、non-tariff barriers と呼びうるような障害に苦情を述べる者もいる、と報じた。

4. By Tracy Dahlby。諸外国での保護主義の backlash を避けるため、自民党が「overly stringent customs, product standards, and testing requirements for a broad range of items, including cosmetics, pharmaceuticals, processed foods, and sporting goods.」の規制緩和策を打ち出し、鈴木内閣の主要通商政策となろうというニュース報道。

5. By John Burgess。本来は、アメリカの失敗に起因する貿易不均衡の責を日本が負わされるのは、「appear to have

created deep resentment in many Japanese officials」。例えば、大河原良雄前駐米大使は日本外国特派員協会で、「If the Japanese people feel the U.S. is asking too much and asking too fast, there could be serious consequences.」と述べた、といった内容だ。

6. By John Burgess。日本の社会経済の国際化を進める具体的処方箋を書いた前川レポートがまとまったという記事。その直後には、「中曽根首相が、Backs Report on Restructuring Economy」(4/8)を出稿している。

7. By Stuart Auerbach。筆者は、80年代から90年代初めにかけて、WP本社で国際経済を担当。米議会や政府の動きを中心に迫った。プラザ合意による円高後も、減らない対日赤字や自動車、東芝機械、半導体などの摩擦案件に業をにやした米側の態度が、見出しにとられている。

8. By Fred Hiatt。日米通商交渉で、「the U.S. again is seeking to restructure Japan's economy」。しかし、「"In Japan, long-term relationships between manufacturers and parts suppliers have been the secret of success."」というのが経団連の幹部の言葉だった。「"If I trade with you because I like you, that is not a trade barrier."」

9. By T. R. Reid。総理就任直前の宮沢喜一氏と外国プレスとの会見後の記事。日米関係を重視し、日本のアジア重視を否定し、真珠湾50周年が悪い結果を産むことはないと断言した氏だったが、コメの輸入問題について、「Japan will not end its ban on rice imports until the U.S. and European countries eliminate their own import controls on agricultural products.」

10. By Paul Blustein。ブッシュ大統領の訪日を前に、主要自動車会社は、アメリカからの部品輸入を増やすと発表。通産省

も主要40社の首脳に外国製品のvoluntarilyな増加を促した。

11. By T. R. Reid and Paul Blustein。ワシントンで行われたPresident Clinton と宮沢首相の首脳会議を受け、「米強硬路線は、has been a clear success at home, winning him greater popularity and editorial support….」という東京の状況を書いた記事だ。

12. By Peter Behr。日本は「to reduce its worldwide trade surplus dramatically over the next three to four years. さもなければ、海外からの重圧に直面することになる」というクリントン政権の警告を記事にしている。筆者は90年代前半、WPの本社で国際経済を担当。

13. By Clay Chandler。カナダ・ハリファックスの先進国首脳サミットでの記事。自動車交渉で、日本の非妥協路線に対し「a series of shifting developments is subtly undermining their position」。President Clinton の対日制裁路線に対する米国民や業界の支持、さらなるドル安の可能性、WTOで日本はそう簡単に支持されないだろう――といった要素である。筆者は、日本語も堪能で、*Wall Street Journal* 東京支局から93年夏、WP本社経済部に引き抜かれた。

賢明な読者の御高察通り、正解は「順序通り」です。手元にある日米経済摩擦関連の記事のうち、個別産品交渉を除いた79本から適当に選んでみました。十年一日。見出しから見れば同じような努力と論議、批判が延々と続いているわけです。以下、それぞれの掲載日です。

```
1 = 77/11/20、2 = 77/12/27、3 = 80/11/23
4 = 82/1/27、5 = 85/3/30、6 = 86/4/4
7 = 87/12/9 (IHT)、8 = 90/4/2
9 = 91/10/19、10 = 91/11/12、11 = 93/4/25
12 = 93/6/8、13 = 95/6/17
```

さて、クイズはこの辺でやめにして、日米間の貿易摩擦の歴史を概観しておこう。70年代初めの繊維交渉はさておくとしても、貿易不均衡がはっきりとした様相を示し始めた77、78年あたりから間断なき紛争が続いている。

　鉄鋼、テレビといった工業製品（対米輸出）や牛肉、柑橘類（対日輸出）などの農産物。80年代初頭最大の課題は自動車で、日本はVoluntary Restraint Agreement（対米輸出自主規制協定）を結ぶ。500〜600億ドルを超える通商不均衡が取りざたされるようになり、円高への流れの中で、日本の金融市場の開放も重要なテーマとなる。電気通信機器、エレクトロニクス、医薬品など個別のMarket Oriented Sector Selective Discussions（市場指向型・分野別協議）。関西空港を初め、日本の建設市場の開放。日米両国の技術の角逐では、東芝機械のココム違反事件、超電導、半導体と対日制裁、FSXなどが80年代最後の数年間を彩る。貯蓄や投資、流通、価格、談合など排他的取引慣行や系列などを俎上にあげたStructural Impediments Initiatives（構造協議）では90年代初めにかけて、日米双方の市場の構造的問題を論じあった。

　バブル経済の崩壊後、日本経済の苦しみが始まるが、貿易不均衡は解消せず、日本の「聖域」コメや、Framework Talks（日米包括経済協議）の一環として取り上げられた、個別分野最大問題の自動車紛争へと発展していくのだ。

　経済紛争は、WP東京特派員の仕事に深く関わっているが、時にはその対日観や心を深く傷つけることもある。自動車や東芝事件、半導体問題に揺れた3年間の勤務を終え、東京を離れるとき、John Burgessは「U.S.–Japan Relationship: Alliance Marked by Paradox / Closer Ties Result in More Dissatisfaction」(87/8/3) を書いた。「The closer that Japan and the United States move together, the more unhappy each becomes with the other.」というのが、80年代後半の、この西側同盟の奇妙な関係だというのだ。事態は、果たしてそれから本質的に変化したのだろうか。

2. Spring 1992

U.S.–Japan Relations Seen Suffering Worst Downturn in Decades

By Don Oberdorfer

March 1, 1992

In the two months since President Bush's troubled trip to Tokyo, U.S.–Japanese relations have suffered their most serious downturn in decades, according to American officials and other observers.

To a greater degree than in earlier crises, the current disputes have spread beyond specific differences over economic and security policies to a broader collision of two dissimilar societies, their leaders and peoples.

Since World War II, the United States and Japan have cooperated extensively in the Pacific and elsewhere, holding in check economic rivalries and cultural differences. Now, however, some of the restraining influences have been shattered by a confluence of developments, including the end of Cold War threats that had cemented the U.S.–Japan alliance, a serious U.S. recession that has deepened American ire about trade frictions, and inflammatory politics that have been fanned by the important elections both nations face later this year.

The complicity of U.S. and Japanese leaders in the current trouble is one of its most unusual and serious aspects.

The Gallup Organization と読売新聞社が行っている世論調査によると、1978年以来、アメリカの対日感情が最悪だったのが92年春前後である。対日評価が「悪い」とするのは通常10％程度だが、この時期のみ約20％になった。3月下旬、アメリカを西から東海岸へと旅し、60人以上にインタビューしたが、日本の政治家の発言を知らなかったのはわずか1人。日本不信の念は広く深く広がっていると感じた（『諸君』92年6月号の拙論「U.S.A.感情摩擦旅行」参照）。Los Angeles Times では、日系人女性論説委員 Nancy Yoshihara から、対日感情の悪化で、大学のキャンパスや市内事務所に、アジア系アメリカ人に対する差別的な落書きがされた、など生々しい話を聞いた。WP で人種問題を担当する Lynne Duke 記者

2. 1992年春

ここ数十年で最悪と見られる日米関係

ドン・オーバードーファー　　　　　　　　　　　　1992年3月1日

2ヵ月前、ブッシュ大統領が多くのもめ事に巻き込まれ、混乱のうちに終わった東京への旅をして以来、日米関係は、ここ数十年で最も深刻な状態にあると、米政府の高官や識者は述べている。

これまでの危機と比べ、今回の対立は、経済面や安全保障政策といった特定領域の違いを超え、異なる2つの社会、その指導者や国民同士の衝突へと広がりを見せている。

第2次世界大戦以来、日米は、経済競争や文化的な違いはひとまず置き、太平洋その他の地域で、大規模な協力関係にあった。しかし、今日、日米同盟を堅固なものにしてきた冷戦の脅威の終結、貿易摩擦をめぐりアメリカの怒りを高めた米国経済の深刻な不況、そして、今年の後半に両国で行われる重要な選挙による政治の扇動化など様々な要素が集まり、これまで対立を抑制してきた一部が、崩れさってしまった。

今回、これまでと一番違う深刻な事態とは、日米両国の指導者が共にもめ事を引き起こしていることである。

は「Panel Links Japan-Bashing, Violence」という合衆国公民権委員会に焦点をあてた記事を書き(92/2/29)、「Much of the bigotry (偏狭さ) is rooted in the belief that Asians are outsiders.」という、アジア系はアメリカ社会になかなか同化できないという偏見に悩む姿を伝えている。

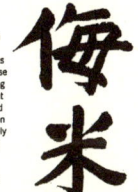

President Cast as Car Salesman

By T. R. Reid

January 8, 1992

In a rebuke that still burns in the memory of Japanese people, the late French president Charles de Gaulle once described a visiting Japanese prime minister as "that transistor salesman." ....

The Gaullist dig and other stings were repeated across the full range of Japanese media....

The most common criticism was that Bush has diminished his own stature by focusing this long-awaited Asian trip on help for the American corporate executives down the steps from Air Force One at Haneda Airport.

By T. R. Reid and John E. Young

January 10, 1992

Miyazawa sought to resolve a controversy that he sparked on New Year's Day when he said he feels "compassion" for America because of its "problems." Some of the American businessmen traveling with Bush found this comment patronizing and reacted angrily.

"What I really tried to say was that we have to understand the other person's position," Miyazawa began. But then he again ticked off a list of American problems: "There are homeless people. There is the problem of AIDS. Education is not as high as in the past. And U.S. industries are not as competitive."

92年初めのブッシュ大統領訪日では、首相官邸の晩餐会で倒れた大統領の姿が記憶に残る。それから、1月もたたないうち、アメリカの労働の質に言及した桜内衆院議長と宮沢首相の発言。そのすべてが米メディアによって詳細にアメリカに伝えられた。加えて上記記事のような出来事もまた、アメリカの誇りを傷つけ、日米関係を曇らせた。アメリカ人にとって「セールスマン」とはある種哀感漂うもので、大統領職の尊厳とは相容れない。さらに、年頭会見で首相の述べた「同情発言」。日米首脳会談後の共同会見で、Tom にこの点を聞かれた宮沢首相の答えが火に油を注いだ。これを知った Bill Clinton は屈辱と衝撃に打ちのめされ、半年後、民主党大統領候補に指名された日、こう演説した。「Our country has

自動車のセールスマンを演じる大統領

T.R. リード　　　　　　　　　　　　　　　　1992年1月8日

日本人の記憶の中に、いまだに燠火(おきび)のように燻り続けている屈辱の思い出がある。故シャルル・ドゴール大統領が、フランスを訪れた日本の首相を「あのトランジスターのセールスマン」と呼んだことだ……。尊大なドゴール主義者の皮肉や嫌みは、日本全土でメディアによって繰り返された……。

最も共通した非難は、ブッシュは、待ちに待ったこのアジア旅行で、大統領専用機エアフォース・ワンから羽田空港に降り立ったアメリカの会社の幹部達の援助に焦点を当てたため、自らの存在を矮小化してしまった、というものだ。

T.R. リード ＆ ジョン・E・ヤング　　　　　　1992年1月10日

宮沢首相は、元旦の日に、アメリカが抱えている「問題」に対して「同情」の念を禁じえないと述べ、物議を引き起こしたが、その事態をどうにかして収拾しようとした。ブッシュ大統領と旅を共にしたアメリカのビジネスマンの一部は、このコメントに保護者ぶった傲慢さを感じ、怒りに満ちた反応を示した。「私が、本当に言いたかったのは、互いに相手の立場を理解しなければいけないということでした」と宮沢は、切り出した。しかし、彼は再び、アメリカの抱える一連の問題を1つひとつ列挙した。「ホームレスの人達がいます。エイズの問題もあります。教育水準もかつてほど高くはありません。そして、アメリカの産業も、充分な競争力をもっていないのです」。

---

fallen so far, so fast that just a few months ago the Japanese prime minister actually said he felt "sympathy" for the United States. Sympathy.」(『Putting People First』より)。「Sympathy」と繰り返した時の、聴衆の重苦しい沈黙はテレビを通じても伝わってきた。自分が大統領になったら世界から蔑まされるようなことは二度とさせない、と語った Clinton の決意が、その後の対日政策の根底に流れているのはまず間違いないだろう。

Japanese on Losing End of U.S. Real Estate Deals

By Michael Abramowitz

March 21, 1992

INDIAN WELLS, Calif.—Just a couple of years ago, Japan's huge investment in American real estate was portrayed by some as a threat to American sovereignty and a blow to U.S. pride. As well-heeled Japanese bought up such national treasures as Rockefeller Center in New York City, there seemed to be no end in sight.

But in this desert playground of the rich and famous near Palm Springs, as well as in Los Angeles, Hawaii, and other centers of the now-busted real estate boom, some Americans are emerging as the wily horse traders while the Japanese appear to have been snookered.

American land owners and developers, it now appears, profited from the Japanese buying spree, unloading their excess real estate to the Japanese, often at inflated prices.

"I expected much more out of the Japanese than they in fact showed," said Christopher Mead, a Phoenix consultant who has tracked Japanese investment in U.S. real estate. "We thought that because they beat us in one field after another, they were going to win in real estate too. But they didn't. It wasn't the Japanese who took advantage of the Americans; it was the other way around."

92年春の危機が鎮まった背景には、日米関係の重要な転機がある。80年代後半からアメリカ全土で、不動産から会社の買収などに荒れ狂ったJapan Moneyの嵐が終わり、風向きが逆転し始めたのだ。3月下旬にWP本社に行った時、Executive Editor（編集主幹）のLeonard Downie Jr.と、日米関係はこれからどうなるのだろうか、といった話をしたが、「We are going to run an interesting story. You'd better read it.」と言われたのが上記の記事である。すでに、アメリカの不動産売買で日本が勢いを失っているという報道が始まっていた。「Japanese Investment in U.S. Real Estate Dips（沈下する）Again」(91/3/28 By David S. Hilzenrath)。「Japanese Slow Real Estate Buying Spree: Investments Tumble By 61

日本人は米国の不動産取り引きで結局損をした

マイケル・アブラモウィッツ

1992年3月21日

カリフォルニア州インディアン・ウェルズ発——わずか数年前、アメリカの不動産に対する日本の莫大な投資は、アメリカの主権にとって脅威であり、合衆国の威信(プライド)を傷つけるものと一部では見なされていた。あり余る資金にものをいわせた日本人が、ニューヨーク市のロックフェラー・センターのような国家的な宝を買い上げた時、こうした光景は今後も続いていくかのように思われた。

しかし、ここパーム・スプリングス近く、金持ちや有名人向けの荒れ果てた遊興施設で、あるいはロサンジェルス、ハワイその他、今でははじけ散った不動産ブームのかつての中心地では、アメリカ人が、抜け目のない商売人として頭角を現す一方、日本人は、だまされた間抜けのような体を呈している。

今となって見れば、アメリカの地主や開発業者は、日本人の目茶苦茶な購入欲を利用し、お荷物となった不動産を高値で押しつけたりして、大儲けしたのだ。

「私は、彼らを買い被っていました」と、日本人による対米不動産投資の追跡調査をしたフェニックスのコンサルタント、クリストファー・ミードは語る。「彼らは、次から次へと新たな分野で我々を打ち負かしていくので、不動産でも勝利をおさめるものと思っていました。でも、勝たなかった。アメリカ人を利用して儲けたのは、日本人ではなかった。事実は、その逆でした」。

Pct. in 1991」(92/2/21 By Kirstin Downey)。"trophy" properties といわれる New YorkのRockefeller Center は三菱地所、米映画産業の華、Hollywood のMCA Inc. は松下電器が買収したが、「Now those days are gone.」と Kirstin は書き、その言葉通り、今や、大規模買収プロジェクトの残骸が次々と横たわっているのだ。

3. Automobiles: Competition and Cooperation

In Japan, Detroit Iron and Different Realities

By Paul Blustein

September 25, 1994

Konen Suzuki, president of Ford Motor Co. (Japan)'s success and frustration are a microcosm of the U.S.–Japan conflict over trade. Suzuki worked for Toyota Motor Corp. for 30 years. Known as a maverick, he stunned tradition-bound Toyota by joining Ford in 1991.

"In the United States, my only job was to persuade dealers how good a future Toyota would have, and their decision was based entirely on whether selling Toyotas offered a good business opportunity or not," Suzuki said. "In this country, there is always the shadow of the manufacture … Getting past that barrier is 90 percent of the problem."

Blurring the Battle Lines

By Paul Blustein

May 21, 1995

The rights and wrongs are less clear cut in the long-simmering spat over automotive trade.…

Behind such endless debates lies the issue concerning the inner workings of corporate Japan, and the question of what measures are justified in prying open the keiretsu system, which bonds parts suppliers to their customers as if they were members of the same family.

95年半ばの自動車協議ほど、日米経済摩擦の広がりと深刻さを感じたことはない。2大経済大国の激突とはこれかと思った。numerical target を回避したという意味で、日本の勝利とみる者も多いが、勝ち負け論争に決して意味があるとは思えない。長らく自国の産業を保護育成するため、高く堅固な障壁を築いてきた日本に対し、アメリカはある種の affir- mative action を求めた。経済原則を超えた要求ではあるが、無理からぬ部分はないか。「In Doing Business, a Deal of Difference: Contrasts Between U.S., Japanese Auto Sales Methods Shed Light on Trade Dispute」(95/6/6 By Paul Blustein and Warren Brown) の取材で会った東京渋谷のディーラーは「外国車を売ろうと思えば、まず社内で決め、それ

3. 自動車：競争と協調

米車の鉄壁の販売陣、日本では異なる現実に直面す

ポール・ブルースティン　　　　　　　　　　　　　　1994年9月25日

フォード自動車（日本）の社長である鈴木弘然の成功と不満は、日米貿易摩擦の縮図である。トヨタ自動車で30年間働いた鈴木は、独立独歩の生き方で知られ、1991年にフォードに入社し、伝統に縛られたトヨタの人々を驚愕させた。「アメリカで（注：トヨタを売っていた時）の唯一の仕事は、トヨタはこれからどんなにすばらしい車になるかをディーラーに説得することでした。彼らの判断は、トヨタを売ることがいい商売になるかどうかの一点にしぼられていたんです」と鈴木は言う。「日本では、いつもメーカーの影がちらついています……。この壁を乗り越えれば、問題の9割は解決します」。

戦線を曖昧にする

ポール・ブルースティン　　　　　　　　　　　　　　1995年5月21日

長期にわたり爆発寸前の状態でもめ続けてきた自動車協議貿易をめぐる争いで、誰が正しく、誰が間違っているのかそれほどはっきりはしていない……。こうした終わりなき論争の背後に横たわっているのは、株式会社日本の内部構造の問題と、自動車部品の供給者とその買い手を家族のように結びつけている系列システムをこじ開けるには、どうしたらよいのかということである。

からうちのメーカーのトップと話す」。あるメーカーの知人は「我社の米工場でアメリカ製部品を扱いたいというけれど、認めると日本の下請けに影響が出るので……」。こうした世界を開放された市場とは言わないだろう。系列をただちに壊すのは暴論としても、国民全体で考え、実行すべきことはないだろうか（『文芸春秋』95年7月号の拙論「日米自動車戦争勃発す」参照）。

For 25 years, Japan has had <u>one</u> word for its market:

CLOSED

Every American President for the past 25 years has heard it from the Japanese government. Four Republican and two Democratic Presidents have tried to negotiate the opening of Japan's markets.

Today, Japan has the second largest auto market in the world, but by

日米が自動車問題で激突を続けた95年5 6月、WPには計11種類の自動車広告が載った。うち6本は日本側、5本はアメリカ側で、それぞれ何回も掲載された。日本側のは上記右頁のように、通商法301条を使って高級日本車の輸入を規制しようという米政府のやり方は、アメリカの労働者に悪影響を与えるというもの。アメリカ側のメッセージはただ1つ、上記左頁のように日本市場がいかに「閉鎖的」か問うことだ。「You're Now Looking at Something Very Few Japanese Consumers Have Ever See」(95/6/20)のように、日本製よりはるかにイグニッション・プラグの大きなイラスト付のもある。WPの読者から見れば「クリントンのやり方は問題だけれど、日本市場はほんとに閉鎖的なんだな」ということになる。

Trade Ban on Japanese Autos? It won't work.

The clock is ticking on the Clinton Administration's threats to stop the sale of certain Japanese cars in the U.S.

Why in the world are they doing it? Because Japanese auto companies won't agree to let the U.S. Government dictate their business plans.

Quite simply, no independent corporation should be strong-armed by a foreign government telling it what to buy and sell.

WHO LOSES?

✗ **U.S. Consumers:** Restricted trade means fewer car models, less competition and higher prices.

✗ **U.S. Workers:** Jobs will be lost all across America in auto plants, dealerships and supplier companies.

✗ **World Trading System:** Unilateral

WHO WINS?

✓ **The Big 3 Automakers:** After making billions in profits in 1994, they now want to close the U.S. market to competition.

この間、日本側の意見をストレートに伝えたのは vice president for Toyota Motor Sales, U.S.A., Inc., C. Douglas Smith による「Myths About the Japanese Auto Market」(95/6/1) という投書だけだったように思う。日本市場は unfair に閉ざされている、といった対日マイナスイメージに果たすマスメディアの役割はきわめて大きいものがある。

Americans Shift Into Toyota Gear

By Fred Hiatt

March 13, 1988

"They work really hard here," Everly had said with admiration. "My main job will be to motivate American workers to work as hard and as fast as Japanese workers. Frankly, I think it's going to be a challenge."

A Concept America Taught Japan Comes Full Circle at Toyota's Ky. Plant

By Shigehiko Togo

January 27, 1994

It was just a small scratch on an interior door panel of 350 to 400 of the 25,000 new Toyota Camrys made here each month, the result of an electric screwdriver slipping in a worker's hand while installing the door lock mechanism....

To find a solution, six American assembly line workers used team techniques pioneered by Japanese companies, closing a loop begun in the 1950s when two U.S. consultants gave a series of lectures on quality control to Japanese executives....

It took team member John Morris, 43, just 20 minutes to come up with an idea—put a plastic plate over the lock to protect the door during the installation. After the team perfected its design over two months, workers eliminated the scratch.

自動車を巡る日米関係は、争いの歴史だけではない。日本の自動車産業は、その成り立ちからして戦前から戦後のかなりの時期まで、アメリカを師と仰ぐものだった。日本の優秀な生産技術、チームワークやガソリン高騰などが対米優位の情勢を形造る中で、「U.S.-Japanese Aid On Quality Control Comes Full Circle」(80/9/17 By William Chapman) では、アメリカに QC を教えるようになった日本を描く。80年代には、アメリカでの現地生産が大きな流れとなり、トヨタの Georgetown の工場で働く米労働者の班長クラスが豊田市の本社で研修を受けることになっ

ギアをトヨタに入れるアメリカ人

フレッド・ハイアット
1988年3月13日

エヴァリー（訳注：ケンタッキーから訪れた David Everly）は尊敬に満ちた面持ちで語ったものだ。「ほんとにみんなここでは、よく働くもんだ。俺の仕事は、アメリカ人の労働者を、日本人と同じくらい熱心かつ速く働けるようにすることなんだ。正直いって、気合を入れてかからないとね」。

アメリカが日本に教えた概念が、ケンタッキーのトヨタ工場で実りの輪を結ぶ

東郷茂彦
1994年1月27日

最初は、小さな傷に過ぎなかった。当地で造られるトヨタ・カムリの新車25,000台のうち、350台から400台のドアの内装部分についた、小さな傷である。それは、ドアに施錠を取り付ける時、電動ネジ回しを持った労働者の手が滑ったのが原因だった……。解決策を見つけるため、組立ラインで働く6人のアメリカ人は、日本企業によって先鞭をつけられたチーム・プレーの技法を用いた。かくして、1950年代に日本に来た2人のアメリカ人コンサルタントが、日本の経営者に品質管理についていろいろと教えて以来の、一連の輪が結ばれたのだ……。チームのメンバーである43歳のジョン・モリスが、そのアイデアを考えるのにわずか20分しかかからなかった。つまり、ドアに施錠を取り付ける時、錠の上にプラスティックの板を置いてドアを守るのだ。2ヵ月かけ、チーム全体で対策案を完成した後は、作業員がドアを傷つけることはなくなった。

たのを取材したのが最初の記事だ。本社勤務中、同工場を訪れる機会があり、そこで、アメリカ人労働者のQC活動が大いに盛り上がっているという話を聞き込み、補足取材をして書いたのが次の記事だ。ホンダの系列工場で働く元空軍将校は「(日本からの) The transfer of technology and management skill is on the way.」と自信に満ちて語り、日本のTQC産みの親と言われる石川馨氏を記念するIshikawa Prize が、アメリカ人のQC活動を対象に新設されたという話などはなかなか感動的だった。

4. Reporting It Fair and Square

The Ties That Bind U.S. and Japan

By Hobart Rowen

January 24, 1988

During the past ten years, the Japanese and American economies have grown increasingly interdependent, not only on trade, but on the investment side.

"Look at the United States and Japan as an integral, coupled economy and the [trade] imbalances you see disappear," said Percy Mistry, a former adviser to the World Bank now teaching at Oxford.

It would be difficult to imagine the United States without Japanese cars and other consumer goods—and without the flow of investment money that helps finance the American budget deficit. Equally, it would be tough for Japan to replace its American market—and the acquisition of new technological ideas.

But the U.S.–Japan relationship goes beyond economic and financial affairs. It is the most important bilateral relationship in the world, as our venerable ambassador, Mike Mansfield, likes to say, because the United States needs Japan, and Japan needs the United States, to provide military security for each other and for the non-Communist world.

That's why it is important to defuse irrational responses here over the huge Japanese trade surplus, as well as the bitterness in Japan over America's seeming inability to put its own economic house in order.

The mutual bashing serves no purpose.

日米経済摩擦に心を傷めている人間で、彼の名前を知らない者はまずいないのではないか。愛称 Bart。米メディアの中の、公平な判断と暖かい心情の象徴だった。その慧眼は、日本の住宅事情と生活レベルの改善こそが「the only long-term solution to correct the huge imbalances between Japan and its trading partners」(86/6/5) と書かせる一方、米貿易赤字の8割はマクロ経済政策による米国内事情に起因し、貿易差額をなくすために「force it (=Japan) to give up unfair trading practice」は間違いだと主張する (90/5/3)。おかげでアメリカ人から「日本びいきの裏切り者」といった類の非難が寄せられたというが、そうした手紙類を、本社の自

4. 公平に報道する

アメリカと日本を結ぶ絆

ホバート・ローウェン

1988年1月24日

ここ10年の間に、日米両国の経済は、通商だけでなく投資の分野でも、互いに依存するようになってきた。

「アメリカと日本を、1つにまとまった経済の結合体と見做すなら、現在のような[貿易]不均衡は消え失せる」と、世界銀行の元顧問で、現在はオックスフォード大学で教鞭を執るパーシー・ミストリーは述べた。

日本車などの日本製品を抜きにして、そして財政赤字の穴埋めをしてくれる日本からの資金投入なしに今のアメリカを語ることは困難であろう。同様に、日本がアメリカに代わる市場を見つけたり、新技術の着想を他の国から得ることは難しい。

今や日米関係は、経済や金融上の枠を超え、我らが高潔なマイク・マンスフィールド大使も好んで言うように、世界で最も重要な2国間関係となった。それも、両国間だけでなく非共産主義世界全体に軍事的な安全保障をもたらすために、アメリカは日本を必要とし、日本もアメリカを必要としているからである。

それゆえに重要なのは、日本の膨大な貿易黒字に対するアメリカ側の不合理な反応や、アメリカの財政状態がなかなかよくならないことに対する日本側の厳しい見方をなくすことである。

お互いに相手を叩きあっても何の益にもならないのだ。

分のオフィスのガラス戸に、外から見えるように張り「I am proud of this stuff.」と嬉しそうに笑っていたものだった。病を得たBartは、95年4月13日に死去。享年76。WPは翌14日の紙面で長文の obituaries のほかに assistant managing editor for business newsのDavid Ignatius が「Indeed, it was Bart who helped make it (= economic journalism) a true profession, one with ethics, integrity, and sophistication.」と書き、その死を悼んだ。

The World Needs U.S.–Japanese Teamwork

By Stephen S. Rosenfeld

April 30, 1990

A week's inspection of official and private thinking in Tokyo does not leave me thinking, with some, that the repeated intensifying disputes on trade and other economic issues are going to produce an explosion or some absolutely intolerable condition of crash between the two countries.

The Japanese and American economies are too intertwined for that. Habits of cooperation are too broad and deep. Japan's security dependency on the United States is now a permanent and treasured fixture of the Asian landscape. Japanese like and admire a great many features of American life: the democratic example, the lifestyle, consumer goods, business services, pop culture....

The real danger, I think, is not a breakdown in relations, let alone a Japanese reversal of alliance, but a grinding deterioration that sours everything and spoils the marvelous potential for cooperation that now exists between these two great nations....

This particular competition is one that no responsible nation would want to win or lose. Such is the connection between the two countries, and their capacity for global impact and service, that it would be a universal loss for either to fall short of its duty to itself and the common good.

半導体摩擦や東芝叩きで日米間に緊張の高まった87年春、Robert J. Samuelson はコラム「Japan Bashing a Gambit」(4/8) で、「It's a perilous gambit: an invitation to bitter, mutually harmful conflicts.」と書き、双方の感情的対応に警告を発した。11年間、駐日大使を務めた Mike Mansfield の引退時、WPは「Japan: The View From Mansfield / As Roles Shift, U.S. Should Become "Less Emotional, More Practical"」(89/1/16 By Don Oberdorfer) と題するインタビューを掲載。その翌年、短期訪日した Deputy Editorial Page EditorのSteve Rosenfeld が書いたのが上記の記事だ。「Fantastic country, Japan ... it has created its own social and economic marvel and its own sort of plausible democracy, too.」。

世界は、米・日のチームワークを必要とする

スティーヴ・ローゼンフェルド

1990年4月30日

私は今回、東京において1週間の間、公私にわたる様々な考え方に接し、調査する機会があった。その結果、貿易をはじめとした経済問題で繰り返される紛争のため、両国関係は暴発するか、激突せざるをえないような条件が形成されることもある、と思わずにはいられなかった。しかし、そうした事態をひき起こすには、日米の経済は、あまりにも相互に入り組み過ぎている。企業の活動領域は、あまりにも広く、深い。日本は、国家の安全をアメリカに負っているが、その体制は今や恒久化し、アメリカは、アジアの地勢の中で、不動の位置を享受している。日本人は、アメリカ式の偉大な生活形態をおおいに好んでいる。例えば、民主主義的なあり方、消費物質、ビジネス上のサービス、ポップカルチャーなどである。……思うに、真の危機は、両国の様々な関係が壊れることではない。日米同盟をやめにしたい日本人がいるなら、そうさせればよい。真の危機とは、現在、ふたつの偉大な国の間に存在している、まことにすばらしい協力の可能性を台無しにし、すべてをじわりじわりと悪化させていくようなあり方である……。このような競争は、いやしくも責任ある国家が、あえて、勝ち負けを問うようなことではない。両国の関わり方は、このようなものである。両国の持つ地球的規模での影響力や役割に鑑みて、己に課せられた義務、並びに共通の善なるものが要請するところに答えなければ、世界的な損失を被ることになるであろう。

日米関係が最悪となった92年春、管理貿易の発想に対して「"Managed Trade": The Worst of Both Worlds / Quotas could come back to haunt us as ceilings on our most competitive exports.」(2/17 By James A. Cramer)。筆者は the University of Maryland の executive director で長く日本の国際企業に勤めていた。

CHAPTER 3

THE GLOBAL ECONOMY AND JAPAN

1. Asia, Japan, and U.S.
アジアと日米

太平洋戦争の前から現在に到るまで、アジアは、日本が思う以上に、世界国家アメリカの重要な後背地なのだ。

Paul Blustein は、東京駐在ではあるが、アジア地域の roving correspondent として、東南アジアを駆け巡った。その結論の1つが、米国とアジアの貿易量は、アジア圏内のそれをはるかに凌ぎ、アジアは、アメリカにとって、EC、カナダ、南米よりも大きな市場であると報じた「Japan's 'Asian Bloc': More Illusion Than Reality / Behind the Rhetoric, Trade Statistics Show Nation's Ties Are Far Stronger to North America」(91/12/8) である。

financial section の一面に、「A LOOK AT THE 'CO-PROSPERITY SPHERE'」(大東亜共栄圏を意識した pun だ)と題し、関係地域間の貿易量を矢印で示した大きな地図を掲載。記事は Bangkok 発で、市内に氾濫する日本車、エアコン、スポーツ器具などにもかかわらず、アジアと太平洋を越えた北米とのつながりの強さを、現地のエコノミスト、ビジネスマン達に語らせている。なかでも、香港の日米両商工会議所の違いについて、米コンサルタント Robert Broadfoot は、こう指摘する。米商工会議所はメンバー数が5倍というだけでなく、地元の企業の参加が圧倒的に多い。「...because the organization is localized. Look at the Japanese membership—it's just Japanese names, which shows what one of their problem is."」。

日本のバブル経済の破綻に伴い、アジア地域の影響力の低下を論じたのが、「Sitting It Out in Asia: Japan's Investment in Region Slows After Economic 'Bubble' Bursts at Home」(92/6/7 By Paul Blustein) だ。

アメリカとヴェトナムの国交正常化に伴い、大使館開設のため Hanoi 入りした Secretary of State Warren Christopher に

第3章 国際経済の中の日本

　同行した現国務省担当、ロシア問題専門家 Michael Dobbs は「U.S. Shifts Goals In Markets of Asia: Failing to Sell its Brand of Democracy, America Now Promotes its Merchandise」(95/8/9) と報じた。「In the old days, we wanted to make Asia safe for democracy. These days, we want to make it safe for American products.」。記事中の米政府高官の言葉である。

　さて、アジアに新しく台頭した経済パワーが中国だ。香港の1997年返還に備え、WP は香港支局を95年春に再開設（米中国交正常化に伴い、北京支局が開設された時に廃止されていた）、Mozambique 紛争で精力的な取材をこなした Keith B. Richburg を赴任させた。96年3月、Keith と Sandy Sugawara（彼女も Paul と同じく、アジアの roving correspondent である）は、「Asia's Dragon: Neighbors Confront China's Power」という3回の連載を掲載した。Sandy は2回目を担当。「China Market Set to Eclipse Its Neighbors: Asian Business Cashes in on Rapid Economic Growth」(96/3/18)。

　共産体制下にあった中国は、経済的には長らく眠れる国だったが、今や、日本を筆頭に、NIES から ASEAN 諸国へと広がった経済成長の波に乗り始めた。「Now China is engaged in a similar process of rapid development but on a scale that dwarfs that of its neighbors.」。記事の結びは、中国でプリンターのリボンを製作している日本企業の役員の言葉だ。「Chinese people are bright; they have a good sense of management.... The coastal area, including Shanghai, has a population of 300 million. If one-third of the people do as well as Japan, that would be a threat, because that is the size of Japan's population."」。

2. Confusian Morality Wins the Day?

You Can't Argue With Asian Success, Only With Confucius' Role

By William Chapman

August 12, 1981

Is there such a thing as a Confucian ethic lurking at the root of Asian economic success stories, something like the good old Protestant ethic that supposedly underpinned the great Western successes of a century ago?

A number of scholars, diplomats and economists think the answer is "yes."

They point to the booming, prosperous countries stretching alongside China and see common threads that just may be traced to the teachings of the great Chinese scholar.

Japan. South Korea. Taiwan. Hong Kong. Singapore. All emerged from devastation and poverty in the past three decades to become textbook examples of economic takeoff. None has any natural resources to speak of. All had been touched, directly or indirectly, by the Confucian tradition....

He recalled a recent conversation in Peking with Premier Deng Xiaoping in which Deng was asked how China will cope with social problems if an economic advance gets under way.

"His reply was not Marxist but Confucian," Watanabe said. "He spoke about the virtues of being orderly and stable and said that is how China will manage."

上記が載ってから約15年後、Tom Reid は「Confucius Says: Go East, Young Man / Many Asians Now Think Their Lives and Values Are Better Than 'the American Way'」(95/11/19) と書いた。President Clinton の APEC 大阪会議不参加が決まった直後のOutlookに載った記事で、ワシントンで日本に関する英文ファックス・ニューズレター『The Japan Digest』を発行している Ayako Doi and Kim Willenson 夫妻の「Overdue Bill: To Asians, Clinton's No-Show Just Shows How Irrelevant the U.S. Could Become」も掲載された。Tom は、東——東南アジアの経済発展の原動力だけでなく、社会に現在も息づくモラルの根底に、儒教を見、それが、アメリカ型個人主義的物質文明に対する「The

2. 儒教社会の功績か

アジアの成功は疑いなし、儒教の役割は不可欠だ

ウィリアム・チャップマン

1981年8月12日

今から1世紀前の西洋の偉大な成功の基礎をなしたとされる古き良きプロテスタンティズムの倫理にも似た、儒教的な倫理なるものがアジア経済の成功物語の根源に潜んでいるのだろうか。

多くの学者や外交官、エコノミストは、答えは「イエス」と考えている。

彼らは、中国沿岸ぞいに展開する豊かで急成長を遂げている国々を挙げ、中国の偉大な賢人の教えに遡ることも可能な共通の糸を見いだしている。

日本、韓国、台湾、香港、シンガポール。いずれも、過去30年の荒廃と貧困から抜け出し、経済的な離陸の教科書的な事例となった。どの国もまともな天然資源にめぐまれず、直接もしくは間接的に、儒教的伝統に浴してきた……。

初代のアジア開発銀行総裁でエコノミストの渡辺武は、先日北京で行われた鄧小平首相との会話を思い起こす。鄧は、経済が成長した場合、中国は社会問題にどのように取り組むのかという質問を受けた。

「答えは、マルクス主義者というより、儒者のものだった。鄧は、秩序だち、安定していることの美徳について語り、それが中国のやり方だ」と渡辺は述べた。

Asian Way」を形成しているとする。住宅の広さやテレビのチャンネル数ではなく、地域の安全や放送内容の健全さこそ「standard of living」を計る基準であり「And it's not just that (西欧文明と) the values are different. Rather, these Asian Neo-Confucianists insist that their cultural values are better than ours.」。Tom は現在、日本での5年間の経験をまとめた『Confucius Lives Next Door』を執筆中だ。

Stephen Rosenfeld
論説副委員長

Part 3

Social News
第三部　社会ニュース

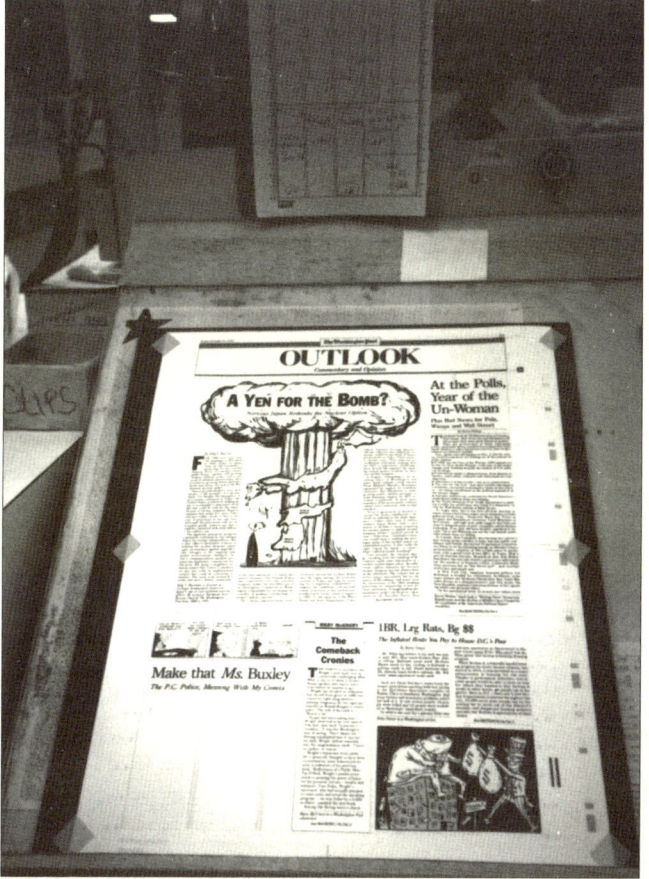

"Beginning to look good."

A New Aristocracy in the Land of the Rising Sun

By Fred Hiatt

April 10, 1988

A new aristocracy appears to be taking shape in Japan, an ancestral elite that is replacing the titled gentry of prewar days and challenging the meritocracy that has underpinned the nation's postwar success.

The rising new establishment, like the old, is based on wealth, inherited power, and strategic marriages linking the two. It is most evident in the Diet, or national parliament, where about one-third of ruling party members—and almost all the party's youngest legislators—are sons or sons-in-law of former politicians.

"A new aristocratic class is being formed," said Takayoshi Miyagawa, a political consultant. "If this trend continues, it will be not just a political problem, but a social problem.... It will sap our social energy."

But the emergence of new class structures in any society usually is gradual and relative. Japan remains an overwhelmingly middle-class society, with universal high-quality education, no real underclass, and ample opportunity for individual initiative. In some sectors, notably big business, the trend is away from inherited authority, most observers agree. But in many areas, the egalitarian, open system created by the U.S. occupation after World War II appears to be constricting....

The phenomenon of power and prominence among the second generation, or *nisei*, stretches from this season's most popular television show to the field of medicine....

More and more bureaucrats in the foreign or finance ministries are sons or sons-in-law of former bureaucrats....

Kabuki actors train their sons to succeed them; the masters of sumo stables marry their daughters to their strongest wrestlers....

新貴族階級が日出ずる国に形成される

フレッド・ハイアット

1988年4月10日

新しい貴族階級が、日本に形成されようとしている。家柄によって決まる選良達が、戦前の名門名跡に取って代わり、戦後日本の成功の土台となった能力主義に挑戦し始めた。

台頭著しい新支配階級は、旧体制と同様、富と世襲の権力、両者を結びつける政略結婚を基盤にしている。この点が最も顕著なのは、国会だ。政権与党の3分の1、若い与党議員の場合、ほぼその全員が、政治家経験者の実の、あるいは義理の息子である。

「新たな貴族階級が形成されつつある」と、政治コンサルタントの宮川隆義は言った。「もし、この傾向が続けば、政治的な問題だけでなく、社会問題となるだろう……。それは、我々の社会の活力を削ぐことになる」。

しかし、いかなる社会においても、新しい階級構造の出現は、まずは緩やかで相対的なものだ。日本の社会は依然として中産階級が圧倒的多数を占めている。高等教育はあまねく行き渡り、真の意味での下層階級は存在せず、個人の自発的行動に大きな可能性が開けている。一部の領域、とくに大企業では、権力を世襲するといった風潮は全くない、と多くの観察者は見ている。しかし、そのほかの多くの領域では、第2次世界大戦後に米国の占領中に形成された平等で開かれた制度は後退している……。

第2世代、あるにはニセイ(二世)に権力と名声が集まる現象は、今季最も人気の高いテレビ番組から、医療の分野にまで及んでいる(訳注:人気俳優や医者の子弟が、親の跡を継ぐようになったのだ)。

外務、大蔵両省では、官僚出身者の息子やその義理の息子達の数がますます増えてきた……。

歌舞伎役者は息子に芸を教え、跡を継がせようとする。相撲部屋の親方は、自分の娘を、部屋の中で一番強い力士に妻合わせる……。

The gradual concentration of power is such, Jin said, that the families of all but three of Japan's seventeen postwar prime ministers by now have linked themselves to the emperor himself, through marriage....

Graduation from Tokyo University's law faculty remains a passport into the elite, and entrance into the university has traditionally offered a "narrow ladder" for smart and hard-working young people with no connections....

Jin said the emergence of a new aristocracy may indicate that post-war democratic reforms did not fully take root. While zaibatsu families of prewar days never regained their power, he said, a new generation is emerging to replace them—with no protest from the public....

Others take a less gloomy view, noting that a free press and other essentials of democracy seem irreversibly ensconced. Second-generation politician Shiina said that, "I think the sense of values is changing. There are more people who don't believe that that is the best way to achieve happiness. They are not interested in that closed society.... I think it's healthy."

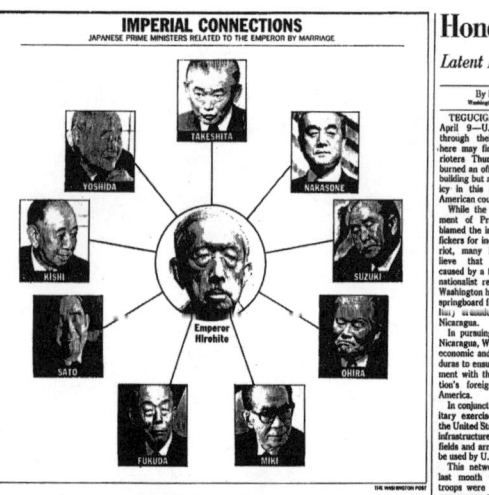

New Aristocratic Establishment

権力の集中は、緩やかに進んでいる。例えば次のように、と神一行（訳注：日本社会の研究家）は指摘する。戦後日本の総理大臣17人のうち、婚姻によって自らを天皇自身に繋げなかったのは3人だけだ……。

東京大学法学部を卒業することは、相変わらず選良へのパスポートを手に入れることだ。同大へ入ることは、これまでは、刻苦勉励型だが縁故のない学生に「狭い梯子」を提供する機会を与えてきた……。

神一行は、新しい貴族階級の台頭は、戦後の民主主義的な改革が日本に根付かなかったことの証かも知れないと指摘する。戦前の財閥がかつての権力を再び手に入れることはなかったものの、それに代わる新しい階級が台頭し、それに対する大衆の反対はない……。

それほど悲観的ではない見方をする者もいる。報道の自由をはじめとした民主主義の核をなすものが、もはや後戻りすることはあり得ないほど、がっちりと構築されているというのだ。「僕は、価値観が変わりつつあると思う。それ（東大をめざす権力志向型）が、幸福を得るための最良の道ではないと考える人たちが増えてきた。彼らは、こんな閉鎖社会にもう興味を抱いてはいない……。

健康なことだと思うよ」。自らも二世議員である椎名素夫は言った。

【解説】

日本社会が、多くの国民がそれと気づかぬうちに変質し、日本の進路がねじ曲がっていることがある。その1つに、自由平等を国是として戦後出発したにもかかわらず、いつのまにか社会の各分野に世襲制がはびこるようになった、というのが本論の指摘である。橋本総理を入れて戦後の総理24人の中、16人が何らかの形で皇室と姻戚関係にあり、世襲候補の割合は、全体の3分の1へと増え続けている（宮川隆義著『選挙の仕組み』より）。Fredは、社会の問題を追いかける報道姿勢にも富み、薬害エイズ問題も外国メディアで最も早く取り上げた1人だ。「Tainted U.S. Blood Blamed for AIDS' Spread in Japan: Hemophiliac Victims Criticize Slow Official Reaction to American Threat」(88/6/23)。アメリカの煙草会社の売らんかな主義を批判した「Tobacco Firms' Sales Effort in Asia Draw Fire」(87/11/13) もある。

CHAPTER 1 | **THE IMPERIAL FAMILY**

1. Emperor Showa
昭和天皇

Hirohito。日本人にとって、今は「昭和天皇」として記憶されるその人は、アメリカ人にとっては、あくまでも Hirohito である。

あらゆる日本人の中で未来永劫、Hirohito ほど、アメリカ人の心に、長く、深く刻まれた名は、おそらくないだろう。本節では、その生涯を、WP などがどう報じたかを検証するが、資料の入手に限りがあり、NYT などを積極的に参照することとした。

Hirohito が、大正天皇の皇位継承者という立場を越えた扱いを、米メディアから受けるのは、皇太子時代の1921年春から秋にかけての欧州旅行と、良子皇太子妃(現皇太后)とのご婚約の成否を巡る「宮中某重大事件」の時である。良子妃の母方縁戚の色盲の問題を懸念した山県有朋公が、この御婚約に疑義を呈した事件だった。

「TOKYO COURT PLOT BEHIND HEIR'S TRIP / Intrigue to Annul Crown Prince's Betrothal to Princess Nagako Is Revealed / MINISTERS FORCED TO QUIT / Newspaper Says Marshall Yamagata Also Will Retire, Accepting Responsibility for "Grave Affair."」(NYT 1921/2/14)

御婚約は滞りなく行われたこともあって、米メディアは以後、伝統に囚われた王国の開明的な若き Prince が、蒙昧なる臣下、とくに守旧派の元凶 Elder Stateman(元老)の圧力をはねのけて己の恋を貫き、国内の民主改革の担い手となったといった趣の報道を、一斉に行うこととなる。

例えば、NYT は「HIROHITO'S NEW PATH / Romantic Marriage of Japan's Prince Regent Sign of His Break with Traditions in Favor of Democratic Ways」(1922/7/23) と書き、『*The Readers Digest*』の前身、『*The Literary Digest*』(1922/1/7) の特集「JAPAN'S SEVENTY

第1章 皇室

DAZZLING YEARS」に掲載された皇太子の写真説明はこうだ。「 CROWN PRINCE HIROHITO: Japan's newly created Regent, who, it is said "will do more for the general cause of democracy in Japan than any other one factor."」。Regent は摂政のことで、御病気がちの大正天皇にかわり、1921年秋に座につかれている。なお、この頃の記事には、まだ Byline は常態化していない。

日本のメディアにとって、摂政宮との会見など考えられなかった当時、*The Saturday Evening Post* は、欧州旅行をも取材した Isaac F. Marcosson 記者による単独会見（正確には謁見というべきか）に成功。「AN AUDIENCE WITH THE JAPANESE PRINCE REGENT」(1922/5/27) は、軍服姿の摂政宮、皇居豊明殿、謁見直後の在京米大使館前で撮った Ambassador Charles B. Warren 大使と Marcosson 記者の写真など計5枚を使っている。殿下の印象については、「No one can meet the Prince Regent without carrying away the impression that he is sincere, earnest, and eager to do his best.」。しかし、「There is still the feeling in Japan…. that the Emperor is not a concrete personality but an incarnation of divine right.」な国では、「Though he has displayed a surprising sense of democracy, he has been obliged to yield in the main to the immemorial (太古からの) traditions of his rank and heritage.」。

1926年暮れ、大正天皇の崩御により、昭和天皇は皇位を嗣がれる。昭和は、Enlightened Peace あるいは Radiant Peace と訳されることが多い。2年後の京都での即位式まで、アメリカのメディアは、この神秘的な国のもっとも神秘的な行事を詳細に報道。あわせて、新天皇の分析記事が度々登場する。基本的には、これまでの開明的な Hirohito 像が描かれる。

この頃、アメリカにあって、日本問題に健筆をふるう日本人や日系人がいた。K. K. Kawakami（河上清）や、Adachi Kinnosuke らである。当然のことながら、皇室についての記

事は多い。彼らの描く Hirohito 像も上記のようなものだった。

「JAPAN'S FIRST MODERN EMPEROR / Who Allows No Traditional Halo of Divinity to Obscure His Human Qualities」(ASIA誌 1928/11 By K. K. Kawakami) や、「A MODERN MIKADO RULES A NEW JAPAN / Hirohito, Who Has Shown Himself Ready to Break with Traditions of the Past, Comes to the Throne at the Moment When His Country Appears Entering an Era of Change」(NYT 1927/1/9 By Adachi Kinnosuke) である。この頃まで、日本の天皇は、Mikado と呼ばれることも多かったのだ。

だが、時代は、次第に軍靴の高鳴りを告げ始め、Hirohito については2つのタイプの記事が散見されるようになる。

1つは、陸海軍大演習の統裁や観兵式、観艦式との関連である。例えば「HIROHITO REVIEWS HIS ENTIRE NAVY / 172 Vessels Assemble at Yokohama for Second Ceremony / Reduced 100,000 Tons by Washington Treaty, the Fleet is a Capable Defensive Unit.」(NYT 1927/10/31) などだ。

そして、34年には、陸軍大演習統裁のため関東地方を回られた昭和天皇の御列を、桐生市の警察官が誤導するという「大事件」が起きる。日本では、当の警察官の自殺(一命はとりとめる)から内閣総辞職まで取りざたされた。WP は、この事件について「The Wrong Turning」と題し、こう論評した。「A simple error, it would have been laughed off in this country and the most dire (悲惨な) result would have been the transfer of the sergeant.… But Japan is another county. The whole affair points up the vast difference between Eastern and Western psychology. It brings out mysterious traditions of an ancient land which are hard for us to comprehend.」(1934/11/20)。

この頃から、Hirohito の呼び方も、しばしば Hitler の Führer (総統) を思わせる Ruler へと変わっていく。「JAPANESE CHIEFS REPORT TO RULER」(NYT 1941/10/15 By Otto D. Tolischus)。

1930年代の後半、米メディアは、いくつか注目すべき日本特集を行っている。Harpers誌（39/2）は、有数のアジア通John Gunterによる「THE EMPEROR OF JAPAN」を特集するが、「Japan is ruled, not by the Emperor, but in the name of the Emperor.」という本質を掴んだ分析が見られる。また、新興ビジネス層に圧倒的な力のあったFortune誌（36/9）も200頁近い大日本特集を行っているが、その中で「WHO RUNS THE EMPIRE」という章を設け、天皇について同様な見方を展開している（同特集については寺島実郎著『ふたつの「FORTUNE」』に詳しい）。

　本格的な写真誌として大きな影響力をもっていたLIFE誌の特集は「SON OF HEAVEN / Japan's Last Liberal, The God-Emperor Hirohito, Is Prisoner of His Own Power」（1940/6/10 By Ernest O. Hauser）。表紙は、白馬に跨り、白手袋も鮮やかに敬礼する大元帥Hirohito——軍事国家としての大日本帝国を世界に象徴する姿だった。

　戦争が始まった。

　「The Guilty」。硬派の大衆誌Colliersは、1944/7/29日号で、細い目、分厚い唇のイラスト付のHirohitoを掲載。内容も、日本人を「the monkey people (as their neighbors knew them)」と呼び、Hirohitoに温情をもって接するべきだ、などというのはとんでもないと論じた。「Viewed honestly, he ranks with the Indian medicine men and African sorcerers of another time and is not more worthy of toleration…」。ただし、米当局は、日本人の戦闘意欲をいたずらに刺激しないためにも、アジア向けの短波放送や戦争関連のプロパガンダから天皇は注意深くはずし、NYTなどの報道も極めて抑制がきいたものとなっている。

　戦いが終わりに近づくにつれ、天皇処刑論がアメリカ内に強まる。WPには、その調査結果が掲載される。「The Gallup Poll / U.S. Public Split on Hirohito; Many Advocate His Execution」（1945/6/29 By George Gallup）。「What do you think we should do with the Japanese Emperor after the war?」という設問に対して、答えは次のようなものだった。

1. Execute him 33%
2. Let court decide 17%
3. Keep him in prison the rest of his life 11%
4. Exile him 7%
5. Do nothing 4%
6. Use him as a puppet to run Japan 3%
7. no opinion 23%

　1945年8月、日本は戦いに敗れ、世界各地から500人にのぼるジャーナリストが東京へ乗り込んできた。Hirohito は、戦犯に問われるか、あるいは、退位するのかが内外で論じられ（日本人の中にあった退位論なども NYT などが盛んに取り上げている）るが、最終的な米当局の意向は、帝位を維持するというものだった。しかし、SCAP (The Supreme Command of Allied Powers) の威光を示すには、Hirohito は、絶好の材料だった。例えば、天皇の General Douglas MacArthur 訪問の時。「Hirohito Calls on MacArthur In Precedent-Shattering Visit / Subject of 40-Minutes 'Social' Talk at U.S. Embassy Not Revealed—Emperor Wears Top Hat, General Lacks Necktie, Medals」(1945/9/27 By Lindesay Parrott)。

　なお、Parrott 記者は、次のような論陣も張っている。「Can We Prevent a Japanese Hitler?」(NYT Magazine 1946/3/10)。「Yes, but we must build up a democratic nation.」（副見出しより）というのが Parrott の答だ。「In any case there is little likelihood of the old military feudal caste (カースト) ever returning. What we have to fear, if the opportunity is lost, is a totalitarianism as much more dangerous than the old regime as Hitler's Germany was that the Hohenzollerns'. To those who say that this could not happen in Japan, it is scarcely necessary to reply that it did happen in Europe.」。

　Hirohito は、今や、日本の民主化のシンボルというのが大勢となる。『LIFE』は「Sunday at Hirohito's / Emperor Poses for First Informal Pictures」(1946/2/4) で、御一

家でくつろがれる天皇を中心に10枚の写真を掲載した。「Imperial family lives in royal bomb shelter」「Japs show emperor as scholarly family man」「Emperor reads "Times" and "Starts and Stripes" near "cherished" busts of Lincoln and Darwin」。

写真といえば、*Newsweek* (1947/10/6) がおもしろい。国民を励まされるための地方の巡幸先と思われるが、白い夏服を御召しの天皇が、右足を靴から出しているスナップを掲載。「Unshod Divinity: In another step to humanize his relations with the public, Emperor Hirohito poses for the first picture showing him with his shoes off.」。

日本は独立する。Hirohito は以後も、米メディアから絶えず注目を浴び続ける。時には強く、時には弱く。主旋律は、平和の時代を生きる円満な老帝。しかし、低音部には、絶えず、あの戦争の影が響いていた。

東京オリンピックや国会の開会式では、Hirohito の様子やお言葉が焦点となる。日本という国のエキゾティズムを出すために、記事の内容とまったく関係なくても、Hirohito の写真が使われることがある。日本の景気拡大のため特別予算決定を報じる記事のカットは、Hirohito の稲刈りのお写真だった (WP 82/10/9)。

1971年のヨーロッパ御訪問と、75年のアメリカ御訪問は、当然のことながら、メディアの注目するところとなる。

WP は、イギリスやオランダで、旧軍人達が、憎悪と不快の念をあらわにしたデモを行い、ブーイングを繰り広げたことなどを報道。東京発では、こうしたニュースは日本では小さな扱いしかされていないと報じている。

アメリカ御訪問では、報道史上、忘れられない出来事がある。*Newsweek* の Bernard Krisher 東京支局長による単独会見だ (75/9/29 日号)。50人を超える関係者への根回しを7ヵ月間にわたって行った結果だった。「I don't think there has been any change, spiritually, in my prewar and postwar roles. I feel I have always acted in strict observance of the constitutions.」と述べられた天皇は、戦争

との関わりについて、開戦時は政府の判断に従わざるをえなかったこと、終戦時は、政府より求められての「聖断」だったことを簡明に述べられている。

また、Washington 滞在中の関連では、WP の辛口の社交記者として知られる Sally Quinn による「Those Dinners Can Be Hard Work」(75/10/4) がおもしろい。アメリカ人あこがれの White House の晩餐会も、当の大統領夫妻にとっては結構しんどいという記事だ。「It's making conversation that's the real killer. Especially when your guests don't speak English too well. And His Majesty, the 74-year-old Emperor of the Chrysanthemum Throne, seemed limited mainly to a number of "Ah so" ("Oh, really," in Japanese).」。

その後、米メディアは、戦前戦中を通じて、日本の支配下におかれた国々の元首や最高指導者と Hirohito との会談に注目する。韓国、中国、フィリピン等々。それぞれに対し、過去をどのように形容されるか。Unfortunate か。Sorrow なのか。「謝罪」をされるのか。

やがて、病を得られた昭和天皇は、1989年1月6日、崩御される。その死をめぐり、日本の反応を含め、膨大な海外報道がなされたのは読者の記憶に新しいと思うのでここでは繰り返さない。ただ、次の点に触れたおきたい。

アメリカの報道は、ヨーロッパのそれにくらべ、はるかに好意的だったことである。日本問題に関わり続けている James Fallows とこの点について、話す機会があったが、(1) アメリカ自身の決断で Hirohito を戦後の占領政策上、残すことにした。(2) 日系人の収容や原爆、空襲など、アメリカの負い目。(3) 戦いで日本を完璧に打ち砕いたという実感（ヨーロッパにはこれがない）。(4) 日米安保を機軸とした戦後の同盟関係、などの理由をあげた。

Hirohito の死に当たり、WP は「The Emperor of Enlightened Peace」と題する社説を掲げた (89/1/8)。「With that choice (to surrender) he saved not only uncounted Japanese lives, but American lives as well. Perceived in this country during the war as a fanatic, he emerged as a man with a surer sense of balance than most of his advisers.」。

若き立憲君主として、アメリカのジャーナリストの共感を勝ち得たHirohitoの人間像は、ここに再び1つに結ばれたのである。

［本論は、1989年3月発行『文藝春秋』臨時増刊号「大いなる昭和」に掲載した拙論「恩讐を乗り越えたアメリカの天皇観」執筆の際に集めた資料と、同論を中心にまとめ、一部は直接引用もしている］

2. The Reigning Emperor and Empress

Japanese Emperor Accosted on Arrival for First U.S. Visit

By William Booth

June 11, 1994

ATLANTA—At a brief reception at the Martin Luther King Center, the rabble-rousing Rev. Hosea L. Williams pushed his large frame before the majesties and told them he considered the Japanese a racist people.

It was one of the few spontaneous moments in this most-scripted of days, filled with careful smiles on both sides as Atlantans put on a lavish display of southern hospitality and the emperor and his wife responded with imperial gratitude and restraint.... Their smiles—constant and encouraging and almost warm—suddenly froze....

"I found the Japanese people to be very disrespectful of African Americans," said Williams. He told them that blacks buy $13 billion in Japanese products—"but not a single black American has a Japanese franchise," he said.

In his soft, almost inaudible English, Emperor Akihito, whose visit to the King Center was designed to demonstrate Japanese respect for black Americans, thanked Williams for his "admirable question."

The moment vanished like a puff of smoke.

文字どおり、people が国を造り、王政とは、最も縁遠いアメリカだが、Royal Family に対するアメリカ人のあこがれには相当なものがある。英王室と並び、日本の皇室は常にニュースの的だ。

今上陛下が即位されるに当たり、神秘的な大嘗祭は、特に米メディアの関心を呼ぶ。WPでは「Sun Goddess Rite in Modern Japan」(90/11/24 By Tom Reid) と RELIGION の section に掲載だ。次に94年6月の訪米時。「The Emperor Who Bowed to Change, Japan's Akihito, Up-to-Date Symbol of Tradition」(94/6/13 同)。世界最古最長の君主制の継承者であり、同時に日本の変化の象徴でもあるとし、「a man of many contradictions」。上記のように Atlanta を経てワシントン入りされた両陛下は、state guest とし

2. 今上陛下，美智子皇后

日本の天皇、初の訪米に際して見知らぬ人に話しかけられる

ウィリアム・ブース　　　　　　　　　　　1994年6月11日

アトランタ発——かつてはアトランタの黒人地区の中心だったマーチン・ルーサー・キング・センターで行われた短いレセプションにおいて、大音声と派手な振る舞いで知られたホセア・L・ウィリアムズ牧師が、両陛下の前に巨軀を進ませた。日本人は人種差別主義者だと彼は自らの見解を述べた。アトランタ側による南部流の惜しみないもてなしに対する天皇夫妻の皇室流の感謝と慎みをもった答礼。双方の注意深く準備された微笑。こうした台本通りのスケジュールの中で、これは自発性の発揮された数少ない瞬間であった……。絶えることがなく、人々を励まし、ほとんど暖かなといってもよい2人の微笑は突然凍りついた……。「日本の人たちは、アフリカ系アメリカ人にまったく敬意を表していないことが私には分かったのです」……。黒人は、13億ドルもの日本製品を購入するが、「日本にフランチャイズのある黒人は誰1人としていない」と、ウィリアムズは述べた。穏やかな、そしてほとんど聞き取れない英語で、アキヒト天皇は、ウィリアムズの「感嘆すべき質問」に対し、謝意を表した。彼のキング・センターへの訪問は、日本人の黒人系アメリカ人に対する敬意を表すために企画されたものだった。だが、この瞬間は、たちまちにして煙のように消え去ってしまった。

て大統領の歓迎を受け、翌14日付は特に Style に記事が満載される。「The Royal Visit: A Bit of Haiku and Hollywood」(By Donnie Radcliffe and Roxanne Roberts) のほか「The Food」「The Fashion」「The Guest List」といった具合だ。1面でも写真を大きく使い「Japan's Silent Majesty」(By Joel Achenbach) という記事を載せているが、「astonishingly substance-free, an almost 100-percent symbolic event」「if there is any news to come from this, it is simply that Washington can still do emperors」といった皮肉も利かせている。

Teatime on Tiptoes

By T. R. Reid

May 28, 1994

"Remember," an earnest gentleman from the Imperial Household Agency hissed, "this is a social occasion."

Well, sort of....

Throughout the 40-minute session with the emperor and empress, an extremely uptight corps of courtiers and palace bureaucrats kept prodding and poking at us to make sure we stood only in the right places and spoke only at the right times.

The royal couple seemed to make everything copacetic. "I wish we could get together more often," the empress said—and sounded as if she really meant it.

The Royal Sound of Silence

By T. R. Reid

October 28, 1993

The royal bureaucracy has traditionally held a firm control over the palace press, with private pressure sufficient to suppress unwanted stories. From now on, however, a different tactic is required, the Imperial Household Agency's Miyao told the parliament today. "After this, with a mind to the empress's feelings, we will correct inaccurate information as soon as it comes out," he said. That too will make for a more open, American-style relationship between press and government.

皇室との接触は、通常は宮内庁記者会の独占事項だが、外国プレスも正式会見にはまず出席できる。皇居はホワイトハウスに比べれば「security measures were minimal」(91/9/21 By Tom Reid) で、金属探知器もなければ、軍の警備もない。「But once we got inside, every step was controlled ... assigned seats, when we should stand, when we could sit, how we should bow, etc.」。こうした雲の上からのニュースには想像も出来ないようなことが起きた。93年夏から秋にかけてのメディアのいわゆる「Michiko-bashing」(93/12/13 同) である。「The Empress's New Clothes In Japan: the Press Is No Longer Mum」(9/25 同)。「Criticized Empress Collapses」(10/21 同)。そして上記第2の記事。

つま先でティータイムを

トム・リード　　　　　　　　　　　　　　　1994年5月28日

「覚えておいてください。これは懇親の場、社交の場です」と宮内庁の生真面目そうな紳士が我々に告げた。まぁ、そうなんでしょう、きっと……。

40分に及ぶ天皇と皇后との会見中、背筋をピンと伸ばしきった、宮廷の吏員や官僚の一団が、我々の立つべき場所、話すべき時が正しくあるよう、こと細かな干渉を絶えず続けてきた。

天皇夫妻は、すべて満足な状態にすることが出来るようだ。「もっと、このような機会をもてたらいいですね」と皇后は述べられた——まるで、本当にそう願っているように聞こえたものだ。

皇室流サウンド・オブ・サイレンス

トム・リード　　　　　　　　　　　　　　　1993年10月28日

皇室を管轄する官僚機構はこれまで、皇室関係の報道をしっかりと掌握し、好ましくない記事は、内輪の圧力をかけるだけで抑えてきた。しかしながら、今後は、違った方法が必要であると宮内庁の宮尾盤(いわお)は今日、国会で証言した。「これからは、皇后陛下のお気持ちをお察し致し、誤った情報は直ちに訂正することにいたします」と彼は述べた。これによって、もっと開かれた、アメリカ式の報道陣と政府の関係がもたらされることになろう。

やがて「The Empress Speaks」(12/13 同)となるが、「It's clear that some elements of Japanese society deplored the new tone in news coverage. On the other hand, the articles seemed to find an audience and sell magazines.」と書いている。この年の天皇誕生日の一般参賀の皇后陛下の御様子はこうだ。「the thin, stately Michiko seemed the least comfortable of the royals」(12/24)。

As Emperor Lays Wreath, Imperial Family's War Role Comes Under Criticism

By T. R. Reid

July 28, 1995

HIROSHIMA, Japan—Protesters? There were indeed—and they represent an important change in Japan's collective view of World War II.

The several groups of demonstrators who gathered as Emperor Akihito came here on his "condolence tour" marking the 50th anniversary of the atomic bombings were arguing that Japan's imperial family itself was responsible for World War II, and thus for the use of the atomic bomb.

This increasingly common line of analysis is itself part of a larger trend to move from the old idea here of "Japan the victim" in World War II to "Japan the aggressor."

"For a long time, it was strictly taboo to suggest that the emperor was responsible for this tragic war," said Daikichi Irokawa, a history professor at Tokyo University of Economics. "But things have changed, and there are many of us saying that Emperor Showa could have prevented the war in the first place and could have brought about a surrender long before the atomic bomb was used...."

The taboo on challenging the conventional wisdom about Hirohito was powerful—as Hitoshi Motoshima, former mayor of Nagasaki, learned the hard way. After he made a fairly mild observation that Hirohito was one of many people responsible for the war, he was shot and wounded by an angry nationalist.

昭和天皇と同じく、今上陛下も究極の政治的な役割を逃げられないようだ。とくに戦争との関わりにおいて。天皇と皇后両陛下は戦後50年の95年春に沖縄、夏に原爆の地を強い御意思の元に訪れられる。Tom Reidはこの時の「The Honorable Words」(お言葉)に注目した。内容というより、形式に。沖縄では「Still, Akihito was quickly shown that old animosities (敵意) toward Tokyo had not died among Okinawans.」(4/24)。従って、お言葉は「Because it was feared that an official imperial speech might grate (いらだたせる) on some Okinawans, it was decided that the emperor should make his remark as informal as possible, with no lectern (聖書などを置く台) and no written text.」。広島の直前に訪問さ

天皇が献花する時、皇室の戦争責任を問う声

トム・リード

1995年7月28日

広島発——抗議する人達？確かにいた。そして、彼らは、第2次世界大戦に関する日本の全体的な見方の重要な変化を象徴している。

アキヒト天皇が「慰霊の旅」で、原爆投下50周年を迎えるここ広島を訪れたのと時を同じくし、集まったいくつかの抗議デモの団体は日本の皇室自体が、第2次大戦の責任を有しており、従って、原爆の使用にも責任があるとの論議をくり広げた。

ますます影響力を増しつつあるこの種の見解は、第2次大戦の「犠牲者日本」という古い考え方から「侵略者日本」という考え方への移行というより大きな潮流の一部である。

「この悲劇的な戦争に関し、天皇に責任があると指摘するのは、長い間、完全にタブーであった」と東京経済大学の歴史学教授色川大吉はいう。「しかし、状況は変わった。昭和天皇はそもそも戦争を阻止することができ、原爆の使用はるか以前に降伏をもたらすことができたと主張する我々のような人間が今では多数いる」……。

ヒロヒトに対する一般通念に異議を唱えるのは厳しいタブーだった。本島等長崎前市長は、身をもってそれを知った。ヒロヒトが、戦争に責任ある多くのうちの1人であるという、比較的おだやかな批判を行った後、彼は、怒った国粋主義者によって狙撃され傷を負った……。

れた長崎では、「Because World War II, and the bombs that ended it, are so sensitive here, it was decided that the emperor would say nothing during his A-bomb pilgrimage.」（7/27）。その代わり、宮内庁が「a one-page statement under the title "The Honorable Feelings"」を発表するのだが、これは「a somewhat less weighty rubric (典礼) than "honorable words"」なのだった。

3. The Crown Prince and Princess Masako

Japan Picking Princess

By T. R. Reid & Shigehiko Togo

January 6, 1993

With the clock running out on the Japanese media's vow of silence regarding the crown prince's marriage prospects, the Imperial Palace is evidently racing to arrange a royal engagement before the news embargo ends....

Once again, many suggested that the new princess may be Harvard graduate Masako Owada, an official in the Foreign Ministry....

Word of court arrangements spread rapidly through media and government circles today, but not a word appeared in Japan's normally vigorous press. For the past year, all media outlets have adhered to a voluntary agreement not to report a word about the prince's long search for a spouse....

Reporters on the court beat, many of whom have waited years to report this one story, are "jumping up and down with frustration" because they cannot report it now, one palace journalist said today. There is no legal restriction on publishing the news, but in Japanese society, the fact of a consensus agreement is strong enough to make everyone go along.

WPの東京支局にとって、皇太子妃決定はニュースである。従って、お妃探しにはそれなりの努力は払ってきた。日本のメディアの熱狂的な取材ぶりと、そのおかげで発足した報道自粛協定は、さらにニュース価値を増す。「The conflict between press freedom and personal privacy comes up in every modern society, but it's unlikely that any other free country could have dealt with it the way the Japanese did.」(92/11/11 By Tom Reid)。FCCJ傘下のThe Foreign Press in Japan（FPIJ、在日外国報道協会）に日本新聞協会から自粛を知らせては来たが、参加要請など全くなかった。しかし、日本のメディアのようにこの件に専念できるわけもなく、「お妃決定」の情報を得てから掲載までは24時間以内、内容の確認

3. 皇太子殿下と雅子妃

プリンセスを選ぶ日本

トム・リード ＆ 東郷茂彦　　　　　　　　　　1993年1月6日

皇太子の結婚の見通しについて、日本のメディアが守っている沈黙の誓いが時間切れに近づくにつれ、宮内庁は、報道管制の終わる前に、御婚約をとりつけようと傍目にも明らかな奔走を始めた。

新たなプリンセスは、ハーバード大学を卒業し、外務官僚である小和田雅子であると、再び多くの者が示唆した……。

宮中の御婚約が取り決められたという話は、メディアや政府の関係機関内に今日、またたくまに広まったが、普段は活発な日本の報道に、この件は一切登場していない。ここ1年間、この国のあらゆるメディアは、長びく皇太子の伴侶捜しについて、一言も報じないという自主協定に忠実に従った……。

この一事のみを報じようと何年も待ち続けてきた多くの皇室担当の記者たちは、この状況下でも報道出来ないため、「フラストレーションで、いてもたってもいられない」と、ある皇室担当のジャーナリストは今日語った。このニュースを報ずることに、法律的な制限はない。しかし、日本社会において、全体の総意によって合意した内容は、全ての人々を従わせるだけの力を持つ。

に最大限の神経を使い、出稿を決断したのは印刷される数時間前であった。天皇陛下の場合、やはり外国メディアがお妃決定を最初に報じたが、日本の主要メディアは解除の予定日まで協定を守った。今回は、日本新聞協会が、ただちに解除を求めて宮内庁に通告する形をとり、6日午後8時45分から一斉にニュースが流れだしたわけだ。

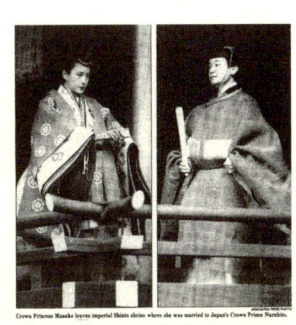

Tying the Royal Knot

Opportunity of a Wifetime

By Elisabeth Bumiller

February 1, 1991

Wanted: intelligent, attractive, athletic, and discreet young Japanese woman from a leading business, diplomatic, or academic family; fluent in English and also, ideally, French; with no ex-boyfriends. Must be no taller, in heels, than 5 feet 4 and no older than 25. Should be prepared to give up considerable freedom in Japan in exchange for ladies-in-waiting, overseas travel, and opportunities to meet world leaders. Independent minded career women acceptable, but no daughters of politicians, please.

Myth of Masako

By T. R. Reid

June 6, 1993

The Japanese media have portrayed Owada as the "Perfect Princess," who will adapt cheerfully to her new life behind the big moat. The U.S. view is darker.

American media have depicted the princess-to-be as a sad case, a successful career woman who was pressured into throwing her job and her freedom overboard. In this view, Owada is a draftee who happened to be in the wrong place at the wrong time....

But among some people here who know the royal bride well, there is a third view, a theory that is less romantic than the Japanese ideal but more uplifting than the American portrayal.

皇太子殿下を「The Charming Prince, a Most Eligible Bachelor」とWPが報じたのは、昭和天皇崩御の直後だった (89/1/14 By Margaret Shapiro)。上記はともに Style 1面を覆う大原稿で、最初のは、小和田雅子さんを含め、お妃候補として名前の上がった3人の写真を使い、お妃がなかなか決まらない要素を「The Michiko Factor」「The Old Daddy Factor」「The Rich Girl Factor」「The Stubbornness Factor」の4つに分けている点が今でも面白い。それぞれを言い替えれば、「嫁イジメ」「オジン」「バブルの令嬢」「恋愛結婚至上主義」といったところか。皇太

妻への扉は

エリザベス・ビュミラー
1991年2月1日

求む。聡明で魅力的、健康で慎み深い若い日本女性。一流の実業家、外交官、学者の家系出身。英語に流暢、望むらくはフランス語も。過去に男性との深い交際経験なし。身長はヒールを履いても5フィート4インチ以下。25歳より若いこと。女官付きの生活、海外旅行、そして世界の指導者たちと会うのと引き換えに、日本の生活で、かなりの自由を犠牲にする覚悟要。自立心のある職業婦人、可。しかし、政治家の娘は、頼むからお断り。

マサコの神秘性

トム・リード
1993年6月6日

日本のメディアは、小和田を「完璧なプリンセス」として描いてきた。皇居を囲む大きな堀と屋根を戴いた白壁の背後の新生活に楽しげに適応するだろうと。しかし、米国の見方はもっと暗い。アメリカのメディアは、未来のプリンセスを、キャリア・ウーマンの道を成功裡に歩んでいた女性が、仕事と自由を投げ捨てさせられた悲しい物語として描いている。この見方によれば、小和田は、誤った時に、誤った場所にいた応召兵である……。しかし、ロイヤル・ブライドをよく知っている人の中には、第3の見方が存在する。日本の求める理想からすれば、さほどロマンチックではないものの、米国の描写よりは上向きである。この見方によれば、小和田雅子は、まさに自分が求めていたものを手に入れたというのだ……。

子妃となられた雅子様は、アメリカの高校とハーバード大学の卒業、完璧なキャリア・ウーマンといった経歴、人柄や容姿もあいまって米メディアの圧倒的な人気の的になっている。第2の記事では、御成婚に対する第3の見方をとる根拠に、名前を明かせない「a Japanese who has known her since childhood」が、結婚を決めたのは、決して犠牲によるものではなく、「because she decided it will make her happy. She is a very intelligent woman who knows what she wants in life and sets out to get it.」と述べたことをあげている。

CHAPTER 2 | **DAILY LIFE**

1. The Mass Media
メディア

日本のジャーナリズムや出版界、なかでも隆盛を極める漫画は、この国の特質を良く顕す分野として、米メディアは注目している。皇室とジャーナリズムとの関わり方がしばしば論じられるのも、両者の関係性の中に、「日本とは何か」をキラリと浮かび上がらせる鍵があると見るからだ。

阪神大震災の時に、こんなニュースが載った。「Rift in Coverage: Japanese and Western Quake Reporting Worlds Apart」(92/2/1 By Tom Reid)。西欧の記者は「the worst scenes of destruction」「the most crushing moments of personal loss」を追い求め、特にアメリカの記者は、「Do you think the government has done enough to help?」といった点をズケズケと聞く。これに対し日本の記者は、破壊の中に建設的な視点を見つけようとし、「focused much more on harmony.... that being, after all, what the Japanese viewer would expect to see.」というのだ。

そんなaggressiveな外国メディアが日本の取材で遭遇するのがあの記者クラブ制度だ。1964年3月、Edwin O. Reischauer 米大使が暴漢に襲われた時、「even when the Ambassador of my own country had been stabbed, I could not attend the press conference held by the police」と、LATのSam Jameson。

1985年当時、すでに日米経済摩擦の象徴だった自動車問題で、日本メーカーの米本土工場進出が最大の解決策と見られていた。しかし、業界最大手トヨタ自動車は慎重な姿勢を崩さない。方針が決まれば「that was certain to be an important news story in the U.S.」(85/11/21 By John Burgess)。ところが「When company president Shoichiro Toyoda announced the plan at a Tokyo press conference, no

第2章 生活

American journalists were present. Many had wanted to attend, but were told they could not, because there was not enough space.」。この決定は会社ではなく、記者クラブがしたもので、「There are about 400 press clubs in Japan, and many foreign reporters see them as the journalistic equivalent of a non-tariff trade barrier.」。

　こうした状況を打開するために、FCCJ の中に、外国メディアだけによる The Foreign Press in Japan（在日外国報道協会）があり、天皇陛下の御成婚以来の過去40年、権利拡張運動を行っている。現在、associate member として、大半の中央省庁の公式会見や、必要に応じてのブリーフィングに出席できる。なかでも、取材をほとんど受け付けなかった東京地検が、足掛け3年越しの FPIJ の交渉の末、90年春、門戸を開いたこと。日本新聞協会が外国記者を各クラブの判断において正会員として認めるべしとするガイドラインを策定したことは大きい。WPは「Foreign Reporters in Japan May Finally Get Equal Access to News」(93/6/11 By Tom Reid) と報じた。

　テレビは宣伝に威力がある故、ときに問題を起こす。貿易摩擦下での faceless Japanese との批判に応えるため、日本が外国へのPRに真剣に取り組み始めた80年代半ば、政府の肝入りで、アメリカのケーブルテレビに日本紹介の番組を送りこんだ。「Japanese Authorities Back Image-Making Effort on U.S. Cable TV」(84/4/26 By William Chapman)。民間のスポンサー付き番組が2シリーズ放送され、「Although the government has sought to remain in the background, three ministries have assisted in arranging the two current shows' corporate sponsorship in a manner that illuminates the traditionally close relationship between business and government.」。こうした番組では「although its sponsors are private」、外務通産運輸など関係省庁のお墨付きがないと「it could not have gotten off the ground」。従って、政府の行為を原則、悪とみなし、民間への関与を極端に警戒するアメリカから見れば「raises journalistic questions」なのだ。記事では、こうした発足時の経緯、直接間接政府の予算が使われている点、editorial control の疑いなどを具体的に指摘している。

来日した President Bush が総理官邸の晩餐会席上で倒れた時、存在しないとされた嘔吐の瞬間の映像が、NHK の無人カメラに映っていた。外国メディアの中で、ほとんど最初に見る機会を得、その存在を報じたが、外国要人に気を使う政府やメディアの一部から、テープの公開はルール違反という声があがったものだ。「Japanese Cameraman Got Crucial Tape by Breaking the Rules」(92/1/10 By Tom Reid)。93年夏の総選挙をめぐる、いわゆるテレビの偏向報道については「concern about a potential threat to freedom of speech grew rapidly」(10/26 By Tom Reid) といった視点を加えた記事になっている。

「In Japan, the Serial Addiction」(92/4/22 By Tom Reid) の書き出しは、「My name is T.R. Reid and I am a mangaholic (漫画中毒とでも訳す？)」。こんな文章は、まさに才能あればこそだ。Tom は来日するとすぐ大変な漫画ファンになった。最初は「ちびまる子ちゃん」で、「At the Crest of Cute: How 'Tiny Miss Maruko' Stole Japan's Heart」(90/10/11)。アメリカで大流行の The Simpsons の「sour and cynical」さに比べると、「sugary sweet」で「traditional values」を全面的に肯定しているという。この記事がちびまる子ちゃんを国際化したというので、Tom はこの年の流行語大賞を受賞した。なお The Simpsons 的な感覚は「クレヨンしんちゃん」に表れたと後になって Tom は話している。

WPで漫画を最初に取り上げたのは Margaret Shapiro だ。「Time is limited and society is moving so fast. Manga are easier. If you can convey the same thing by picture, why not?」(90/3/24) という編集者の言葉を紹介。宗教、政治、文学から外交、宣伝などあらゆる分野が漫画化されていると報じた。

その3ヵ月後、Atlantaで日米混合のbilingual雑誌『漫画人 MANGAJIN』が創刊された。副題は「Japanese Pop Culture & Language Learning」。日本で評判の漫画5、6編とアメリカの漫画1編を取り上げ、言葉の訳から言語的、文化的背景について詳しい解説をつける「manga」コーナー。あるいは、日本語の重要基本単語（「知る」「わかる」など）を漫画のシーンに即して具体的に説明する「language learning」。話題の商品や新刊書を紹介する「departments」など凝った企画が並んでいる。年10冊。96年新年号が第51号。評判は上々のようで、日米計3万部を確保している。

　日本の漫画と言えば、ポルノや過激なイメージもある。NYT「In Japan, Brutal Comics for Women: Mass-Market Rape Fantasies」(95/11/5 By Nicholas D. Kristof)で、「the growing independence of Japanese women is reflected not in stories of assertive women, but rather of passive women being brutalized」と書いている。

　日本の漫画の過激性を強調するのは「In a word, this is baloney」（漫画関連冒頭の記事で）というのがTomの見方である。とくに評価するのがサラリーマン社会を描いた劇画（dramatic comicという訳もある）で、現代日本を理解する最良の教科書扱いだった。「But for most of us addicts, the manga that really matter are the "story comics," which introduce a setting and a panoply（見事な一式の）of characters, and set forth a story line that spins out for years or decades. In their depth and plotting, and particularly in the cinematic quality of their art, these manga serials are strikingly different from what Americans think of as comics.」。『課長島耕作』はその代表例。作者の弘兼憲史氏には、仕事場までお邪魔してインタビューをし、記事のイラストは大町久美子とのラブシーンだった。Tomがアメリカへ帰国後も愛読漫画は雑誌の頁を破って送っている。『三丁目の夕日』『加治隆介の議』『釣りバカ日誌』『龍RON』『みのり伝説』『この女に賭けろ』『OL進化論』などだ。

2. Living Tradition

A New Year for Reflection

By Kevin Sullivan and Mary Jordan

January 2, 1996

New Year's is the most important and widely observed day of the year in Japan. There is no Times Square countdown, no champagne-tinged kisses at midnight. It is a quiet family time of reflection and renewal, and a showcase of the Japanese emphasis on group behavior....

American New Year's celebrations fade quickly after midnight, but that is when things get started here....

Red-cheeked and bubbling with a 10-year-old's energy, Yoji Otsubo, 10, stood before the altar, tossed a few coins, and clapped his hands. Then he energetically bowed, his hands together in front of his Donald Duck ski hat.

"This is fun," he said.

"Every year, the cycle is repeated," said Tomoharu Fukunaga, the shrine's chief priest, watching the old and the young gather to mark the new year. "There's some sense of eternity there."

飛驒の山深い神岡の正月は、雪に包まれていた。大晦日の夜、低い家並みの続く街は人っ子一人なく、屋号や家紋をあしらった大きな提灯が、それぞれの軒先にひっそりと掛かっている——それが、除夜の鐘近くになるにつれ、あちらこちらから、老若男女が初詣へと白い道を向かい始める。丘の上に建つ神社の深い木立の下では、焚き火の炎が燃え盛り、お神酒が振るまわれる。そんな中に、ディズニーのキャラクター付きの帽子をかぶった元気な子供の声。日本の正月を初めて迎えるKevinとMaryは、「Jesus, it's something.」「We really have to be here to feel it, to understand it.」と実に興味深そうだった。年賀状 (94/1/3 By T.R. Reid) や書き初め (91/1/6 同) も含め、お正月が外国メディアの関心を強くひくのは、伝統的な行事に加

2. 伝統生活

熟考するための新年

ケヴィン・サリバン ＆ メアリー・ジョーダン
1996年1月2日

お正月は、日本で1年のうち、最も重要かつ様々な行事が広汎に見られる日だ。タイムズ・スクエアのカウント・ダウンもなければ、年越しの深夜零時、シャンペン・グラスを合わせてのキスもない。家族と共に過ごす静かな時の流れ。来し方行く末、新たな生を熟考する。それは集団行動を重くみる日本人のひな型でもある……。

アメリカの新年の祝いは、深夜零時を過ぎると急速に色あせていく。しかし、当地では、まさにその時から、全てが始まる……。

頬を赤くし、10歳の子供らしく、元気いっぱいの大坪頌児は、神社の拝殿の前に立ち、小銭数枚を投げ、柏手を打つ。それから、元気いっぱいにお辞儀をすると、両手をドナルド・ダックのスキー帽の前で合わせた。

「楽しいな」と彼は言う。

「来る年も来る年も、全てが繰り返されます」と神主の福永朝治は、新年を祝うために集まって来た老いや若きを見ながら述べた。「ここにはある種、永遠の感覚があるのですよ」。

え、日本人の最大の特徴とされるgroup-oriented society の姿がはっきり現れる、と見るからだろう。日本では「anything worth doing is worth doing en masse」(92/12/30 同)。しかし、民族を挙げて祝う行事のある国は多いのに、なぜ日本についてこの点が協調されるのか。見方がオーバーなのか、一理はあるのか、などと考えてしまうのだ。

The Glorious Moon of the Rising Sun

By T. R. Reid

September 12, 1992

There were "Tsukimi karaoke" parties at nightclubs all over Japan tonight, and McDonald's of Japan chose to introduce its new "Tsukimi burger," a hamburger with a fried egg yolk on top representing the moon....

The thing that these three natural phenomena have in common, the thing that really appeals to Japanese sentimentality, is that they all pass away quickly. In most of Japan, the fallen snow will melt away within one day or two. The cherry blossoms are famous for falling at the height of their beauty. And the full moon will start to wane just one night later.

Shaky Japan Turns to Drama of Ancient Values

By T. R. Reid

December 14, 1994

In Western terms, the "Chushingura" is something like a combination of the Alamo and "Hamlet"—a dramatic historical event that was turned into the greatest theatrical masterpiece of the culture. Although the story of the loyal samurai has always been immensely popular here, neither new movie is breaking box-office records.

This modern, increasingly Westernized society is changing so fast that people no longer respond uniformly to the antique values upheld by the loyal 47.

なんといっても、春はお花見。「Cherry Blossoms, the Japanese Way」(94/4 WEEKEND Section) で、Tom Reid は「Everybody heads out to a park, plaza or pond for flower viewing.」「The ritual of hanami gets to the very core of Japanese aesthetics (美学).」と書き、カラオケ片手の花見の宴、新入社員の席取りの苦労などを紹介。この記事の隣は、ワシントンはthe Tidal Basinの桜を撮る写真術「Getting Those Fleeting Buds on Film」(By Frank Van Riper) だ。「an enduring gift from the government of Japan」の桜はあまりにも美しく、「almost impossible not to take a good picture」という。夏は花火。最近の日本列島の過熱ぶりは、はかなさを愛する日本人の心情にも通ずると思うのだが、a fire-

日出ずる国の壮麗な月

トム・リード　　　　　　　　　　　　　　　1992年9月12日

今夜は、日本中のナイトクラブで「月見カラオケ」パーティが開かれ、日本のマクドナルドはハンバーグの上に目玉焼きをのせ、黄身を月に見立てた「月見バーガー」を新たに発売した……。

　この3つの自然現象に共通していること、そして日本人の感傷的な心を真に揺さぶるのは、どれも瞬く間に消え去ってしまうということである。日本の大半の場所では、降り積もった雪は一両日のうちに融けてしまう。桜の花は美しい盛りに散っていくことで有名だ。そして満月は次の夜には、かけ始める。

古い価値観のドラマに頼る不安な日本

トム・リード　　　　　　　　　　　　　　　1994年12月14日

西側の表現で言えば、「忠臣蔵」は、アラモと「ハムレット」を組み合わせたようなものだ。それは、ある国の文化を代表する芝居の最高傑作を生み出した、劇的な歴史的事件である。忠実な武士の物語は、常に、たいへんな人気を博してきたが、今回新たに作られた2本の映画は、ともに過去の興行成績の記録を塗り替えるには至っていない。ますます西洋化しつつある現代日本社会は急激に変化しているため、人びとは、47人の義士が掲げた価値に対してもはや一様には反応しなくなったというのだ。

---

works display はアメリカにも有り、いまだ記事にはなっていない。秋はお月見。そして、年末に、忠臣蔵やベートーベンの第九、紅白歌合戦(「Japan's Auld Lang TV」・91/1/1 By Tom Reid) と続く。第九は「A Japanese New Year's Tradition: Beethoven Sing-Alongs」(87/1/1 By John Burgess)。カット写真がなんと「Prime Minister Yasuhiro Nakasone marks New Year's at his residence with a tea ceremony.」—Oh, Jesus!

3. Modern Life

Snug in Their Beds for Christmas Eve

By T. R. Reid

December 24, 1990

For young people all over the Christian world, this evening will be a night of magic and wonder. Here in Japan as well, Christmas Eve has become immensely important—but for rather different reasons. It has become the sexiest night of the year.

Japanese popular culture has made Christmas Eve a night when every unmarried person must have a date, and it is now *de rigueur* for the date to include an overnight stay.

For whatever reason, the new view of *eebu* has increased the Japanese people's belief that they are unique. "In the whole world," said the lead-in to a TV talk show last week, "only Japan has turned the day before Christmas into a day for sex."

Something Borrowed, Something New

By T. R. Reid

February 25, 1993

Rather, the Christian wedding has caught on here for the same reason so many other aspects of American culture have been absorbed into Japanese life: If it's Western, it's cool. It's glamorous. It's romantic....

The aisle of a Christian church—or, for that matter, of a hotel meeting room designed to look like a church—is known in Japan as "the Virgin Road" (a term people here think they learned from Americans).

テレビのトレンディードラマが、年末近くになると、やけにクリスマスを強調するのがちょっと気になりだしたのが1988年秋「君がうそをついた」(麻生祐未、鈴木保奈美ら)辺りだったか。イヴを彼、または、彼女と過ごせるか——ドラマはその1点に向けて盛り上がっていく。周りを見回せば、Eveの狂想曲。これはニュースと思ってからWPの記事になるまで3シーズンかかった。男性からちやほやされる代償に、独身女性には「Christmas Eve enhances the fear that they are not rooted to society.」との分析がある。同じくトレンディードラマの結婚式は、まずキリスト

3. 現代人の生活

クリスマス・イブにベッドにもぐり込む

トム・リード
1990年12月24日

世界中のキリスト教社会に住む若者にとって、今夜は、奇跡と驚きの夜である。ここ日本でも、少々異なった理由からではあるが、クリスマス・イブはきわめて重要な日となった。1年で最もセクシーな夜になったのだ。日本のポピュラー・カルチャーは、クリスマス・イブを、すべての未婚の人がデートしなければならない夜にしてしまった。そして今や、そのデートでは、一夜を共に過ごすことが絶対条件となった……。理由は何であれ、新しい「イブ」観は、自分たちがユニークであるという日本人の信念をより強めることになった。先週、テレビのトークショーの冒頭で、「世界中を見渡しても、クリスマスの前日をセックスの日にしたのは日本だけだ」と述べていた。

借り物だがどこか新しい

トム・リード
1993年2月25日

キリスト教式の結婚式は、じつに多くのアメリカ文化が日本に吸収されたのと同じ理由で、人気を博している。即ち、西欧風なら、かっこいい。魅惑的で、ロマンティックだ……。教会――それは教会に似せて設計されたホテルの会議室でもよいのだが――の通路は、日本では、「バージン・ロード」として知られている（日本人は、この言い方をアメリカ人から学んだと信じている）。

教スタイルだ。信者は1％にも満たない日本で結婚式の3割以上。「We have to take the chance to plant a seed.」というのがプロテスタント系 the Christian Bridal Mission の面々。その司る都内ホテルのチャペルでの式を取材。それに対し「This is not a religious choice.... This is a matter of what's fashionable.」との批判の声もあった。それにしても、チャペルの中央通路を「バージン・ロード」（断じて英語ではない）と呼ぶだけは、語感からいっても勘弁してほしい――Tom ではないけれど。

The Puckering Stops Here

By T. R. Reid

November 8, 1994

You must remember this: A kiss is still a kiss—except in Japan, where it has become a social problem.

The Japanese have been raised to greet friends, spouses, and lovers with a polite bow. Even soldiers coming home from months overseas are welcomed by their wives at the airport with nothing more than a smile and a bow.... Even in mainstream publications, pictures of naked women are so common.... There are stores where men can buy used lingerie packaged with a photo of the high school girl who reputedly wore it. Why, then, would anybody care about kissing on the corner? The difference seems to be the public nature of the kiss.

It is commonplace here that shame in front of others—rather than a private sense of guilt—is the chief restraint on bad conduct. It follows that if people no longer restrain themselves in public, the whole society may soon go to pot.

Japan's No-Tell Hotels

By T. R. Reid

August 13, 1995

With characteristic efficiency and ingenuity, the Japanese have brought the full force of modern technology to bear on a timeless human endeavor: the secret afternoon tryst.

All over the country, a special breed of hotels exists just for couples who want a quick fling in complete confidentiality.

「ねえ、チュウしてよ」というテレビのCMが話題になるお国柄、人前でキスをするカップルの是非が、日本のマスコミを賑わした。日本は、今や世界に冠たるヘア解禁国。アメリカでも解禁だが、それは純粋ポルノの世界でのこと。日本のように、一般の週刊誌にヌードやヘアのグラビアが堂々と掲載されるなど考えられない（WP本社で、日本から届く週刊誌は、どうにも恥ずかしくて、というより、こちらの人格を疑われそうで、社内では開けなかった）。ブルセラショップの類がまかり通る国で、なぜ、人前のキスが問題にされるのか――最初の記事は、Tom のそうした疑問

唇を突き出すのは、ここで終わり

トム・リード

1994年11月8日

以下のことを覚えておかなければならない。所詮、キスはキスに過ぎない。ただし、社会問題にまでさえなってしまった日本は別として。……日本人は、友達、配偶者、そして恋人に対してさえ、丁寧なお辞儀で挨拶するように教育されてきた。何ヵ月も国外にいた帰還兵さえ、空港で、妻は微笑みとお辞儀で迎えるだけだ……。主要な刊行物に女性のヌード写真が掲載されるのはごく普通のことだ。男どもが、女子高校生の使い古した下着と、それを身につけたとされる少女の写真をパックで買える店もある。ではなぜ街頭でのキスを気にかけるのだろうか。両者の違いは、キスの社会的な性格によるようだ。ここでは、個人的な罪の感覚ではなく、他人の面前で恥をかくことが、悪い行いを抑制しているとはよく言われるところである。それゆえに、もし、人々が公共の場で自らを抑制しないならば、社会自体がまもなく堕落してしまうと人びとは考えている。

日本の秘密のホテル

トム・リード

1995年8月13日

その効率の良さと工夫の巧さによって、日本人は、近代テクノロジーの威力と、いつまでたっても変わることのない人間の行ない、即ち、午後の密かな逢い引きとを結び付けた。

日本中どこに行っても、いっときのお楽しみを密かに行いたいカップルだけのための特別なホテルがある。

が出発点になったものだ。第2の記事で、渋谷のラブホテル街をルポすれば、経営者は、ラブホテル興隆の一因には日本の貧困な住宅事情があるものの、かつて利用者は、人目を忍んで入ってきた。それが最近は、「Kids today—can you believe it? They come into a love hotel, and they have no shame about it at all.」と叫んだ（もちろん日本語で、だが）。ともに、Ruth Benedict がかつて『The Chrysanthemum and the Sword: the Pattern of Japanese Culture』で指摘した「恥」の文化に異変が起きているという視点である。

Hot-to Koh-hee, but Hold the Creap

By Margaret Shapiro

January 11, 1988

How about a nice, cool Pocari Sweat? Or a cup of coffee lightened with some Creap?

If neither sounds particularly appealing the reason is probably Janglish, the peculiar Japanese adaptation of English that is flourishing here on T-shirts, signs, magazine covers, storefronts, and in everyday speech.... Janglish is supposed to make a product sound chic and modern, and therefore desirable. To the English speaker, however, it sometimes sounds bizarre. Take the slogan for a major cosmetics company: "For beautiful human life...." A restaurant offers "God hamburgers."

Not all is nonsensical; in fact, Janglish is now so widespread that foreigners floundering to make themselves understood often find they can use an English word, provided it is pronounced in a Japanese way.

Thus, department store becomes "de-pah-to." A carton of milk is called "miru-ku." A cup of hot coffee becomes "hot-to koh-hee." .... Even rice is often called "raisu," instead of *gohan*, the term that served the nation for hundreds of years. And remember *sayonara*? Well, today, "by-ee by-ee" will do....

Today, there are those who view the Janglish phenomenon as a threat not only to the language, but to the culture....

But others see Janglish as a sign of Japan's internationalization, a natural development for this once-isolated island country.

タイトルの「Creap」は英語ではないが、印象としては「creep」——はい回る、よろけるといった語感が漂い、飲み物に入れるにはなんともはやでholdとなるわけだ。Janglish にはTom Reid も注目。在任中のほぼ隔週、電話出演していた National Public Radio（米公共ラジオ放送）の日本コラムでも取り上げた。東京支局のOffice Manager 丸田康子も友情出演して Janglish 部分を担当。自動車摩擦がピークとなった95年6月末とあって「one item Japan does import in quantity is American words」と司会者が述べた後、「my favorite English adjective in Japanese is アンビリ」

ホットー・コーヒー、でもクリープはいりません

マーガレット・シャピロ　　　　　　　　　　1988年1月11日

ちょっと一杯の冷たくてしゃれたポカリスエットはいかがですか。それともクリープで薄められたコーヒーがよろしいでしょうか。もし、このいずれも特に魅力的に聞こえないとしたら、それは、おそらくジャングリッシュのせいでしょう。ジャングリッシュとは、Tシャツ、看板、雑誌の表紙、店先、そして日常会話で盛んに用いられている独特の英語風の日本語です……。ジャングリッシュは、製品をシックにし、モダンに見せるとされており、それゆえに望ましいものなのです。しかし、英語を話す者にとっては、時として、あまりに奇妙に聞こえてしまいます。たとえば、一流化粧品会社のスローガンは「フォア・ビューティフル・ヒューマン・ライフ」だしレストランに行けば「ゴッド・ハンバーガー」が出てきます。すべてが無意味な言葉というわけではありません。事実、Janglishは今やあまりにも普及しているので、自分を分かってもらおうと四苦八苦している外国人は、しばしば英語を使えるのに気がつきます。ただし、日本式に発音すればですが。ですから、百貨店は「デパート」、牛乳カートンは「ミルク」、一杯の熱いコーヒーが「ホット・コーヒー」というわけです。……あのお米さえ、この国で何百年も使われてきた「ご飯」ではなく、「ライス」と呼ばれることが多いのです。それから「サヨナラ」を覚えてますか。なんと今では「バイバイ」でいいんですよ……。ジャングリッシュ現象は、言葉だけでなく、文化に対する脅威だと見る人がいます……。しかし、日本の国際化の印、かつては孤立していたこの島国にとっては自然な流れと見る人もいるのです。

「something the politicians often do is イメージアップ」といった具合に2人で語った15語ほどを司会者に当てさせる趣向だった。正解率はざっと半分。NYTもJanglishをテーマとした記事 (95/2/21 By Nicholas D. Kristof) で「LANGUAGE ON LOAN: English Made in Japan」という表を作り、Shirubaa shiito, Romansu gurei, Patokaa, Kosuto daun, Wetto などを Japanese word, English source, Meaning に分けて示している。

A Gifted Society

By Fred Hiatt

December 18, 1989

When it comes to the calculations and complications of gift-giving, no one out-figures the Japanese. According to *Nikkei Gifts* magazine, Japanese will spend more than $90 billion on gifts this year—a sum considerably larger than the U.S. Japan trade deficit....

Gift-giving is a key component of personal relations here. Japanese give presents on almost every imaginable occasion and have invented a few simply so they can give more.

If you go to a wedding, naturally you must bring a present, but if it's your wedding you have to give presents to all the guests, too. Funeral guests bring gifts, usually money; the bereaved family offers gifts in return.

If you go away, even for a day, you must bring back presents, usually edible, for your office mates....

A number of politicians and businessmen are currently on trial for allegedly carrying the gift-giving tradition a bit too far in the so-called Recruit Scandal. The former chairman of NTT said his acceptance of cut-rate stock from the Recruit Co. was not a bribe but part of a normal exchange of favors. "Rejecting such an offer is considered rude in Japan." ....

"Price and prestige, not product, count most when decisions are made," the *Japan Economic Journal* recently said, noting that wrapping from a prestigious department store is essential.

日本のクリスマスを描いた「Dashing Through The Dough (現ナマ)」(95/12/22 By Kevin Sullivan) で、Christmas presents の交換は、今世紀初め日本にもたらされ「in the 1930s, department stores held the first Christmas sales」という。それが年末のボーナスシーズンと偶然重なるが「If workers spend their bonus on gifts, they're much more likely to be buying *Seibo* gifts than Christmas presents.」。年を越して2月のValentine's Day。「Like many other successful imports from the West ... it is being adapted in decidedly Japanese ways.」(88/2/13 By Margaret Shapiro)。具体的には「This day is as much about duty and

贈り物社会

フレッド・ハイアット　　　　　　　　　　　　　1989年12月18日

贈り物をする際の計算や煩雑さに関し、日本人の右に出るものはいない。日経ギフトによれば、日本人は、今年900億ドル以上もの額を贈り物に費やす。日米間の貿易赤字を、かなり上回る額だ。……ここでは、贈り物をすることは、人間関係を構成する基本的な要素である。日本人は、想像できる限りのほとんど全ての機会に贈り物をし、さらにその数を増やすため、いくつかの機会を発明さえした。……結婚式に行けば、当然贈り物を持参していかねばならない。たとえ、自分の結婚式であっても、ゲスト全員に贈り物をしなければならない。葬式に参列する人も、通常現金ではあるが、贈り物を持っていき、遺族は、そのお返しをする。1日でも旅行に出かけた場合には、職場の仲間のために、お土産──それは通常食べ物である──を持って帰らねばならない……。かなりの政治家やビジネスマンが、この贈り物の伝統をちょっとやり過ぎたとされる、いわゆるリクルート事件で、現在、裁判にかかっている。NTTの前会長は、裁判の証言で、リクルート社から割安株を受け取ったのは、賄賂にはあたらず、ごく一般的な好意による贈り物の交換の一端に過ぎないと述べた。「そのような申し出を断るのは、日本では、無礼なこととされる」と彼は証言した……。
「何にするか決める時に一番大事なのは、品物ではない。値段と権威なのだ」とジャパン・エコノミック・ジャーナルは最近述べている。評判の高い百貨店で包装してもらうことが肝心だ、とも付け加えている。

---

obligation ... as it is about ... love. And unlike the U.S., only women do the gift giving.」。そして "duty chocolate" の贈り先は「Mr. Wheels, Mr. Meals, Mr. Real, and the Boss」(91/2/14 By T.R. Reid) に分かれるのだ。包装社会の日本だが、省資源時代の過剰包装追放については「Wrapped in Environmentalism: Japanese Retailers Cutting Down on Layers of Packing」(91/4/23 By Paul Blustein) がある。

In Japan, ATMs Clean Up

By Evelyn Richards

November 17, 1994

The latest technology from Japan: money laundering.

Newly installed bank automated teller machines here sanitize and press bills before customers withdraw funds. The "Clean ATMs," as they are known, dispense yen notes that, while not quite as crisp as newly minted ones, are nearly wrinkle-free. Customers can even insert bills and get them back laundered. In certain ways, Japan is obsessed with cleanliness.

Japanese are known for scrubbing their bodies two or three times during their daily hot bath ritual. Young women keep kits in their office restrooms stocked with cosmetics, lotions, and toothbrushes. There are bathroom ceramics said to fight bacteria, as well as germ-combating socks and slippers.

Japan Is Crawling with Insect-Lovers

By Fred Hiatt & Margaret Shapiro

September 29, 1988

Bug museums, bug zoos, bug exhibits in department stores, street-corner vendors selling crawling, flying and creeping creatures: Much of Japan may have been paved over, but the Japanese retain a special fondness in their hearts for the insects of yesteryear.

These days, Japanese schools still often assign summer homework to collect a certain number of beetle or butterfly species. But Tokyo children often do their collecting at the nearest department store.

日本人の感性の中で、第一にあげるとすれば「清潔好き」かもしれない。原因には、「Partly that's because Shinto, Japan's indigenious faith, features purification rituals」と「a tidy personal appearance has a lot to do with being accepted in Japan's group-oriented society」を上記最初の記事はあげる。昆虫好きも、外国人の目には奇異な感を与えることがあるが、ときに馴染みにくいのが和風朝食だ。1996年の正月、本社は、数人の記者にそれぞれ headline を与え、8時間以内に電話取材だけで原稿を書く企画を考えた。皮肉な見方や高尚な表現、palindrome（回文）を

日本ではATMで洗います

エヴリン・リチャード
1994年11月17日

日本からの最新テクノロジー、それはマネー・ロンダリング、即ち貨幣の洗浄である。ここ日本で新たに設置された現金自動払出機は、利用者が、現金を引き出す前に、お札を消毒し、プレスする。「クリーンATM」として知られているその機械は、円の紙幣を、新札ほどではないにしろ、ほぼしわのない状態にする。利用者は、紙幣を機械の中にいれ、洗浄された状態で受け取ることさえ出来る。……ある意味において、日本は、清潔さに取り憑かれている。日本人は、毎日入浴する時、体を2～3回洗うことで知られている。若い女性は、オフィスの洗面所に、化粧用具、ローション、そして、歯ブラシなどが入ったキットを置いておく。バクテリアに効くという浴室のタイルや、細菌と闘う靴下やスリッパまである。

昆虫愛好家と一緒に這い回る日本

フレッド・ハイアット & マーガレット・シャピロ
1988年9月29日

[日本よりの手紙]
昆虫博物館。昆虫園。デパートでの大昆虫展。這い回り、飛び回る生物を売っている街角の自動販売機。日本の国土のほとんどは開発され、舗装されてしまったかもしれないが、日本人は、過ぎ去った年月の昆虫たちに対する特別な愛着を持ち続けている。……いまだに日本の学校は、甲虫や蝶の採集を、よく夏休みの宿題に出す。しかし、東京の子供たちの多くは、近くのデパートで、採集をすることになる。

入れ、最後は「end」で終わる条件付き。Kevin Sullivan も選ばれ、見出しは「Breakfast Epiphanies」。日本は大好きだが、起き抜けの和風朝食は苦手という Kevin は「but to the Western eye, a Japanese breakfast looks as though someone dumped the contents of a large frog onto a table, chopped it, pickled it, and served it in an impossible number of very small dishes」(1/7)。回文は Enid and Edna dine, Akasaka と too hot to hoot。最後は「What time does McDonald's breakfast menu end?」。

No Sympathy Here: Japanese Advice Columnists Tell the Troubled: Shape Up!

By T. R. Reid

November 19, 1992

Mrs. T. became so upset that she recently wrote a letter about her problem to the *Yomiuri Shimbun* newspaper's "Jinsei Annai" (Guide to Life) column—Japan's version of Ann Landers. But the answer she got was hardly in the Ann Landers style.

"Please, be patient with your husband," the newspaper replied....

The most common piece of advice offered to the long-suffering questioners is that they practice the stoic virtue Japan loves must: *gaman*, a word that means endurance, tolerance, and bearing pain without complaint.

In Tokyo, Too, the Homeless Seek Food, Shelter From Winter Chill

By John Burgess

January 20, 1985

Japan has tackled crime, illiteracy, unemployment, and other social ills with a success envied in the rest of the non-Communist world. Yet homeless people, their possessions bundled into shopping bags, still walk its streets, a reminder that in some cases, Japan is as impotent as other nations....

Some older people see them as proof that the ethics that made Japan great are on the decline.

阪神大震災の時、外国人を感嘆させたのも、やはり被災者達の「gaman」だった。「For many survivors, the key word ... was *gaman*. This Japanese term means "enduring something difficult," and it is a cherished virtue here.」(95/1/19 By Tom Reid)。タンスの上の棚から物が全部落ちてきて、もう死ぬかと思った西宮の被災者は「So now there's nothing to do but gaman—get to work, clean up the street, rebuild the shop.」と語るのだった。

homelessについては、上記第2の記事から11年目の96年初めに扱った(1/22 By Mary Jordan)。ある駅で彼らに食事を供給する慈善団体のアメリカ人は「It's amazing how polite they are.」という。食事がなくなっても、待っていたhomelessは「No

同情なし「ちゃんとしなさい」とアドバイスをする日本の人生相談

トム・リード

1992年11月19日

思いあまったT子さんは、最近悩みをつづった手紙を、アン・ランダースの日本版である読売新聞の「人生案内」欄に送った。しかし、彼女に対する回答はアン・ランダース流とは、ずいぶん違うものだった。「ご主人に対して辛抱強くなりましょう」と新聞は回答した……。長い間悩んできた依頼者に対する最も一般的な回答は、日本人が最も好む禁欲的な美徳である「我慢」をなさいというものだ。「我慢」とは、耐え忍び、寛容であり、不満を申し立てずに痛みをこらえるという意味である。

東京でも、ホームレスは食物を求め、寒さをしのぐ場所を捜している

ジョン・バージェス

1985年1月20日

日本は、犯罪、識字、失業その他の社会的な病に果敢に取り組み、成功を収め、非共産圏の国々から羨望の的となってきた。しかし、ホームレスたちが、持ち物をショッピング・バッグにまとめ、今でも、住みかとしている街頭を歩いているという事実は、日本も、場合によっては、他の国と同様に無能な国だということを思い起こさせる……。一部の年長者は、ホームレスを、日本を大国にした倫理の凋落の証だと見なしている。

problem」。「In America, I might have gotten banged over the head.」。新宿駅西口の地下通路の「Cardboard Alley」に住む約200人が、動く歩道建設のため立ち退きを迫られた事態を取材した記事だが、Maryが何より驚愕したのは、都が総計費2億円で新たに港区芝浦に仮設住宅をつくり、それを2ヵ月で壊してしまうという税金の使い方だった。

4. Company Life

In Japan, Unwilling Exiles

By T. R. Reid

April 18, 1991

That so many families can live apart for years at a time—with little increase in the nation's low divorce rate—also says something about how distant husband and wife are in a normal Japanese marriage. In Japanese family life, the father generally plays a small role, making cameo appearances when his job permits.

In Any Language, Move From Yokohama to South Dakota Is Major

By Shigehiko Togo

November 26, 1993

When Mitsuo Komai told his teenage daughters, Momoe and Hana, that they would be moving from populous Yokohama to this small town, they had never heard of South Dakota....

Momoe concurred: "In Japan, we only saw Dad on Sunday. We were busy with school, study, and clubs. He came home very late and left early in the morning, always wearing a suit. He didn't even know that I really hated onion. But here he actually noticed that I had changed my pierced earrings."

日本とアメリカの新聞社で一番違うのは、仕事ではない。記者達と家族との関わり方だろう。東京に来るWPの特派員達は、夕食はまず家でとる。育児は夫婦で分担。学校関係の行事は、極力最優先だ。北海道の単身赴任者を描いた第1の記事が「Something pretty unusual happened at the Kakuyama household outside Tokyo the other day: Dad came home from work.」という皮肉を利かせて始まるのも、こうした違いが根底にあるからだ。そして、単身赴任は「Generally it is not a corporate dictate」で、教育や住宅問題、その背景にある東京第一主義などによって決まると見る。第2の記事は、Mount Rushmore の大統領頭像群で知られる South Dakota 州唯一の日本の企業を訪れ、駐在員とその家族の

4. 会社生活

日本の不本意な亡命者

トム・リード
1991年4月18日

こんなにも多くの家族が、何年にもわたって別々に暮らせるということは、通常の日本の結婚で、いかに夫と妻の間に距離があるかを示している。しかも、それがこの国の低い離婚率を上昇させることもない。日本の家族では、夫の役割は一般的に小さく、仕事の都合が許す範囲内で、これはという場面に登場するに過ぎない。

何語だろうが、「横浜からサウス・ダコタへ」は大変だ

東郷茂彦
1993年11月26日

サウス・ダコタ州、ミッチェル発――駒井光雄が10代の娘、百恵と華に、人口の密集した横浜からこの小さな町へ引っ越すことを伝えたとき、2人はサウス・ダコタなど聞いたこともなかった……。

百恵は、こう結論した。「日本では、おとうさんと会うのは日曜日だけ。私たちは、学校や勉強、部活で忙しく、おとうさんは夜遅く帰っては朝早く出かける。着ているのは、いつも背広だけ。私が玉葱が大嫌いということさえ知らなかったの。でも、ここでは、私がピアスを変えたらちゃんと気がついてくれました」。

生活をルポしたものだ。突然、アメリカ社会のど真ん中に投げこまれた駒井一家は、試行錯誤しながら言葉と文化の壁を越え、会社、学校、教会など各コミュニティーへ溶け込んでいった。日本と違い、御主人の通勤時間はほぼゼロ、深夜の帰宅、週末ゴルフなし。「Here, the American lifestyle has given me a chance to have a new, fuller relationship with my family.」という感想だった。

Corporate Worship Day

By T. R. Reid

January 5, 1994

"Oh sacred spirit Daikoku-sama, we humbly ask you to watch over *The Washington Post* Company and take diligent care that the honorable *Washington Post* newspaper not lose out to its competitors in the year to come."

That's how it went today at the altar of Kanda Myojin shrine.

Western visitors to Japan are often struck by the strong sense of shared responsibility, a collective feeling of "membership" that produces a highly civil society largely free of crime and violence.

But as the Japanese know the nation's leadership, public and private, works hard to produce it.

Ghostly Lore Fascinates the Japanese

By Tracy Dahlby

October 31, 1981

Amid the towering glass-and-steel structures of the city's downtown business district in Otemachi, a tiny Japanese garden with a stone tablet marks the spot where, according to legend, Masakado's head came to rest.

To the frustration of Tokyo real estate developers, the 300-square-meter patch of ground has remained untouched because of a widespread belief that tampering with it would rekindle the ancient rebel's fury.

日本人最大の特徴とされる、共同体意識を positive なものとして捉えるのが、Tom の特徴だ。新年の企業参拝式は、「the concept of the community」「the idea that each person … must act with the group in mind」を形成する無数の行事の先陣を切る。成人式(厚木市で取材)は「that common spirit」を「inculcating(注入する)」することが最大の眼目で「this annual holiday turns into a great national pageant of Japaneseness」(93/1/16)。入社式「The Company Wedding: Bowing into a Japanese Firm Is for Life」(92/4/2)では、企業の新人教育のテキスト中の、お辞儀の漫画をイラストに使っている。こうした日本的合理主義に基づいた共同体意識だけではない。その底に流れる宗教観にま

企業参拝式

トム・リード　　　　　　　　　　　　　　　　1994年1月5日

「ああ聖なる御魂のダイコクさま。ワシントン・ポスト社をどうかお見守り下さいますよう、よろしくお願いいたします。さらに、本年におきまして、ワシントン・ポスト紙が、ライバル紙に負けることのないようくれぐれもよろしくお願いいたします」。神田明神の祭壇でこのような儀式がきょう執り行われた……。

　西欧から日本を訪れる者は、責任を分かちあう感覚や、「組織の一員である」という集団への帰属意識がいかに強いことか、また、そのおかげで、犯罪や暴力のほとんど蔓延しない高度な文明社会を作りだしたことに、しばしば驚かされる。しかし、日本人ならわかるように、国全体が共有するこの感覚は、指導的な立場の人々が、公私両面の懸命な努力で造りあげたのだ。

「霊魂の世界」に曳かれる日本人

トレイシー・ダルビー　　　　　　　　　　　　　1981年10月31日

都心部のオフィス街大手町にあまたそびえるガラスと鉄の建物の真只中に、小さな日本庭園がある。その庭園に置かれた石碑こそ、伝説によれば将門の首が安置された場所なのだ。……この300平方メートルの区画は、まったく手がつけられておらず、東京の不動産業者をいらだたせている。もしいじろうとでもしようものなら、古(いにしえ)の反逆者の怒りに再び火をつけてしまうと多くの人が信じているからだ。

で踏み込んだのが第2の記事。東京大手町の三井物産本社内に祭られている「将門塚」の由来と現状をルポしている。平将門——WP東京支局が参拝した神田明神の祭神の1人である。

In Japan, the Buck Stops at the Top

By Sandra Sugawara

October 10, 1995

It's an age-old Japanese ritual as well-scripted as *seppuku*, the samurai's rite of suicide. Scandal shakes a major Japanese company. Its reputation is on the line. So its top executive announces he takes full responsibility for the misdeeds, even if he was unaware of them, and resigns. Going out his way wouldn't occur to most U.S. corporate leaders.

Many Americans, tired of what they see as buck-passing in society's upper echelons when things go wrong, might welcome a system of high-level responsibility. But critics say that in Japan it has a hidden cost: The public sacrifice may become cover for nothing being done to correct the problem that caused the crisis.

Faulty Workmanship on Train Injures Japan's Pride

By T. R. Reid

May 8, 1992

The 1985 crash undermined Japanese confidence in the quality of American workmanship. Ishihara said it would be "unthinkable" for a Japanese company to make such a mistake. Apparently, though, a Japanese company did.

With national prestige at stake, the loss of a motor because of sloppy workmanship has become a serious concern.

「The Buck Stops at the Top」と、キスはダメの「The Puckering Stops Here」は、ともにPresident Trumanのモットー「The buck stops here.」のもじりだ。buckとは、ポーカーの親にbuckhorn（鹿の角）柄のナイフを置いたことから「責任」のこと。大統領職に最終責任有りといった意味だ。日本では、会社という組織の中で誰が責任をとるのか。いかにも

日本的な引責辞任の習慣は、武士の血、落城寸前に、城主の「underlings were saved if he killed himself by *seppuku*」という伝統に起因すると第1の記事では解説。事件や事故、スキャンダルが起きると、組織のトップが「over misdeeds ... that largely had occured before he took the post」によって辞めることに驚きの目を注ぐ。仕事べったりの生き方は

日本では、トップが責任をもつ

サンドラ・スガワラ

1995年10月10日

サムライが自殺する時の儀式である切腹同様、それは、きちんとした筋書きのある古い日本の儀式なのだ。スキャンダルが、日本のある大企業を直撃し、今やその名誉が問われてきた。すると、企業のトップが、たとえ事情を知らなくても、全面的に不正の責任をとると述べ、辞任する。このような辞め方は、アメリカ企業のトップにはまず考えられない。不祥事が生じた際の、上層部における責任のなすり合いに嫌気がさしている多くのアメリカ人は、トップクラスが責任をとるというシステムを歓迎するかもしれない。しかし、日本では目に見えぬ損失が伴う。公職から身を引くという自己犠牲は、危機が発生した原因を少しも正さないうちに事態が覆い隠されてしまう危険性を生む。

規律のゆるみによる電車事故が日本の誇りを傷つける

トム・リード

1992年5月8日

1985年の日航機墜落事故は、アメリカの労働者の質への日本の信頼を低下させた。石原慎太郎は、日本の企業がそのようなミスを犯すことは「まったく考えられない」と述べた。しかし、日本の企業もどうやら同じようなミスを犯してしまったようだ。

今や国家の威信が問われる事態となった。作業現場での規律の緩みのために起きたモーターの脱落事故は、深刻な懸念を呼んでいる。

---

workaholism への非難ともなるが、余暇を楽しもうとしても「Japan is now working hard at the notion of working less hard」(91/6/9 By T.R. Reid)。Casual Friday まで「Japanese Firms Try Boosting Worker Morale With a Change of Clothing」(95/9/30 By Kevin Sullivan and Mary Jordan)。そんな鉄壁な日本人の仕事への取り組みに、変化有りとしたのが第2の記事だ。

日本企業の行動といえば、米国三菱自動車のセクハラ問題をWPは連日、大きく取り上げている。96/4/29付紙面では Front page のトップのほか、8、9両面を埋め尽くす記事が掲載された。

CHAPTER 3 | ISSUES AND OPINIONS

1. Education
教育問題

江戸時代の寺子屋以来の伝統を背景に、戦前戦後を通じ、日本が近代国家として成功した秘訣はその教育にあり、というわけで、日本の「教育システム」は海外で賞賛の的となった。その反面、マイナス面にも米メディアの目は注がれる。

1985年秋、日米の教育会議が京都で開かれ、WP本社教育担当 Keith Richburg(現香港特派員)も長期来日した。その報告が「Japanese Education: Admired but Not Easily Imported」(10/19)。「When Americans look with envy at Japan's education miracle, they see an academic side that emphasizes high standards and a human side that instills (徐々に教え込む) discipline and moral values. But Japan's impressive educational system—rooted in the national culture and reinforced by society—cannot be so easily transplanted to American shores.」。教師の給与水準の高さと社会的な尊敬、統一された教育目標と基準、規律と倫理の存在などを指摘したうえ、現場での子供達も「There was order but not lack of humor」「they do it without excessive rigidity」という、こそばゆいほどの暖かい見方だ。学校だけでなく、家庭では「every house is equipped with a study table where children are expected to sit every night for at least two hours of homework」、社会的背景では「structural, political, and societal advantages」として「centralized society」「homogeneous country」を長所にあげている。日本では「uniformity」への批判が生まれていることに触れてはいるが、記事の主眼ではなく、アメリカの教育改革の課題である、教師の待遇改善、教師テストや「a uniform curriculum (統一要綱)」の実地、「the shift in power from local school

第3章 問題提起と批判

boards to the state capitals」などについて「"We can, but the question is, will we?"」というthe Department of Education高官の言葉で記事を終えている。

　日本の教育に追いつけ追い越せというアメリカについては、現東京特派員の Mary Jordan が本社で教育を担当した頃、「On this side of the Pacific, hundreds of educators who are tired of losing to Japan in international academic and economic competitions are pushing for a Japanese-style longer school」(92/3/4) と報じた。年間の授業日数を180日から210日に。逆に日本では243日を11日減らし、「more well-rounded and less-pressured students like those in America」を育てようとしている——。

　日本の中学で1年間英語を教えた Bruce S. Feiler は、日本の1クラスの生徒数はアメリカより3割以上も多いが、「regimented seating plans」「strict dress codes and rigorous work schedules」のおかげで勉強が続けられる。「extracurricular duties」でも、親より学校の役割が大きく、非行の場合、警察はまず教師を呼び出すし、学校は「teaching students how to obey traffic rules, to pour tea, even how to bow」とop-ed 欄に報告している。そして、アメリカでも、子供達に「spend more time in teaching them our common civic values while they are at school」と提案する。(93/2/11)

　日本のような人口過密で自然資源に恵まれない国が戦後、成功したのは「a single resource: its people」のおかげで「For that reason, education is viewed as a crucial national enterprise.」と Tom Reid は報じ、その頂点としての東大入試発表をルポした (93/3/11)。「and diligent young people such as Mayuko Toyoda—who spent all of her high-school vacations in a special "cram school"—are seen as the country's finest product」。

しかし、受験戦争をはじめ、日本の教育がいかに子供達へ過大な圧力となり、社会構造が個性を圧殺しているかという批判的な記事の方が圧倒的に多い。

幼稚園の入試に備える2歳児のための予備校 The Growing Buds（伸芽会）を1970年代の終わりに、William Chapman は早くもルポした。校内暴力の嵐「Japanese Schools Suffer Wave of Classroom Violence」(81/8/3 同)。中学生による横浜の浮浪者殺し「Frustrated Juveniles Spread New Terror in Usually Staid Japan」(83/3/15 By Tracy Dahlby)。校則地獄「School Days, Rigid Rule Days: Harsh Discipline Restricts Japanese Students」(89/5/8 By Margaret Shapiro)。校門圧殺事件「Girl's Death Sparks Debate on Discipline in Japan's schools」(90/7/15 By Fred Hiatt)。そして、いじめと自殺。なかでも「In Japan, Reading, Writing, Bullying: Student Suicides Follow Harassment for Being Different」(96/1/15 By Mary Jordan) は、いじめを受け、自殺を考えた子供のルポを含め、全力投球の取材の結果である。

世界中、どこでも子供は残酷なものだ。「Children around the world taunt, jeer, tease, hit, mock, and ignore others, especially those who are weaker. In many places, bullies are simply one of life's unpleasant realities.」。だが「In Japan, there is a common reason for children to refuse to attend school, sink into depression, and end lives barely begun.」。アメリカの学校で横行するいじめとは違い「bullying here involves more than just a small group of rogues（悪餓鬼）inflicting abuse. Rather, it is often an entire group that ostracizes（排斥する）someone who is somehow different: a newcomer, a slow reader, a very bright child, one with different eye or hair color.」。

とにもかくにも、子供1人ひとりの個性を伸ばすのを眼目とするアメリカの教育。「It's so different」と Mary が何回もため息を

漏らした。集団によるいじめに遭い、登校拒否となった子供達の通う「an alternative school (フリー・スクールなどといわれる) Tokyo Shure」を主催する奥地圭子。受験、画一化といった構造的圧力のなかで、いじめる子もいじめられる子も同根と見る。「"It's unnatural pressure.... and they lash out at others」。Shure で会った17歳の少女は、中学時代のある日、学校で誰も口をきかなくなった。理由は分からない。最初は親友、次に女子、次が男子。「"I asked many times, 'Why are you doing this?' No one would answer."」。包丁を手首に当てた時、親も事態の深刻さを理解する。「I several times thought seriously about killing myself. You feel pushed in a corner. I tried to do my best.... You lose perspective. You think, there is no place for me.」。事態をなんとかするため、私立探偵に助けを求め、暴行、精神的な辱め、性的いじめの実態を初めて知る親。輪をかけて実態に疎い教師達。なお、法務省は全国で1万2000人の中学生対象に調査を実施、いかに多くの学校にいじめが蔓延しているかを発表、原稿にも入れたが、軽度のいじめも混じっているかもしれない、などの理由で、この部分は削除になった。重要なデータと思うので、ここに再録しておく。「The Justice Ministry recently issued a report that said one in three Japanese students reported being bullied, and more than 40 percent said they had bullied others.」。

2. Woman's Place

In Japan, the Son Still Rises

By Margaret Shapiro

February 9, 1988

In a country where wives are often addressed by their husbands as *oi* ("hey you") or *gusai* ("dumb wife"), and the term "woman's wisdom" means shallow thinking, career-minded women are a rarity.

Women make up about 40 percent of Japan's work force. But those who venture outside the house usually are given the lowest paid, least significant work, often wearing office uniforms with aprons to run errands and pour tea for bosses and male colleagues. On average, they earn half of what men do....

Yet there is no question that many women feel some dissatisfaction with the traditional arrangement, particularly once their children are out of elementary school....

"Women are changing, they've started to think that household and housework should be shared by husband and wife," said Itsuyo Karakuni, a mother of three who works in an accounting office and whose husband is a salaried office worker. "But men don't want to change things, and for good reason: it's more convenient."

アメリカのメディアにとって日本の女性は興味深い。伝統と先進的な現代が共存する（とされる）日本で、高い教育を受けた女性の人権や男女平等はどうなっているのか——。この記事では、産業戦士を支える good wives and wise mothers 型から、受験体制下の教育ママや結婚退職の風潮、さらにはキャリアを積み、社会のトップに躍り出る女性、若い女性の外資系志向などについて触れている。しかし、アメリカと比べると変化の歩みは遅いようで、男女雇用機会均等法が施行される時には、「many of its proponents (支持者) concede that old practices regarding women's rights will not die quickly」(85/7/3 By John Burgess) と書いた。１０年たった９５年、ＮＹＴは「Downturn (不況) Hurts Women: In

2. 女性問題

日本では、"男子"はまた昇る

マーガレット・シャピロ　　　　　　　　　　1988年2月9日

妻が、しばしば「おい（ヘイ・ユー）」もしくは「愚妻（馬鹿な妻）」と夫から呼ばれ、「女性の知恵」が浅知恵を意味するこの国では、キャリア志向の女性は依然として珍しい存在である。

女性は、日本の労働人口の40％を構成している。しかし、家の外で働こうとするものは、通常、低賃金で重要でない仕事を与えられ、制服を着用し、雑用をさせられたり、上司や男性社員のお茶汲みのため前掛けを着けている。平均では、彼女たちは、男性社員の半分しか稼いでいない……。

だが、多くの女性が、伝統的なあり方にある種の不満を感じているのは疑いない。とくに、子供が小学校を卒業してからはそうだ……。

「女は、変化してますよ。家庭の問題や家事は、夫婦で分かちあうべきだと考え始めました」と唐国稜代は言った。彼女は3人の子の母親で会計事務所に勤め、夫は、サラリーマンである。「でも男って、物事が変わるのを望まない。ちゃんとした理由があるの。その方が便利だからよ」。

Japan, Still Getting Tea and No Sympathy」(8/27 By Sheryl WuDunn)の中で、女性の待遇は一応上がったが、税制面や年金の差別もあり、「Moreover, many discriminatory attitudes linger in hiring, salary and promotion, particularly among the male-dominated upper and middle ranks of management」と批判している。その一方で、96年春の米大統領夫妻来日を機に、WPは橋本久美子総理夫人を単独インタビュー。日本の女性全般に言及した記事中、ジャーナリスト下村満子の「Japanese women have their own tradition, and have accumulated their own power their own way.」という発言を紹介している (96/4/15 By Mary Jordan)。

Japan, Land of the Rising Daughter

By T. R. Reid

May 31, 1995

The firing of Connie Chung has raised new questions as to whether a talented woman can ever reach the very top in television news. The answer may be iffy on American networks, but in the world's second-richest TV market, the issue is settled. On Japan's network news shows, women rule the airwaves....

But the female anchors who dominate the network news here now are experienced, opinionated journalists. Most of them speak English. They are also generally older than the male reporters on their programs—a crucial distinction in a Confucian society where seniority and respect generally go together.

All this has happened in a country that is not exactly famous for gender equality....

Japan has a more egalitarian economy than the United States, with fewer very poor people and fewer making huge incomes. TV newscasters here reportedly make about one-tenth to one-fourth what their counterparts in America command.

"Connie Chung made $2 million per year?" gasped a Japanese TV reporter in disbelief. "That's about, what, 200 million yen? In one year? Nobody in our TV networks is looking at money like that."

Connie Chungと言えば、Dan Ratherの向こうを張るCBSの超人気キャスターだった。それが降番というのだからアメリカでは大変な話題になった。その直後に書かれた記事である。田丸美寿々、桜井良子、安藤優子、野中ともよ、国谷裕子が登場（同順）。依然として男性が職場の中心にいる日本で、女性キャスター活躍の理由は「ratings」。同じくテレビの人気番組「ねるとん紅鯨団」で、最後の決定権を握るのが女性であるのにヒントを得たのが「In Japan's Singles Scene, Women Rule」(93/9/17 By T.R. Reid)。番組では「it's almost painfully cruel」だが、社会学的には重大な力関係の変化を反映し、「in matters of the heart and home, Japan's single women today are taking direct advantage of a

日本、令嬢出ずるの国

トム・リード

1995年5月31日

コニー・チャンの降番は、才能ある女性が果たしてテレビ・ニュースの頂点を極めることができるのかという疑問を提起した。アメリカのネットワークについて言えば、答えはかなり疑わしいが、世界で2番目に大きなテレビ市場においては、決着はついている。日本のネットワークのニュース番組では、女性が、電波を支配している……。

当地でニュース番組を圧倒している女性アンカーたちは、経験を積み、自分の意見をきちんともったジャーナリストである。ほとんどが英語を話す。年齢も、番組に出る男性のレポーターたちより上なことが多い。この点は、年長者であることが一般的には尊敬の対象となる儒教的な社会では、重要な区別である。

これらはすべて、男女の平等に関し、評判が良いとは必ずしも言えない国で起きたのだ……。

日本は、アメリカよりも経済的に平等である。極端に貧乏な人と、極端な金持ちは、アメリカよりも少ない。伝えられるところによれば、この国のテレビのニュース・キャスターの稼ぎは、アメリカの同業者の10分の1から4分の1だ。

「コニー・チャンは年に200万ドル稼ぐんだって」。日本のテレビ・レポーターは、信じられないといった様子で息をのんだ。「というと、なに、2億円？ たった1年で？ うちの局で、そんな金額を考える奴なんて1人もいないよ」。

---

buyer's market for boyfriends」とする。男性は結婚したがっているのに、女性はそうではない。かつてなく、独立志向が増え、それを許す環境が出来てきたからだという。夫婦別姓の流れを扱った「In Right to Maiden Names, Japan's Women See Independence」(95/9/14 By Kevin Sullivan and Mary Jordan) も、そうした変化に焦点を当てている。

3. Population Growth

Birth Dearth Bears Worries for Japan

By T. R. Reid

October 29, 1990

While its efficient factories and financial firms have made Japan an economic superpower, this rich country faces a potentially disastrous shortfall in one vital area: The Japanese are not producing enough babies....

The *Asahi Shimbun* recently reported on an exchange at a women's college here in which a professor urged her students, for the sake of their country, to marry and have three or more children. "But Professor," the students reportedly replied, "if you have three children, you'll ruin your figure."

Japan Nearing Crisis in Care of Elderly

By Mary Jordan

October 31, 1995

OHME, Japan—People here live so long—longer than anywhere else on Earth—that their children, often in their fifties, sixties, or seventies themselves, cannot cope with them.

Nursing homes, frequently more comfortable than hospitals and generally half as expensive to operate, are not common here because the Japanese view them as sinful places where children abandon their duty to care for their elders. But hospitals do not have the same reputation, so aging Japanese are flooding them, placing an enormous financial burden on the national medical insurance system.

日本の人口問題は2つある。若者が子供を産まなくなったことと、長寿社会になり、お年寄りの割合が激増したことだ。最初の記事は「fertility rate—the number of babies an average woman will bear in a lifetime」が world's lowest の1.57となったこと（1989年）を取り上げた。1993年には1.46にまで下がっている。原因は「the failure to turn enormous national wealth into an acceptable standard of living」であり、教育や仕事の圧力が家庭にかかる上、史上初めて「My life is none of your business.」と叫ぶようになった女性の意識の変化をあげる。第2の記事は、

3. 人口問題

出生率低下に悩む日本

トム・リード

1990年10月29日

日本は、効率のいい工場や金融機関のおかげで超大国へと発展したが、この豊かな国は、ある極めて重大な領域で、壊滅的な不足を招くおそれに直面している。即ち、日本人は、赤ちゃんを充分に生産していないのだ……。朝日新聞に、ある女子大学での教授と学生のやりとりが載った。教授が学生たちに、結婚して国のために子供を3人以上産みなさいと勧めた。学生たちはこう答えたという。「でも先生、子供を3人も産んだら、体の線がくずれちゃう」。

お年寄りの介護問題で日本に危機迫る

メアリー・ジョーダン

1995年10月31日

青梅発──日本人の寿命はきわめて長い。地球上のどの国よりも長いので、しばしば50代、60代、そして時には70代の子供たちは、年老いた親たちに対応することができない。たいていは病院より居心地がよく、運営に半分の経費しかかからない老人ホームは、あまり一般的ではない。子供たちが年老いた親の面倒を見る義務を放棄する罪深い場所と見なされているからだ。しかし、病院は、そのような評判は立たないので、お年寄りで溢れかえり、この国の医療保険の財政を深刻に圧迫している。

世界の最長寿国となった日本では、お年寄りを家族が面倒みるという「traditional Japanese family life is changing drastically」。自ら老人ホームを経営する滝上宗次郎氏や厚人省とのインタビュー、病院とホームの中間のような青梅慶友病院のルポ、高齢の両親を持つ家庭の苦悩を描いた『黄落』の著者佐江衆一氏の自宅訪問などの取材を経ている。「a government study paper said, "... we often hear elderly people say, 'I have lived too long' or 'I would like to die suddenly.'"」(記事の結びより)。

4. The Law

D.C. Police Import Japanese Method

By T. R. Reid and Lena H. Sun

December 22, 1994

Tokyo police are curious to see whether the D.C. cop on the beat can be converted into an "Honorable Mr. Walking-Around." Yesterday, the District held a grand opening for its first *koban*, a Japanese-style police booth.

The koban concept, in turn, is part of a broader American movement toward "community policing."

Japan's famous postwar "miracle" usually is defined in economic terms. But there has been a social "miracle" as well; the Japanese have built a free and prosperous society with crime rates far lower than what Western nations have come to accept.... Just as other countries learned manufacturing and financial lessons from Japan in the 1980s, many Americans are turning to Japan in the 1990s for lessons on creating a safe society. They have found various explanations for Japan's social stability, including an egalitarian economic structure, a national commitment to full employment, the traditional Confucian respect for authority, and the widespread sense that every person has a stake in making society work....

But another factor in Japan's success seems to be the community police system, and particularly the citizens' trusting relationship with *Oh-mawari-san*.

アメリカの特派員にとって、日本社会の安全は、最重要なテーマの1つ。犯罪や銃の氾濫といったアメリカ社会最大の課題への答えが見つかるかも知れないからだ。その鍵はKobanか。「Police in Washington and Tokyo Patrol Vastly Different Worlds」(81/6/9 By Tracy Dahlby) は、赴任前に、ワシントンで取材し、東京と併せて書いた。犯罪多発地区をパトカー以外で巡回するなど考えられないワシントンから見れば、徒歩と自転車で巡回するのが当然の東京の警官は新鮮だ。「Japanese Respects for Authority Takes a Big Bite Out of Crime」(87/8/20 By Margaret Shapiro) は、六本木と新宿の派出所のルポ。オウム事件もあって The Asia Pacific Economic Cooperation (APEC) で厳戒体制を

4. 司法問題

ワシントンDC警察、日本方式を取り入れる

トム・リード ＆ リナ・H・サン
1994年12月22日

東京の警察は、ワシントンDCを巡回する警察官が、「尊敬すべきお巡りさん」になれるかどうか、興味しんしんである。昨日、DC市当局主催による、初のコーバン、即ち、日本式ポリス・ボックスの開所式が盛大に行われた。

コーバンとは、万事を交替で行うという考え方なのだが、広い意味で、アメリカにおける「コミュニティー警察活動」の一環といえる。

戦後日本の「奇跡」は、通常、経済的な次元で語られる。しかし、そこには、社会的な「奇跡」も存在していた。日本は、西側の国々が許容しているよりはるかに低い犯罪発生率の中で、自由かつ豊かな社会を築き上げた……。1980年代に、他の国が、製造業や金融に関して日本に学ぼうとしたのと同様に、1990年代においては、たくさんのアメリカ人が、安全な社会を創るための教訓を日本から学ぼうとしている。彼らは、日本の社会が安定している様々な理由を発見した。公平な経済構造、完全雇用を実現するための国をあげての取り組み、儒教的な伝統に基づく権威に対する尊敬、さらに、一人ひとりが社会を動かす役割を担っているという広く行き渡った感覚などである。

しかし、安全面で日本が成功した今1つの要因は、警察の地域活動、とくに市民と「お巡りさん」との信頼関係にあるようだ。

とる日本の警察。「Japan, in Name of Security, Disarms 40,000 Carpenters」(95/11/15 By Kevin Sullivan) では、工事に電気銃を使う大工さんや暴走族にも、低姿勢で協力を呼びかける警察や「And in typically Japanese fashion, the bikers, carpenters … don't seem to be complaining about being inconvenienced.」と、それに不満も漏らさずに応ずる人々の姿を、半ば感嘆、半ば呆れた調子で描いている。

Japan's O.J. Trial

By Mary Jordan and Kevin Sullivan

October 5, 1995

When cult guru Shoko Asahara walks into court for Japan's most notorious trial in 50 years, there will be no jury, no celebrity lawyers, no scrutiny of the prosecutor's hairdo. And virtually no doubt about the outcome: It is a near-certainty that the bearded leader of the Aum Supreme Truth sect will be convicted and sentenced to hang....

Like the trial that just ended in Los Angeles, the one unfolding here has stretched Tokyo prosecutors, police, and courts to capacity. And while many Japanese say that the Simpson case highlighted weaknesses in the American jury trial, the Aum case has turned an international spotlight on a very different kind of judicial system, one in which judges, not juries, decide guilt or innocence—and one that critics contend systematically ignores defendants' rights.

Police can hold suspects before indictment for weeks and interrogate the detainee daily for 12 hours or more without the presence of an attorney. During this time, most suspects confess, a key reason that Japan's conviction rate is almost 100 percent.

犯罪は、人間の極限の姿を顕わにするが故に、それを裁く司法制度は、その国の民族的特徴や国民性と切り離せない。オウム事件を巡って、その点を様々に考えさせられた。日本では、最終的に有罪に判決を取るに足るだけの証拠がなければ、警察も検察も、軽々しく逮捕、起訴に着手しない。アメリカの場合、beyond reasonable doubt があれば逮捕して調べ、容疑が晴れれば釈放する。そうした制度に慣れた目から見れば「Japanese Police Probe of Gas Attack Moves like Tortoise, Not Bullet Train」(95/4/23 By T.R. Reid)。教祖逮捕となり、事件の凶悪性はそれとして、被疑者の人権問題をどう扱うかが支局内で議論となった。取り調べ時の弁護士の同席や、頻繁な保釈は当然のアメリカから見

日本のO.J.裁判

メアリー・ジョーダン ＆ ケビン・サリバン

1995年10月5日

カルトの教祖麻原彰光が、過去50年、日本でもっとも悪名を轟かした事件の裁判で法廷に入る時、そこには、陪審員も著名な弁護士もいなければ、検察官の髪形をあれこれ詮索する者もいない。そして、その結末に疑念をはさむ余地は事実上ない。オウム真理教の髭面の指導者は、有罪を宣告され、絞首刑となるのは、ほとんど確実と言ってよい……。

ロサンジェルスで、ちょうど終わった裁判のように、当地で展開されている裁判にも、東京の検察官や警察、裁判所が総動員されている。シンプソン事件は、陪審制をとるアメリカの裁判の弱点を明らかにしたと多くの日本人は主張しているが、オウム事件は、それとは全く異なる司法制度に国際的なスポットライトを当てた。陪審員ではなく、裁判官が有罪か無罪かを決め、批判的な人に言わせれば、被告人の権利が組織的に無視されているような制度である。

警察は、起訴の前に、容疑者を、何週間にもわたって拘留することができ、弁護士の立ち会いなしに、拘留者を1日12時間、あるいはそれ以上も訊問できる。この間に、ほとんどの容疑者は、自白をするが、まさに、日本の有罪宣告率が100％に近い理由である。

れば、日本はあまりにも調べる側に有利に見える。理不尽な調べを受けたという女性を取材した「Police Violence, Flip Side of Japan's Low Crime Rate」(90/4/30 By Margaret Shapiro) を出稿したこともあった。だがオウム事件は確信犯による組織犯罪であり、地下鉄事件以後の警察の捜査に、国民から基本的な批判は出ていないことなどから、人権問題を前面に出すのは適当でないとし、検察のトップとのインタビューも含めて原稿をまとめたのだった。

Doc Deals Gangsters a Full Hand

By T. R. Reid

October 5, 1992

Here's an item to file in the category of necessity as the mother of invention. A Japanese doctor has popularized a procedure to replace fingers sliced off by Japan's *yakuza* gangsters.

The necessity that motivated this medical breakthrough is a tough new federal law—the first comprehensive anti-gang law in Japan's history—that took effect in March. Facing increased pressure from police, hundreds of gang members have decided to go straight.

That's where the finger problem comes in....

An ex-yakuza member who wants to look like a normal Japanese "salary man" can let his hair grow so he no longer has the tightly curled crewcut standard for gangsters here. He can wear clothing that covers the elaborate tattoos that mark yakuza members. But the lost finger is hard to hide, given Japanese social customs.

On first meeting here, it is common for people to exchange business cards. In a society where the form of things always matters, it is essential that the card be held in both hands when it is passed to a new acquaintance. For ex-gangsters, this rite calls attention to the missing fingers.

福井県の整形外科、吉村光生医師はヤクザの救世主だ。詰めた手の指に、足の指を切断してつけ代える手術に成功したからで、今も希望者は跡を絶たない。だが、アメリカの目には、組織や組員を明らかにする日本的なヤクザは実に奇妙に映る。「The yakuza operates like every other big business organization here. Members proudly wear yakuza lapel badges and pass out business cards....Gang leaders hold press conferences. They ... flaunt their famous corporate logo on the front door of their office buildings.」(92/2/29 By T.R. Reid)。それが、92年春の暴力団対策新法の施行で組織的な活動は大幅な制限を受けることになる。だが「The tough new law may backfire by driving Japan's highly visible organized

ヤクザの指をもとどおりにするお医者さん

トム・リード

1992年10月5日

　ここに、必要は発明の母なりというファイルに入れるべき項目があります。日本の医者が、ヤクザによって切り落とされた指をつけ直す方法を実用化したのです。

　この医学的大躍進は、今年の3月に施行された厳しい新法によって、必要性が生じたためにもたらされました。それは、日本史上初の包括的な反ヤクザ法です。警察からの圧力は増えるばかりとあって、何百人ものヤクザの組員が普通の市民になろうと決心しました。

　ここに指問題が登場するのです……。

　日本の普通の「サラリーマン」のように見られることを願う元ヤクザは、髪をのばし、典型的なヤクザの髪形であるきつくカールしたクルーカットを、やめることはできます。組員の証ともいえる、入念な入れ墨を隠すため、服を着ることもできます。しかし、日本の社会慣習を考慮するならば、失った指を隠すのはとても難しいのです。

　当地では、初めての出会いに際し、名刺を交換することが一般的です。形式を重んじる社会においては、初対面の人に名刺を渡す際、両方の手で差し出すことがとても大事なのです。元ヤクザにとって、この儀式は、失われた指に注目を集めさせてしまうことになるのです。

crime families underground.」と、ヤクザを水面下に追いやる危険性にも言及している。

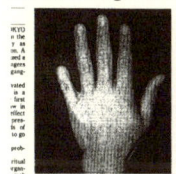 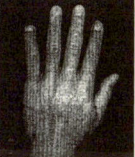

CHAPTER 4 | JAPAN AND AMERICA

1. The Land of Guns and Violence

Image of U.S. Affirmed in Student's Death

By T. R. Reid

October 20, 1992

For the American news media, it was just another accidental killing. In Japan, though, the real-life Halloween horror story quickly became a major national concern.

The case is newsworthy mainly because it tends to confirm all the worst impressions the Japanese people hold in their intense love-hate relationship with the colossus across the Pacific....

Man Acquitted of Killing Japanese Student

By William Booth

May 24, 1993

Peairs testified that Hattori appeared to him as a grinning, potentially crazed intruder who was brandishing a weapon and refused to stop when Peairs yelled "Freeze!" ....

The district attorney told jurors that Peairs's character was not on trial but that his behavior was wrong. The jury apparently disagreed, and returned its "not guilty" verdict in less than three hours.

Louisiana 州 Baton Rouge での服部剛丈君の殺害は、アメリカでは、ごくありふれた銃による殺人事件で地元だけの小さなニュースだったが、日本の反応はまったく違っていた。その点に着目したWP東京支局が第1報（上記最初の記事）を送り、本社が1面で取り上げ、事件は全米の問題となった。しかし、裁判で犯人のRodney Peairs は無罪。Peairs 宅で服部君は、いったん道路側まで戻ったのに、拳銃片手の被告がバタンとドアをあけ、それにつられて服部君が再び玄関へ向かったなど肝心な点は無視され、記事でも報じられてさえいない。「Japanese Media Disparage（誹謗する）Acquittal in "Freeze Case," Commentators See America as a Sick Nation」(93/5/25 By Tom Reid)。久米宏は「銃を認め

第4章 日本とアメリカ

1. 銃と暴力の国

対米イメージ、生徒の死によって確認される

トム・リード

1992年10月20日

アメリカのメディアにとっては、よくある不慮の殺人にすぎなかった。しかし、ここ日本では、本物のハロウィンの惨劇は、瞬く間に国をあげての関心事になった。

この事件が大ニュースとなったのは、太平洋対岸の巨人との激しい愛憎関係において、日本人の抱く最悪の印象が確認されたからにほかならない……。

日本人留学生を殺した男に無罪

ウィリアム・ブース

1993年5月24日

ピアースは、ハットリはにやにやした笑いを浮かべた、頭のおかしそうな侵入者に見えた、と証言した。それが武器を振り回し、「フリーズ」と叫んでも止まるのを拒絶したというのだ。地方検事は、陪審員に、ピアースの性格が裁かれているのではなく、行いが間違っていた点が問題なのだと述べた。陪審員は、検事には明らかに同意せず、3時間もたたないうちに無罪の評決を下したのだった。

るかどうかは文化の違いというけれど、how can you call it a "culture"」。しかし、民事裁判では被告に過失が認められ、「Ruling Softens Japan's Image of Violent U.S. After Monetary Award in Exchange Student's Murder, "There Is a Sense of Justice in America" After All」(94/9/18 同)。結びは「"The commitment to justice is rewarded."」という産経新聞見出しの引用だった。

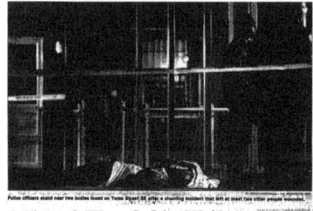

Parents of Slain Japanese Student to Meet Clinton With Anti-Gun Message

By Shigehiko Togo

November 16, 1993

The many letters sent to the Hattoris by Americans included these comments:

- "The influence your son demonstrated in Baton Rouge is beginning to be felt across our nation. It showed that, for the first time in our history, more Americans favored stricter gun control than did not. No, Yoshi did not die in vain."
- "The USA will never achieve a high level of culture without the careful and strict control of these weapons."

A Heart-to-Heart on Gun Violence

By Charles W. Hall

November 20, 1993

In more than an hour of discussion about violence in America, many at the session said they accept the presence of firearms as a grim necessity....

Their message had an effect. Macoto, who earlier said that guns give their owners a sense of power, said he had realized that killing his father's murderer was not the answer. "She made me realize I would become exactly what I despise," Macoto said.

剛丈君の死後1年、服部夫妻は、銃反対の署名を集め、President Clinton に渡すため、ワシントンを訪れた。Yoshiのhomestay先だったHaymaker夫妻と、銃反対の団体 The Coalition to Stop Gun Violence が夫妻の受け皿となった。当時、私は本社に勤務中でこの件を担当。当日の朝、The Coalition の集会は、銃反対の総決起集会の観を呈し、宗教団体などが次々と激しい言葉を連ねた。上記第1の手紙はこの記事中に引用したものだ。夫妻は数日後、Arlington の Wakefield High School を訪ね、高校生と語った。「わが子を殺した相手を殺しはしない。Even the killer has people who love him, and it would simply bring much grief to another family.」。この言葉が Macato を動かしたのだ。銃の所有者の資格を調べ

殺害された日本人生徒の両親、銃反対のメッセージを携えてクリントンと会見へ

東郷茂彦　　　　　　　　　　　　　　　　1993年11月16日

アメリカ人から服部家に送られたたくさんの手紙の中には、次のようなコメントも含まれていた。

■「あなたの息子さんが、バトンルージュで示した感化は、いまや全米に広がり始めています。我々の歴史上初めて、銃を厳しく規制することに賛成するアメリカ人が、反対派を上回ったことを示しているのです。いいえ、ヨシの死は、無駄ではありませんでした」。

■ アメリカ合衆国は、こうした武器を注意深く、かつ厳しく規制しないうちは、文化的に高いレベルに達することはできません」。

銃の暴力を本音で語り合う

チャールズ・W・ホール　　　　　　　　　1993年11月20日

アメリカの暴力についての1時間以上にわたる討論中、会場にいた多くが、火器の存在を必要悪として受け入れると言った……。

　2人（訳注：服部夫妻）のメッセージには効果があった。先程、銃を持つと強くなったような気になると述べた（ホセ）マカートが「自分の父を殺害した犯人を殺しても、問題は解決しない」と言ったのだ。「服部夫人が目覚めさせてくれなければ、もう自分が軽蔑する人間になってしまうところだったよ」。

るという、それでもこの国では画期的な Brady Bill が、The National Rifle Association の強い反対にもかかわらず議会を通ったのは2週間後の12月3日だった。式典で Clinton は「We have taken this important part of the life of millions of Americans and turned it into an instrument of maintaining madness. It is crazy.」と声をふり絞るように叫んだのだった。

Yoshi の死はアメリカの銃反対運動にじつに大きな影響を与えた、というのが現地で取材して得た実感である。

2. African Americans

Arrogance or Ignorance?

October 3, 1986

Black America is outraged. Outraged and insulted by the negative reference to minorities attributed to Japan's Prime Minister Yasuhiro Nakasone.

LEST YOU FORGET

Immediately after World War II, it was the black GIs, segregated in the U.S. Army, stationed in Yokohama, Kobe, Nara, Gifu, and many, many other cities who adopted hospitals, orphanages, schools, and the homeless. We fed your people and clothed them. Many Japanese survived—because of us.

A NATION OF MINORITIES AND PROUD OF IT

The people of the United States have just spent a summer celebrating the restoration of the Statue of Liberty, the symbol of our uniqueness as a nation whose citizens, including millions of Japanese Americans, all contribute to the cultural, political, social, and economic diversity that makes us strong.

A CHANGE IS IN THE MAKING

Japan must reach out for greater understanding of black people and institutions in America. It is commonly believed that the Japanese intolerance for differences is rooted in that nation's isolation from people of different backgrounds or cultures.

1986年9月22日、静岡で開かれた自民党研修会での中曽根首相の知的水準発言は、日本のメディアではほんの雑報扱いだった。しかし、これを受けた米メディアの報道が、アメリカ国内での怒りに火をつけた。上記の全面広告は、ひび割れた日章旗をイラストに「The Black Community Responds to Japanese Prime Minister Yasuhiro Nakasone」とし、主張に共感する読者は、松永信夫駐米大使、在米日本商工会議所、Congressional Black Caucus、Your Congressperson or Senator 宛に手紙を出そうと呼びかけている。発起人団体は「Concerned African-American Business Leaders」。Rev. Jesse Jackson ら政治家や出版団体、黒人系企業計40余が名を連ねている。米国内では、怒りを基調とする報道

2. 黒人問題

傲慢か無知か？

1986年10月3日

ブラック・アメリカは、激怒している。日本の総理大臣中曽根康弘が言ったというマイノリティについての否定的発言に、我々は、ひどく侮辱され、激怒している。

夢忘るるなかれ 第2次大戦直後、米陸軍内で差別されていた黒人GIこそが、横浜、神戸、奈良、岐阜など多くの都市に駐留し、病院、孤児院や学校、さらには浮浪者の面倒を見たのだ。私たちが、あなた方を食べさせ、衣服を与えた。たくさんの日本人が、我々のおかげで生き延びることができたのだ……。

マイノリティーの国家を誇る アメリカ合衆国の人民はこの夏、自由の女神の復元を祝ったばかりだ。この像は、我が国の独自性の象徴なのだ。そこでは、数百万人の日系アメリカ人も含め、市民全てが、文化、政治、社会、経済の多様性に貢献している。それこそが、我々を強靭にしている……。

変化は起きている 日本は、黒人、ならびにアメリカ社会のあり方をもっと良く理解しなければならない。物事の差異に対する日本人の不寛容さは、異なった文化や背景を持つ人々と長く接してこなかったためだと一般には見なされている。

が圧倒的ではあったが、「The Real Issue Nakasone Raised」(10/7 By Carl T. Rowan) のように、アメリカ人は minority 問題をもっと直視すべきだという論調もあった。この年以来、政治家のいわゆる問題発言は、2年おきに、渡辺美智雄（88年）、梶山静六（90年）両氏から桜内宮沢発言（92年）へと続き、WPはそのいずれも重要事件として報じている。

Old Black Stereotypes Find New Lives in Japan

By Margaret Shapiro

July 22, 1988

Little Black Sambo, the racist caricature that most Americans thought had died a well-deserved death years ago, has been resurrected across the Pacific as the mascot of a hot-selling line of Japanese toys and beachwear.

Sambo and other stereotypical depictions of blacks—some with grotesquely fat lips and ethnic dialect—have become something of a fad here this summer in what appears to be an attempt at internationalization gone gravely awry....

Despite the recent trend toward global travel and overseas investment, the Japanese remain a strongly insular people, with little understanding of or empathy for foreign cultures.

One Small Force Against Racism

By Phil McCombs

August 12, 1989

What his dad, Toshiji, read that summer day last year was shocking: Japanese companies were selling dolls and other toys, purses, clothing and other items imprinted with stereotypical depictions of blacks to an eager Japanese public.

Hajime was genuinely upset. "It's really terrible," he said in the Thursday press conference. "The stereotypes are so exaggerated."

有楽町の百貨店に展示されていた黒人のマネキン。六屑貝売り場の「Sambo & Hanna」のキャラクター商品。それがアメリカでは典型的な黒人差別のスタイルと名前を持っている――この取材に関わるまで、問題の根の深さは十分にはわからなかった。記事の出た翌日、軽井沢での渡辺美智雄発言があり、ことは一挙に政治問題化した。このニュースを正面から受け止めたのが堺市の有田さん一家3人だった。黒人グッズの収集から始まって「The Association to Stop Racism Against Blacks」の結成。その活動により、差別的な絵や図が、多くの広告、商品、漫画から消え、絵本『ちびくろサンボ』も姿を消した。おかげで、何百万という日本の子供が「Sambo」という最悪の差別用語に親しみ、黒人のイメー

黒人の古いステレオタイプ、日本に新生する

マーガレット・シャピロ
1988年7月22日

ちびくろサンボといえば、もう何年も前に、亡びるべくして亡びたとほとんどのアメリカ人が思っている、人種差別的なカリカチュアである。それが太平洋を越え、ここ日本の売れ筋のおもちゃとビーチウエアに、マスコットとして復活した。サンボをはじめ、ステレオタイプな黒人の描写は、この夏、当地ではちょっとした流行（はやり）となり、なかには、グロテスクなほどの厚い唇や、強い黒人なまりも含まれている。おかげで、国際化に向けての努力も台無しになってしまったようだ……。最近の外国旅行ブームや、海外投資熱にもかかわらず、日本人には依然として島国根性が強く、異文化を理解し、共感することは少ない。

人種差別に対抗する小さな力

フィル・マッコム
1989年8月12日

去年の夏のある日、父親の有田利二（はじめ）が、太に読んで聞かせた内容は衝撃的だった。黒人をステレオタイプに描いた人形やおもちゃ、図柄をプリントした財布、洋服など様々なグッズを、日本の会社が、貪欲な日本の大衆に売っているというのだ。

太は、心底驚き、悲しんだ。「本当に、ひどいんだ」。木曜日に行われた記者会見でこう述べた。「黒人のイメージが、ものすごく歪んで誇張されているんだもの」。

ジと直結させながら育つという恐ろしい状況に陥らずにすんでいる。中曽根発言で結成された「Concerned African-American Business Leader」の Albert L. Nellum さんが一家のことを知り、お礼にアメリカへ招待した時に書かれたのが上記第2の記事だ。日本の国際化と人権擁護の観点から勲章ものの働きをしている有田さんだが、堺市は人権関係の仕事から外し、駐輪場の管理などの職につけている… Jesus!

3. Japanese Americans

House Votes Apology, Reparations

By Tom Kenworthy

September 18, 1987

The House offered the nation's apology and $1.2 billion in reparations yesterday to thousands of Japanese Americans who were forced into relocation camps during World War II....

The measure declares that the justification for the mass internment—that Japanese Americans posed a security risk—was unfounded and that the relocations were "motivated in part by racial prejudice and wartime hysteria."

Japanese American Pride Wins Battle

By Shigehiko Togo

March 18, 1994

After five years of struggle, a Japanese American who charged that racial discrimination kept him from becoming a Marine Corps officer finally has won his case and will be formally commissioned as a captain in the Marine Corps Reserve today.

Bruce Yamashita, whose grandparents left Japan for Hawaii nearly a century ago, had never doubted his identity as an American when he entered the Officer Candidate School at Quantico, Virginia, in February 1989. That is why the verbal and physical abuse he encountered from school instructors was all the more shocking for him.

太平洋戦争で、日系アメリカ人の強制収容は、今日に至るまで深い傷となって残っている。その償いを決めた議会決定を報じたのが上記第1報の記事だ。法案を推進した1人、Norman Y. Mineta 議員はこの日、「"We lost our homes, we lost our businesses, we lost our farms, but worst of all, we lost our basic human rights."」と演説した。この年の夏から The Smithsonian Institution の the National Museum of American History で日系人強制収容の展覧会が始まった(その後常設)。国威を傷つけるという反対論も台頭したが「1787–1987—and 1942」と題する論説 (87/5/7) は「We think the museum is right to go ahead with the exhibit...」と開催を支持した。こうした流れにも関わらず、海兵隊士官

3. 日系人問題

下院、謝罪と賠償を可決

トム・ケンワージー　　　　　　　　　　1987年9月18日

下院は、第2次大戦中、強制的に収容所に移された無数の日系アメリカ人に対し、謝罪と120億ドルの賠償金の支払いをすることを昨日、決定した……。

この法令は、大規模な抑留の正当化——日系アメリカ人は、安全保障上危険とされた——には根拠がなく、移住は「人種偏見と戦時中の興奮状態に基づいて行なわれた側面がある」ことを宣言している。

日系アメリカ人の誇り、闘いに勝つ

東郷茂彦　　　　　　　　　　　　　　1994年3月18日

人種差別が、海兵隊の将校になるのを妨げていると訴えていた日系アメリカ人が、5年間の法廷闘争の後ついに勝訴し、今日、正式に海兵隊の大佐に任命される。

ブルース・ヤマシタ——およそ100年前に祖父が、ハワイに移住するために日本を離れた——は、1989年の2月にバージニア州クァンティコにある幹部候補生校に入学した際には、自らのアメリカ人としてのアイデンティティを疑ったことはなかった。それゆえに、学校の教官に受けた言葉と物理的ないやがらせは、なお一層の衝撃であった。

を志した Hawaii 出身の Bruce Yamashita は「We don't want your kind around here. Go back to your country.」「Yamaha」「Kamikaze-man」などの蔑称で呼ばれ、ごみ箱をぶつけられるなど様々な人種差別を受け、将校になれなかった。闘いに勝利した Bruce は「This case is not just for Asian Americans. This is for all Americans.」と謙虚に語るアメリカ人らしい好青年の lawyer である。

4. From America with Love: America's Place in Japan
アメリカ発日本へ、日本の中のアメリカ

日本人はアメリカをどう見ているか。WPにとっても興味深いテーマである。

暴力、銃、麻薬といったマイナスイメージが先行している、というのが Tom Reid の見方だ。日本へ赴任してまもなく Foreign Journal に書いたのが「Good Morning, Japan! Here's Ameripop!」(90/8/6)。「The Japanese draw their current image of the U.S. largely from television. And the picture of America portrayed on Japanese TV, by and large, is of a country mired in crime, drugs, corruption, and greed.」。

直接的には、テレビ朝日の早朝番組「デイブレイク」の流すアメリカは「"Stupid American Tricks (特技)"」に偏っていると噛みついた記事だ。例えば、プレスリー博物館から盗んだトイレの紙を祭る部屋を作った Louisiana の男、Florida では裸のお尻を見せる憲法上の権利を情熱的に論じる女性、障害児を虐待した California の教師など「strange American happenings」が主に登場するというのだ。「On Sunday, many many Americans go to church. Most of the Americans are healthy, hardworking, and family loving people. でも、そういうアメリカ人がぜんぜん出てこないよ」という Tom の歯ぎしりするような持論が滲み出たような記事だ。しかし、この番組は、CNN の報じたアメリカに関する報道を素材にしており、日本人が意図的に偏った内容にしているわけではない、という抗議が東京支局と本社に寄せられたものだ。

こうしたイメージは、日本人の留学生が射殺される事件が相次いだことから、実証され、増幅されたかのごとくだ。「Journey Into Fear: Japanese Courses Teach Travelers How to Guard Against U.S. Crime」(92/12/19 By Tom Reid) のカット写真は『VIEWS』誌92年12月23日号「フリーズ事件の街を現場検証する：銃とアメリカ人」の、何丁ものライフルを手にす

るアメリカ人一家の写真だ。フリーズ事件の民事での勝訴判決の記事でTomはこう書いている。「Opinion polls show that most Japanese idolize the U.S. as the world's leader in pop culture. American movies, music, fashion, and fast food are the very definition of "cool"（かっこいい）for young people here. But these feelings are coupled with a sense of disillusionment, even disdain（軽蔑）, for a society that has been seen here as riddled by crime, drugs, and fatal shootings in suburban backyards.」(94/9/18)。

さて、日本での「最もアメリカらしい」ものを、WPはどのように報じているか、見てみよう。

まず、場所。なんといっても米軍基地だろう。そのアメリカ性は計画的に作られたものだ。少女への暴行事件で揺れる沖縄を訪れた時、海兵隊のMWR—morale, welfare, and recreationを担当する大佐はこう述べたものだ。「I try to make this look and act like the good old USA."」(95/10/1 By Mary Jordan)。「His job is to "replicate America" for the Marines and their family members....」とこのやり方にある種の違和感を持ったMaryは書いている。

そして、普通の日本人の行ける場所でいえば、東京ディズニーランド。「the Tokyo version is aggressively American...」(89/8/23 By Margaret Shapiro)。入場者の大半は「looking for an escape from typically tiny houses, non-existent backyards, and noise and congestion.」なのだ。

運動では、アメフトだ。その大学選手権Rose Bowlの出場権をかけた試合が、東京ドームで行われた。Wisconsin's Badgers対Michigan State team。その応援ぶりがまた極めて日本的だった。決して自然発生的ではないのだ。「To boost morale in the stands, the announcers did their best to get the crowd involved. But this too was done with characteristic Japanese courtesy. "We humbly call on our honorable patrons," the announcer would say, "to offer their esteemed cooperation for another effort at the *way-bu*"」(93/12/6 By Toshihiro Nakayama)。アナウンサーが「みなさんウェーブをお願いします」などと放送しているのをとらえての表現だ。中山俊宏記者は、私がWashington本社で勤務中、東京支局でピンチ・ヒッターを務めた気鋭の若い政治学者だ。

音楽といえば無数だろうが、ロック・ギターのPaul Gilbert。愛知の電気ドリルメーカーの「マキタ」を演奏に使ったことから、同社がスポンサーとなっての日本公演だった。赤坂のホテルでの記者会見に行った中山記者はBaltimore Sunの女性記者の質問に注目した。Baltimoreに工場のあるBlack & Decker社の製品をなぜ使わないかというのだ。Gilbertは「B&D社はもうイギリスの会社で、自分のマキタはアメリカで作られている」と反論した後、こう言った。「"In this international world, we are economically interdependent. With free trade, everybody wins. Makita makes a darn good drill, and we use it. And Makita has been good to us, so we can come over here and sell records."」(93/11/4/ By Tom Reid)。

食事では、アメリカ風のファーストフードが日本でどう変わるか。「When it comes to fast food, however, U.S. marketing here has been the stuff of genius.」(93/10/4 By Tom Reid)。イカのピザ。カレーのドーナツ。ライス・バーガー。テンプラ・ホットドッグ。BST(ベーコン、海藻、トマト)のサンドイッチ等々。そして「In Japan, it's not just the food but also the style of the stores that has been adapted to local preferences.」。

宗教では、キリスト教、それもプロテスタント。Evangelistの世界的な説教師Billy Graham「Faces Land of Many Faiths」(94/1/15 By Tom Reid)。来日したGrahamはホテルの部屋の引き出しから、The Sayings of Buddhaを見つける。「... he said, "Many of the sayings of Buddha are almost exactly the same as the teachings of Jesus Christ."」。

アメリカ人ということになれば、コマーシャルで有名なタレントに日本ではお目にかかれる。「In Japan, a Yen for Yankee Pitchmen: Why American Stars Consent to Appear in Advertisements They'd Never Do Here」(89/3/11 By Margaret Shapiro)。here とは、もちろんアメリカのこと。記事中、日本の広告会社員の言葉が紹介される。「"They want the money from appearing in the commercials but they don't want it known in the U.S. They want to hide as much as possible that they are appearing in commercials in Japan."」。

アメリカ人で最も有名な人——大統領ということになろうか。現職中の公式訪日についてはさておくとして、辞任後の訪日には、とかくケチがつく。「Muttering in Tokyo Over Reagan's Tour: Ex-President Being Paid \$2 Million by Media Giant」(89/10/7 By Fred Hiatt)。日本のメディア・グループが多額の謝礼のもとに呼んだということで、東京発で5回ほど記事になったが、批判的なトーンが消えていない。Geroge Bush 前大統領の場合は、統一教会との関連だ。「Moon Group Paying Bush for Speeches: Foes of Church Criticize Japan Tour」(95/9/6 By Kevin Sullivan and Mary Jordan)。

最後に、日本で暮らすアメリカ人の素顔に迫ろうとする記事も。「Tokyo's Young American Imports: Those With a Yen for Business Enter a World of Differences」(89/11/5 By Elisabeth Bumiller)。日本で1年前に仕事についたアメリカ人女性は「sometimes thinks that working for a Japanese company as an American is like having a Ferrari and every day driving it 180 miles an hour into a brick wall.」。異文化の中で日々起きる衝突を、こう表現している。

CHAPTER 5 | THE JAPANESE IMAGE

1. From Japan with Love: Japan's Place in America
日本発アメリカへ、アメリカの中の日本

日米間には、情報ギャップがある、という。この分野では、世界に悪名高い日本の貿易黒字とは反対に、圧倒的なアメリカの出超である。

平たく言えば、日本人はアメリカを知っているけれど、アメリカ人は日本を知らない。というわけで「Be honest now: Without digging out a World Almanac, and without peeking further down into this story for hints, how many prominent Japanese people can you name?」とTom Reidは同胞に問いかける。「How the West Was Dumb: TV News Doesn't Fill Info Gap on Japan」(94/3/24) の書きだしだ。記事によると、民間の調査で若いアメリカ人に聞いたところ、Yoko Ono, Bruce Lee, and Godzilla がトップ3だった。92、3年の7ヵ月間のテレビ報道では、日本がアメリカのニュースを1121回、アメリカは日本のニュースを92回しか扱っていない。Ellis Kraus, a University of Pittsburgh political scientist はこう分析する。「"Aside from an occasional disaster or election, Japan has not been a very dramatic story. Japan gets defined as a 'business and economics' story, and economics gets a low priority for a good, visual television news item."」。

こうしたギャップを埋めるために、日本から情報発信をしなければ、というわけで官民の努力ということになる。「Japanese Seek to Fund Cultural Exchanges」(90/6/16 By Fred Hiatt) では、安倍晋太郎外相の名を冠した「Abe Fellowship」の創設を取り上げ、「The proposals reflects deep anxieties here that Japan is increasingly viewed as

第5章 日本人の顔

different and even menacing by other nations in the developed world.」と書いた。「Japan's Literary Trade Deficit」(92/8/27 By Tom Reid) では、日本文学の英訳を進めるための The Association for 100 Japanese Books に焦点を当てる。1990年には、3000冊以上の英語の本が和訳されたが、アメリカで英訳された日本の本はわずか82冊。「The works of a new wave of Japanese novelists, which deal not with cherry blossoms and tea ceremonies but rather with air pollution, entrance exams, and alienation, are also starting to appear in English. The best known is Haruki Murakami, whose novel *A Wild Sheep Chase* made some Western bestseller lists in 1990.」。現在、全米の図書館、日本関係の専門家に計4000冊の需要があり、「"That's getting close right there to paying back the costs."」と上智大学の Gregory Clark 教授はコメントしている。

　日本文化の発信という点から、映画を抜きに語れない。日本映画といえば、黒沢明は巨大である。しかし、最近の作品の評価は高くない。「'Dreams' Never Wakes Up」(90/9/14 By Hal Hinson) や「The Setting Sun of Akira Kurosawa」(93/12/28 By Tom Reid) などだ。日本の庶民を代表する映画キャラクター「寅さん」や伊丹十三監督の作品が注目される一方、味のある新作は肯定的に評価される。金に踊らされる現代の家族を描いたコメディー「木村家の人々」は「'Yen family': The Perils of Profits」(92/6/19 By Rita Kemply) となり、「an aggressively ambivalent comedy on Japanese affluence, can't decide whether to water the money tree or poison the root of evil」。江戸川乱歩の生涯を神秘的耽美的に描いた「Rampo」は「Rich Rewards of 'Rampo': From Japan, a Splendid Mix of Illusion & Reality」(95/6/2 By Hal Hinson) だ。「Japanese writer-director Kazuyoshi Okuyama … constructs a quicksilver universe in which nothing seems solid, where objects, characters, even history itself appear whimsical and fluid.」。

ファッションの分野も日本人のデザイナーの活躍が目立つ。むしろ NYT の方が取り上げる機会が多いが、WPでは「Japan's Madame Couturier: Hanae Mori, Designing a Fashion Empire in which East Meets West」(90/2/28 By Elisabeth Bumiller) という Style を埋め尽くすような長文の記事を掲載している。

伝統芸能では、御存知歌舞伎。天井桟敷から声をかけ、芝居を盛り上げる「大向こうさん」を取り上げたのが「Theater Of the Shout」(82/6/18 By Tracy Dahlby) だ。能の世界ではWashington公演での幽玄な所作はこんな理解だ。「But Otoshige Sakai is doing something else, something more obscure, something that surely must be more meaningful that fidgeting. Or maybe not.」(88/10/27 By Elizabeth Kastor)。

Washington の the National Portrait Gallery で催された細川家の肖像画展は「If Americans are ever to understand Japan, it will be in small sips—as if from a rare, ancient tea bowl—or in luminous little exhibitions such as "Noble Heritage: Five Centuries of Portraits From the Hosokawa Family,"…」(92/7/29 By Jo Ann Lewis) と報じられている。

現代の世界では、スポーツは重要な共通言語だ。日米間になじみ深いのは相撲と野球。相撲は、日本の国技として伝統の色濃く残る特殊な世界だけに外国メディアの関心を容易にひく。千代の富士が大関に昇進した時は「Aggresive 'Lightweight' Battles to the Top of Sumo Wrestling」(81/3/6 By William Chapman)。写真説明は「Superstar Chiyonofuji, known as "Wolf" to fans of sumo, in a training session」だ。貴の花の婚約破棄や結婚も、日本社会の明暗にからめて報じられるが、当然のこととして、高見山、小錦、曙らハワイ出身者の活躍は、WPにとって必須重要なニュースで報道量も多い。

野球は日米双方、共通のルールの上に立っている。一応はそうなのだが、微妙な所ではそうでもない。その差異に着目した報道もあるし、アメリカの野球記録を日本が抜く時は、ニュースだ。王貞治のホームラン世界記録達成直前には、John Saar 支局長と王選手のお宅までお伺いしたものだ。衣笠祥雄選手の連続出場記録に関しては「Japanese Baseball's Iron Outcast: The Forgotten Mixed-Blood Slugger Who Is Still Ahead of Ripken」(95/9/17 By John B. Holoway)。そして Los Angeles Dodgers の Nomo だ。オールスターに出場した野茂英雄選手をWP はこう報じる。「Johnson clearly is not Tuesday's top attraction, however, Nomo is … Nomo mostly shrugged off questions today about being the Japanese savior of America's pasttime … Nomo said through an interpreter: "I love baseball. If I do my best, I hope that will be the best for the game."(95/7/11 By Mark Maske)。Nomo 1人の存在が、自動車摩擦など日米関係にたちこめた暗雲を吹き飛ばしたかのようだったのを鮮明に記憶している。アメリカのメディアが Nomo をどう報じたかについては、『WE LOVE NOMO! / How Did the American Press report Hideo Nomo? アメリカの現地紙はこう報じた・文藝春秋編』が興味深い生の材料を提示している。

　イチローの活躍、ゴルフの岡本綾子や青木功、テニスの伊達公子、松岡修造らがWPの紙面に登場する。こうしてみると、元気印の女性が目につくようだ。政治の世界でも、元気印の女性はニュースになりやすい。

　土井たか子社会党委員長(もう、党名も変わってしまったが)の誕生時には「Japanese Embrace New Political Star」(89/6/26 By Paul Blustein)。その直後、海部政権が誕生すると「The Political Bow of Japan's Top Wife: First Lady Sachiyo Kaifu」(89/8/31 By Fred Hiatt and Margaret Shapiro)。政治家ではないが、Washington 駐在の日本大使夫人をWPが取り上げることがある。日本経済交渉が決裂した94年2月、Style に栗山昌子夫人の記事が載った。「An official delegation of 70 Japanese bureaucrats failed to make any headway in trade talks in Washington this week, but a couple of miles away on Nebraska Avenue（大使公邸がある）, one woman is making inroads—in understanding if not tariffs.」(94/2/12 By Judith Weinraub and Shigehiko Togo)。Washingtonの社交界で、彼女の個性的積極的な活動ぶりが前々から話題になっており、2ヵ月近い準備を経たものだが、細川総理訪米に合わせて掲載されたこともあって、日本のメディアの一部などに批判が起きた。内容は、政治家対官僚、首相夫人は載っていないのに等々、言ってみれば「内輪の村社会の論理」以外のなにものでもなかった。WPのStyleに前向きな記事が出る（辛らつなことが多いStyleとしては異例なほど好意的だった）インパクト、それをぎくしゃくする日米関係のなかでどう評価していくか、という姿勢の欠如は「出る杭を打つ」の典型ではないだろうか。栗山夫人についてWPは、離任時にも記事にしている。

最後に、日本人全般に関わる報道を2つ。

まず、血液型。「Red-Blooded Romantics: In Japan, Finding a Compatible Mate Is as Simple as A, B, O」(95/12/29 By Kevin Sullivan)。ボーイフレンドを決める時に血液型がものを言う若いOL。「Japan has an obsession with blood types. The blood in your veins is supposed to determine how well you live and love, how well you manage money, whether you will succeed at marriage or sumo wrestling. Great marriages or lousy careers are attributed to blood type.」。血液型を言わないのは日本人の間では疑念を呼び起こす。「"It's like you're withholding information."」。

そして、名前。なぜ日本人は英語表記の時、西洋式に姓と名を逆にするのか。「As the Japanese began dealing with the outside world, they "moved west" in terms of nomenclature. In the 1870s, they started writing their names Western-style (family name last) when dealing with Americans and Europeans. They never stopped.」

(92/8/23 By Tom Reid)。これほど世の中が変わった今、なぜ日本は、中国や韓国などほかの漢字文化圏のように母国語と同様に「姓・名」通りの順番で英語表記をしないのか、というのがTomの発想だった。この記事を書くに当たって、支局でミニ調査を行ったが、現状維持と改革派はほぼ半々、どちらかといえば著名人に現状維持派が多かった。それから3年後、Tomは週刊新潮のコラム「聞いた日本　見た日本」で2回 (95/7/25と9/21) この問題を取り上げ、テレビのニュースショーでも話題になった。反響は大きく、支局に寄せられた約400通は圧倒的に賛成派だった。すでに一部の英語教科書、個人の名詞、パス・ポート、日本発の英語雑誌などで「日本式表記」が定着実行されていることもわかった。時代は変わっている。「I'm starting to believe that the question of Japanese names is going to stretch on indefinitely, like some of those U.S.–Japan trade disputes that seem to come back every single year. But I'm not giving up. I'm telling you, we'll settle this question eventually, or my name isn't Reid T.R.」(前出同)。

　以下、ここに登場したゴジラ、オノ・ヨーコ、村上春樹、小錦らを含め、WPが取り上げた、日本の文化を代表する12人（？）の記事を紹介する。

Japan's Interpreter with Punch

By Elisabeth Bumiller

March 14, 1991

Today, the person best suited to head off such flaps is Ken Yokota, the number one English-Japanese interpreter in Tokyo. When Japan speaks to America, Yokota is often in between....

Yokota, who is the American Embassy's first choice for any job, says he simply signs up with whoever calls first, and rejects the implication that his nationality undermines his objectivity or effectiveness. "I'm very conscious that other people would question my loyalty or conscience," he says. "But my job is to translate as accurately as possible."

On at least one occasion, though, his sympathies were clearly with Japan. Yokota was interpreting for a powerful member of Japan's ruling Liberal Democratic Party when the politician told a crude, off-color joke to a woman cabinet member from another country. Yokota cleaned the joke up, and the politician never knew. "I guess I did it for myself, and that's very unprofessional. But I think I did it for the image of Japan too." ....

Throughout history, interpreters have always had the potential for influencing events and creating catastrophe. "It's scary," Yokota says. "One slip of the tongue at a press conference and it can be carried electronically around the globe." ....

But Yokota says he wasn't interested in promoting Japan's national interest abroad; to him, interpreting was the real intellectual challenge. Was he drawn by the secrets, the behind-the-scenes power? "I didn't look at it as power," he says. "It was more like working on a puzzle—and having to work on that puzzle right then and there." ....

Yokota says his politics are "center-right," and admits that over the years he has formed "distinct opinions" about the substance of his work. On the trade talks, he says, "the U.S. side ought to be a little more tactful. The Japanese side ought to be a little more ... hmmm ... a little more what? Aggressive in

パンチの効いた日本の通訳

エリザベス・ビューメラー

1991年3月14日

今日、こんな（言葉による）混乱を防ぐのに最適なのが横田謙だ。東京における英語と日本語の通訳の第一人者である。日本がアメリカに向けて発言するとき、横田はしばしば両者の間にいる……。通訳する内容のいかんにかかわらず、横田は、アメリカ大使館第一のお気に入りだ。だが横田は、仕事は、相手のいかんにかかわらず、依頼してきた順番で契約する、と語る。自分の国籍によって、通訳の客観性や効果が妨げられたり、薄められたりすることはない、というのだ。「僕の忠誠心や良心に疑念をはさむ人がいるのはよくわかっている。しかし、僕の仕事は、可能な限り正確に訳すことなんだ」。そうはいっても、少なくとも1回は、彼の気持ちは明らかに日本に向けられていた。与党自民党の有力政治家の通訳をしていた時、ある国の女性閣僚について、むき出しのいかがわしいジョークを述べた。横田は、そのジョークを、さっと消してしまったが、当の政治家は、そんなことは夢ご存じない……。「たぶん、僕自身のためにしたと思う。プロとはとても言えない行いだけど。でも、考えてみれば、日本のイメージのためという面もあるかもしれない」……。歴史のなかで、通訳者は、常に、物事に影響を与え、破滅的な状況を作り出すことも可能だった。「実にこわいことだ」と横田は言った。「記者会見でほんの一言、口を滑らすだけで、世界中のオンラインにのってしまうことになるかもしれないんだ」。……しかし、横田は、海外における日本の国益を喧伝することに興味はないという。彼にとって、通訳は、真に知的な挑戦だった。では、権力の裏舞台や秘密の花園に曳かれたのでは？「そうした世界は、僕には権力とは見えなかった。むしろ、パズルを解くようなものだった。その瞬間に、その場で解かなければならないパズルと格闘するんだなあ」……。横田は、自身の政治的な立場は「中道右派」で、仕事の内容についても、時がたつにつれ、「明確な意見」を持つようになった、という。日米の貿易交渉については、こう述べる。「アメリカ側は、もう少し臨機応変にやったほうがいい。

certain cases? Speak out more clearly. I guess the Japanese way of negotiating, of going around in circles, is a good way of evading certain points. But there ought to be more direct communication."

Who are the better negotiators? "Honestly speaking," he says, "I don't think either side is really that"—he pauses, thinking—"skillful. But on balance, probably the U.S. side, knowing that they can always push. The Japanese side usually gives in, inch by inch."

Japan's Hero Barks from Beyond the Grave

By T. R. Reid

June 3, 1994

If a national election were held to pick America's favorite dog, the votes would probably be split among such diverse candidates as Lassie, Snoopy, Goofy, Beethoven, Old Yeller, and Millie Bush. But in this more homogeneous nation, where everybody tends to agree with everybody else on these big cultural questions, there would be no such confusion.

Unquestionably, unequivocally, the choice for Japan's favorite dog would be Hachiko....

The Culture Broadcasting Network obtained a hitherto unknown recording of Hachiko's bark.

Hachiko said, "Wan-wan."

"Wan-wan" is how the Japanese render the sound of a dog's bark, rather than "bow-wow." For the matter, cats in Japan say "nyaah-nyaah" instead of "meow," and frogs here say "kero-kero." The Japanese word for what a rooster says is "ko-kek-ko-ko," which is, if you think about it, a lot closer to the real thing than "cock-a-doodle-doo."

Having a hefty "wan-wan" is considered a sign of health and good karma for a dog here. And to everyone's relief, Hachiko had a healthy, hearty *wan-wan*.

日本側は、もう少し、えーと、もう少しね、なんといったらいいかな、積極的になる方が良い場合もあるというか、もっと、はっきりとしゃべったほうが良い。日本的な交渉の仕方、堂々巡りの議論はある種の論点を避けるにはもってこいだけれど、もっと、直截に意見や感情を伝えることがあっていいと思うんだ」。交渉者としてどちらが優れていますか?「率直に言って、どちらも、それほど……」。しばらくの沈黙の後、「優れているとは思わないな。でも、全体的に見れば、アメリカかな。いつも、押せ押せでいけるのを知っているから。日本は後退することが多い。それも、1歩ずつ」。

日本のヒーロー墓のかなたから吠える

トム・リード

1994年6月3日

もしアメリカで一番人気のある犬を選ぶ国民投票が行われたら、票は、おそらくラッシー、スヌーピー、グーフィ、ベートーベン、オールド・イェラー、そしてミリー・ブッシュなどさまざまな候補に割れるだろう。しかし、万事がはるかに均質的なこの国では、このような文化的に重要な諸問題についても、互いに意見が一致することが多く、アメリカのような混乱は起きないだろう。間違いなく、そして、明らかに、日本一の人気犬は、ハチ公となろう……。文化放送は、今まで誰も聞いたことのなかった、八公の鳴き声を手に入れた。

ハチ公は、「ワンワン」と言った。日本人は、犬の鳴き声を「バウワウ」ではなく「ワンワン」と表現する。そうした点について、一言言うなら、日本の猫は「ミャウ」ではなく「ニャーニャー」と鳴き、蛙は、「ケロケロ」と鳴く。日本語の鶏の鳴き声は、「コケコッコー」であるが、ちょっと考えてみるならば、「カッカドゥールドゥー」よりも、よっぽど本当の鳴き声に近い。

ここでは、力強い「ワンワン」という鳴き声は、健康で筋の良い犬の証とされている。ハチ公が情のこもった元気な「ワンワン」と鳴いたことでみんな心からほっとした。

Haruki Murakami's Homecoming

By Fred Hiatt

December 25, 1989

Japan's best-selling, millionaire novelist steps into the room hesitantly, like a child expecting the worst, and sits on the sofa's edge, feet together, knees apart. His blue deck sneakers are half-tied, his blue jeans frayed, his flannel shirt buttoned at the collar, as if his mother had insisted on at least this one concession.

Murakami may be the first Japanese writer since the days of Mishima and Kawabata to break through to the general reading public outside Japan. He represents "the new international voice of Japanese youth," said one reviewer....

He has returned, at 40.... "I want to reconstruct a morality for this new world, this economic world," he says. "My generation, we are in a way disappointed, but we have to survive. We have to survive in this society, so we have to establish a new morality."

Japanese Writer Oe Wins Nobel

By David Streitfeld

October 14, 1994

"I have sensed from informed readers a fair amount of disappointment," Nathan, the translator, said yesterday. "He has become the big honcho, the dean of Japanese literature, but people see a pedagogical, didactic streak. He's become harder and harder to read." But if his influence has waned, his commitment hasn't....

The man who published Oe's first book in this country, tells the story of what happened when he went to visit the writer in 1991: "He insisted on meeting us at the airport. We got there about four o'clock, but Oe didn't show up.... It turned out that on the way to the airport he saw this demonstration about the treatment of students in China. Oe got out of cab and make a speech—in favor of the students, naturally."

村上春樹の帰郷

フレッド・ハイアット

1989年12月25日

日本のベストセラー作家で大富豪の小説家は、まるで最悪の事態を覚悟した子供のようにおずおずと部屋に入ってきた。そして、足元をそろえ、膝はちょっと開き気味にしてソファの端に腰かけた。青色のデッキ・シューズの紐は半ばほどけ、ブルー・ジーンズは色あせている。フランネルのシャツのボタンだけは、まるで母親がこれだけは言うことをきかせたかのように、襟元までとめられていた。

村上は、三島と川端以来、初めて海外の一般読者に読まれるようになった日本の作家かもしれない。彼は「日本の若者の新しい国際的な声」を代表している、とある評論家は指摘した……。

そして、40歳にして、彼は(海外の生活をやめて)帰ってきた。「この新しい世界、この経済の世界に、倫理を再建したい」と彼は言う。「私たちの世代は、どこか絶望している。でも、生きてゆかなければならない。この社会を生き抜くためには、新しい倫理を構築しなければならないんだ」。

日本の作家大江、ノーベル賞を受賞

デーヴッド・ストライトフェルド

1944年10月14日

「熱心な読者は、かなり失望しているようだった」と翻訳者のジョン・ネーサンは昨日述べた。「彼は日本文学界の大親分、つまり長老になったが、教訓的で説教的だとみんな感じている。ますます読みづらくなってきた」。しかし、たとえ影響力は衰えても、世の中にコミットする姿勢は一向に衰えない……。

アメリカで初めて彼の本を出版したバーニー・ロセットは、1991年に作家を訪問した際のエピソードを語っている。「彼は、我々と絶対に空港で会おうと言った。4時頃到着したんだが、大江は現れない……。あとでわかったんだが、大江は空港へ来る途中、中国の学生の扱いに抗議するデモを見かけたんだ。それでタクシーから降り、演説を始めた。もちろん、学生側に立ってね」。

After 51 Years, a Temple Is Restored

By John Burgess

December 26, 1985

IKARUGA, Japan—At age 4, Nishioka began learning the craft's manual skills and oral traditions....

"The old builders were people of art who approached their work with religious devotion...." he said.

"In our craft, we have a set of unwritten principles," he explained in his home, located just outside the temple's walls. "One is, 'Don't buy trees, buy a mountainside.'" A temple's wood should come from a single site. Wood should be positioned in the orientation at which it grew as trees, with beams from the mountain's north side on the north, and so on.

Each tree, shaped by its soil and decades of wind and rain, has a unique personality, artisans say. The builder, then, must understand and exploit these traits.

The Ando Dynasty

By Benjamin Forgey

October 5, 1991

NEW YORK—For his succinct retrospective exhibition at the Museum of Modem Art, Japanese architect Tadao Ando went all out.... The result is a breathtaking show, splendidly installed, that firmly establishes Ando, 50, as one of the preeminent living architects in the world....

The belief that architecture operated outside of national or regional norms was one of the great failings of the ideology of the modem movement. Though by no means alone in his awareness of this failing, Ando has made the tension between his own and the "other" culture a profound source for architecture in the late twentieth century. In his work, Ando gives immutable expression to a world in which modernity collides inevitably with tradition, West with East, the collective with the individual, noise with silence.

51年かけて復元された寺院

ジョン・バージェス

1985年12月26日

斑鳩発——西岡常吉は、4歳から、職人の技術の基本と口伝を学び始めた……。「かつての大工は、宗教的献身の気持ちをいだき、仕事にあたった芸術家だった」と彼は言う……。「我々の技には、暗黙の決まりがいくつかある」。法隆寺の壁のすぐ外側にある自宅で、こんな説明をしてくれた。「例えば、"木を買うな。山腹を買え。" お寺に用いられる木材は、同じ場所から伐ったものでなければならない。木材は、実際に木が生えていた時と同じ方角で用いなければならない。山の北側で光を受けていれば北側に、という具合に。

木は、育った土壌や、何十年にもわたる風雨によって形成される。1本いっぽんが個性をもっている」とこの職人は言う。従って、大工はこうした特徴を理解し、活かさなくてはならない。

安藤王朝

ベンジャミン・フォージェイ

1991年10月5日

ニューヨーク発——ニューヨーク近代美術館(MOMA)における、簡素な回顧展で、日本の建築家安藤忠雄は、遺憾無くその実力を発揮した……。結果は、作品が見事に配置された、息もつけないほどの会であった。それは、50歳になる安藤が、現在、生きている世界の建築家のうち、傑出した1人であることを確かなものとした……。

建築家が、民族や地域の枠外で活動しているという思い込みは、近代思想の大きな誤りの1つであった。その点に気づいたのは彼1人ではないにせよ、安藤は、自らの文化と「他者」の文化との緊張関係を、20世紀末の建築の深遠な源泉と見なした。自らの作品において、安藤は、近代が、伝統と不可避に衝突する世界に、不変的な表現を与えた。すなわち、西と東、集団と個人、雑音と静寂と。

A Monster Hit

By T. R. Reid

February 2, 1992

As if George Bush, Lee Iacocca, and the U.S. Congress weren't making enough noise themselves, this country's biggest movie star has suddenly gone on the rampage over Japanese exports....

Why is it, you may ask, that an entertaining but otherwise unremarkable grade-B monster film concerns itself with global politico-economic issues like Japan's balance-of-trade surplus?

The answer lies in the history of Godzilla movies.

Since the mutant's debut in the 1954 hit *Godzilla*, the films have always dealt with controversial topics. That first Godzilla movie was, in fact, an anti-nuclear protest, with its fantastic plot based—well, loosely based—on actual events.

Japan's Porno Preoccupation

By Elisabeth Bumiller

November 12, 1989

The pornography demonstrates that beneath the pastel vision of a Japan of tea ceremonies and cherry blossoms, or of Nikon cameras and Sony Walkmans, there exists a throbbing modem culture producing its own contradictions and jagged picture of humanity....

Here on this afternoon is Tooru Muranishi, the nation's leading porno director, who says he has made 400 adult videos, starred in 200, and been arrested four times....

"In working in the front lines of this industry," he says, "I have learned about the formidable sexual powers of women. Women have immense power compared to men. They can have multiple orgasms. A man has only one, and he is finished...."

Muranishi, however, contends that "abnormal sex" and rape scenes are part of the old days. He argues that actresses are now encouraged to participate as equal, responsive partners who should "show their joy."

怪獣大ヒット

トム・リード　　　　　　　　　　　　　　　　　　1992年2月2日

あたかもジョージ・ブッシュ、リー・アイアコッカ、そしてアメリカ議会が、充分に騒いでいないかのごとく、この国最大の映画スターが、突然、日本の輸出をめぐって大暴れを始めた……。確かに面白いかもしれないが、それ以外は、さしてとりたてるほどのこともないB級怪獣映画が、なぜ日本の貿易黒字などという世界的政治経済問題に関わっているのか疑問に思われるかもしれない。

その答えは、ゴジラ映画の歴史の中にある。1954年のヒット作『ゴジラ』で、ミュータント（突然変異体）がデビューして以来、このシリーズは、常に、論争の的になるテーマを扱ってきた。ゴジラ映画第1作は事実、反核の抗議であり、奇想天外な物語は、かなり大雑把ではあるが、現実の出来事に基づいていた。

ポルノにのめりこむ日本

エリザベス・ビューメラー　　　　　　　　　　　　1989年11月12日

しかし、ポルノは、お茶やお花見のような淡い色調の日本、あるいは、ニコンのカメラ、ソニーのウォークマンの日本の背後に、この矛盾や猛々しい人間の姿を産み出す、胸躍る現代の文化が存在していることを示している……。

今日の午後、我々の目の前にいるのは、日本のポルノ監督の第一人者村西透である。400本のアダルト・ビデオを制作、200本に出演し、4回逮捕されたという……。「この業界の最前線で働いて、私は、女性の驚くべき性の力を知った。女性は、男性と比べ、ものすごい力を持っている。繰り返しオルガスムを体験することができるんだ。男はたった1回、それで終わり」……。村西は「異常なセックス」やレイプ・シーンは、古いと断言する……。女優は、「自らの喜びを表現」すべき、平等かつ責任のあるパートナーとして、作品造りに参加することが求められるようになった、と彼は主張する。

Sumo Exports

Editorial

May 29, 1987

Defenders of Japan's trade practices sometimes argue that if an import measures up to the high standards of the Japanese, they will accept it. Perhaps there's something to that. Consider the case of Salevaa ("Sally") Atisanoe, an American, a former high-school football player in Hawaii and, as of this week, the first foreigner in 13 centuries to be admitted to the champion ranks of Japanese sumo wrestling....

And as he approaches the very pinnacle of that sport, let the Japanese purists beware: there are many more like him in America....

Should enough of them follow Sally Atisanoe to Japan, his case may someday be a chapter in texts on international economics.

Lennon's Widow Faces Mobs and Memories

By Paul Hendrickson

November 16, 1987

What could a woman, perhaps the most famous Japanese face in the West, hope to tell a stranger in 12 minutes about her life that would seem meaningful? That she didn't really break up the Beatles? That she was never the self-aggrandizing, dragon-lady, calculating bitch that her detractors always wanted to make her out?

The wonder is she could say anything at all, given such a roil around her, given all the kibitzers and leaners-in....

And yet, despite all this, she seemed eager to try to say something that would establish a real if momentary contact with another human being....

Yoko passed. The phalanx directed her back toward the escalator. Halfway up, she turned and blew kisses to the crowd. She was smiling. "I love you!" she called, and this time she didn't mouth the words, she shouted them.

相撲の輸出

社説　　　　　　　　　　　　　　　　　　　　　　　1987年5月29日

日本の貿易慣習を擁護する者は、この国の高い基準に見合っているなら、日本人は輸入品を受け入れる、といった議論を展開することがある。おそらく、一理はあるのだろう。サリヴァ(サリー)・アティサノエの場合を検討してみよう。彼はアメリカ人であり、ハワイの高校でフットボールの選手をしていた。そして今週、過去13世紀中、初めて日本の相撲の、大関の座につくのだ……。

このスポーツの頂点に彼が近づくにつれ、日本の純血主義者は、用心をしなければならない。アメリカには、彼のような者がたくさんいるのだ……。

こうした巨漢のうち、かなりの数がサリー・アティサノエに習うなら、彼の例はいつの日か、国際経済の教科書の1章となるかもしれない。

やじ馬と思い出に対面するレノンの未亡人

ポール・ヘンドリックソン　　　　　　　　　　　　　1987年11月16日

おそらく西側における最も知られた日本人の顔を持つ彼女が、見知らぬ人に、わずか12分で、自らの人生についてなにか意義のあることを語れるだろうか。ビートルズを解散させたのは、本当は、彼女ではないというのだろうか。あるいは、彼女を悪く言う人たちが仕立て上げたように、自己拡大に取りつかれた猛女、計算高いあばずれ女だったことは一度もないとでもいうのだろうか。

驚くべきことは、周囲が混乱し、おせっかい屋やたかりがいようとも、彼女はなんでも話せるということだった……。

このような状況にもかかわらず、彼女は、たとえそれが一時的なものであっても、ほかの人間と本当に触れ合える何かを熱心に述べようとしていた……。

ヨーコは通り過ぎていった。警備の集団が、エスカレーターまで案内する。途中まで上がったところで、彼女は振り返った。群衆への投げキス。満面の微笑。「アイ・ラヴ・ユー！」もはや、口ごもってはいない。ヨーコは叫んでいた。

The Modern, Misunderstood Geisha

By Elisabeth Bumiller

October 29, 1991

In the world of the geisha, Chiyogiku and Shizuka are the essence of discretion, femininity, and power. Between them they have poured sake for every Japanese prime minister since 1959....

In recent years especially, the geisha has in her own fashion adjusted to the modern world....

All in all, Shizuka concludes, "What we do is not that different from the new career woman in Japan." ....

Chiyogiku is pretty and delicate, with exquisite manners and a quiet sense of self-possession. She is excited about an upcoming three-month trip to Paris to study French....

Shizuka is striking. "I think of myself as a liberated woman. I am free, but I also have a strong notion that I belong to the Shimbashi Geisha Association. So I know I can't do stupid things."

"The Power of People, the Love of Baseball"

By Kevin Sullivan

September 13, 1995

TAKAMIYA, Japan—Dream Field opened on a misty morning in the Japanese mountains when 12 baseball players in new white uniforms emerged from the cornstalks growing in deep left-center....

Hori had been so moved by Kevin Costner's 1989 film, *Field of Dreams*. So when Hori started talking about his project in workshops and homes from Hiroshima to Takamiya, it took off. About 30 people—carpenters, salesmen, designers, and furniture makers—began donating their time....

Playing third base, he fielded a ground ball gracefully and threw the runner out to end the inning. As he bounded like a little boy toward the bench, across the field he had imagined and built, he shouted: "There's nothing more I need to do. Now I can die."

誤解されている現代の芸者

エリザベス・ビュミラー　　　　　　　　　　　　　　1991年10月29日

芸者の世界にあって、千代菊と静香は、慎み深さ、女らしさ、そして権力の「華」である。2人で一緒に1959年以来、日本のすべての総理大臣にお酌をしてきた。とくに近年、芸者は、自分なりの流儀で現代の世界に自身を合わせるようになった……。あれやこれやで、静香は、こう結論する。「私達のすることは、日本の新しいキャリア・ウーマンと、たいして違いませんのよ」……。

千代菊は美しく、繊細で、優雅な振るまいとものの静かな冷静さを兼ね備えている。フランス語の勉強のため、まもなくパリへ3ヵ月ほど行くのを、とても楽しみにしている。静香は、実に印象的だ。「わたくしは、自分が解放された女だと思っています。わたくしは自由。でも、新橋芸者組合に属しているということも、強く意識しています。ですから、みっともないことはできないって、わかっていますよ」。

「みんなの力、野球への愛」

ケヴィン・サリヴァン　　　　　　　　　　　　　　1995年9月13日

高宮発――霧深い朝、純白の新しいユニホームを身にまとった12人の野球選手たちが、左中間奥のトウモロコシ畑から出て来た時、「ドリーム・フィールド」が、日本の山中にオープンした……。堀治喜は、ケビン・コスナーの1989年の映画『フィールド・オブ・ドリームス』に心の底から感動した。その感動が広島から30マイルほど北のこの村に、自分の球場を造る決心をさせた……。こうして堀が、仕事場や家庭で、広島から高宮で自分の計画を語り始めたとき、すべてが動き始めた。約30人の人たち――大工、セールスマン、デザイナーや家具職人――が時間を提供するようになった。

堀は三塁を守った。ゴロを華麗にさばきランナーをアウトにし、その回を終わらせる。頭の中に思い描き、自ら造ったフィールドを横切り、ベンチに向かって少年のように飛びはねながら、こう叫んだ。「もうしなければいけないことはないんだ。死んでもいいや」。

Don Graham 社主

About
The Washington Post

Katharine Graham WP 会長と著者

WP 本社正面玄関

も し、あなたが、WP の本社に勤務している記者へ電話したとする。
本人が不在なら、そのデスクの留守番電話が、本人の吹き込んだ声で応対してくれるだろう。「This is Xxxx Yyyyy at *The Washington Post*....」。日本なら「○○新聞の××ですが」、つまり「of」だろうが、そうではない。「at」なのだ。短い前置詞の違いではあるが、私には、日米ジャーナリズムの違い、2つの文化の違いを象徴しているように思える。すなわち、記者1人ひとりの主体性と個性を最大限に活かそうとするのか、組織自体により大きな価値を置こうとするのか、である。

WP の News Room は、本社5階に広々と広がる大部屋だ。editor や columnist のガラス張りの個室、高さ上半身ほどのパーティション、記者やデスクの机、コンピュータなどがひしめき、計ざっと200人が働く場所だ。全体の色の基調は灰色で、日本の新聞社の大部屋とよく似ている。

その南側の News Conference Room は、まったく趣が違う。約30畳ほどの室内は、ベージュ色の絨毯が敷き詰められ、中央には、楕円の膨らみを持った長方形の大型テーブル。椅子は赤い布張りで、三方の壁には薄茶のベンチ型ソファ、全体がやわらかな暖色系で統一され、ダウンライトが明るく室内を照らす。

正面奥の壁には、Watergate 事件で President Nixon が辞任した日の front page の本物の活字版が額装されている。字も写真も裏返しだ。その横には President Ford から送られたサイン入りのリトグラフ。「I got my job through *The Washington Post*」という文字がデザインされている。

毎日、午後2時半、この部屋で、翌日の front page を決める News Conference が開かれ、議論、ときに激論が交わされる。出席するのは、各 Desk(日本の各部に当たる)から Assistant Managing Editor (AME 編集局次長)や Editor(部長)ら幹部、その日の担当 desk、さらにオブザーヴァーも含めて約30人。budget と呼ばれる出稿簿には、150前後の記事が載っているが、1面に行くのは、6、7本。全体のざっと半数は積み残される。

Publisher(社主)の Donald (Don) Graham が「That's what we want, strong personality.」と言うように、WP には、強烈な個性を持つ記者が多

く、各部同士の競争も当然、激しくなる。会議をリードするのが、Executive Editor（編集主幹）Leonald (Len) Downie, Jr. と Managing Editor（編集局長）Robert (Bob) G. Kaiser の2人だ。それぞれ National や Metro の幹部、London、Moscow などの特派員もつとめた WP 生え抜きだ。

「American reporters are very competitive in most cases with each other, even in the same newspaper. Japanese reporters are very competitive by organizations, but aren't they in the same organization?」と Len。

「O'brien!」「George!」「Michael!」……気合の入った声で、Len（あるいは、Bob）が、各部のデスクを first name で呼び、それぞれが出稿計画、記事のねらい、背景、注意点、scoop かどうかなどを説明。少しでも疑義があると出席者から質問や意見が出る。ただし、発言は、担当デスクか部長以上に限られ、他のスタッフは緊張した表情でやりとりに聞き入っている。

3時過ぎから、各部での出稿内容の再調整、News Desk（記事のレイアウトや見出しなどを決める、整理部）を交えての編集トップによる議論を経て、front page の素案 dammy が作られ、夕方6時から再度 News Conference が開かれるのだ。

こうした会議に出ていて感じるのだが、世界を揺るがすような大ニュースから、身近な生活の香り高い出来事までを扱い、議論と瞬時の判断を繰り返しながらも、じつに余裕があるというか、明るいというか、常にユーモアと笑いが絶えないのだ。「This is probably the culture that Ben Bradlee did, we literally grew up there.」と Bob Kaiser。

Ben Bradlee。President Kennedy との交遊や、Watergate 事件の指揮で知られ、4半世紀にわたって WP の Executive Editor を務め、91年9月に Len に道を譲っている。現在は、Vice President の肩書で、メモワール『*A Good Life / Newspapering and Other Adventures*』を出版したばかりだ（95年秋）。「I tried very hard to encourage everybody to have a good time and to be absolutely free to criticize. Don't be scared to say to your boss or to me,… So there developed a kind of an openness, a camaraderie, if you want, say a teasing. Oh, we like to tease each other.」。

ここで、WP を世界的に有名にした Watergate 事件、それをきっかけに注目されるようになった investigative news（調査報道）について触れておきたい。

WP には現在、Investigative report 専任の記者が約10人いる。そ

の1人 Athelia Knight は、93/10/24 から4回にわたり「Murder on Trial」という連載を書いた。1988年から3年間に Washington D.C. 地区で起きた殺人事件を William Casey, director of computer-assisted reporting とともに綿密に分析した記事だ。1286件の殺人事件のうち、犯人が起訴されたのは4分の1で、被害者も犯人も、9割以上は黒人であるといった劇的な内容だった。驚いたのは、Athelia の調査報道に対する WP の待遇である。「I was allowed not to write even single line for two years. Two years. Just preparing for this series.」というのだ。なお、アメリカの調査報道の現状については下山進著『アメリカ・ジャーナリズム』に詳しい。

Investigative News 担当の AME が Watergate 事件で White House を追い詰めた1人、Bob Woodward だ。週末や休みで、Downie や Kaiser が不在の時、Woodward は News Conference を主催するが、通常は、自らのテーマを決め、それに専念している。数ヵ月、数年かけての取材が終わると、WP に概要を書き、本はベストセラーという、Bradlee に言わせれば「Woodward himself is an institution.」の生活を送っている。

その彼が、WP の編集局で、庶務的な仕事をする若い copy aide 達と話し合う会に出た。後輩にいろいろと語る中、最も印象的だったのは次のエピソードだ。ある上院議員が、なぜ Woodward に話をしてしまうのかと聞かれ、こう答えたというのだ。「The answer is, if you are interested in journalism, grain in your head. "Because he asked." ……That simple.」(文藝春秋誌94年11月号拙論「『大統領の執務室』の内幕」参照)。

マンモスが己の牙で滅びたように、WP を WP たらしめた調査報道の過熱によって悲劇が生まれた。1981年の Pulitzer 賞報事件である。受賞対象となった、麻薬禍に冒された黒人少年のルポ「Jimmy's World」が、女性黒人記者による完全な創作とわかったのだ。WP は、直ちに事態を徹底的に調査。Ombudsman の Bill Green による今後の対策を含めた詳細な報告「Janet's World」を掲載している。

さて、冒頭のエピソードで記したように、個性を尊重する WP だが、アメリカのジャーナリズム全体を踏まえ、その特質を具体的に見てみよう。

第1に、Byline 制。アメリカでも、その本格的な導入は、第1次世界大戦の戦争特派員の活躍以降とされているが、アメリカ人の国民性からしても、この制度無しに、現在のように、多様で強い個性の持ち主が集まり、ジャーナリズムが、The Fourth Estate と呼ばれるような影響力ある存在とな

るのは不可能だと思う。書く方からいえば、記事に対する責任と励みとなる。読者にとっては、誰が記事を書いたのか、知る権利のある重要な情報だ。これによって、新聞と読者の健全なコミュニケーションもまた可能となるのだ。「If you don't have the guts to put your name on your story, then why should readers believe you?」と Kevin Sullivan は話している。

1988年7月、WP では会社と組合が対立し、ほとんどすべての記者が Byline を拒否したことがあった。「By a *Washington Post* Staff Writer」という「署名」だけの紙面は実に味けなかったものだ。日本では、最近、署名記事が増えてくる傾向にあるものの、まだ外国からの特派員、解説などに限られている。その中で十勝毎日新聞が昨年11月、全面的な Byline 制に踏み切ったのはすばらしいことで、おおいに注目されて良い。

第2が news source、あるいは attribution の明示だ。WP には、原稿の書き方や記者の行動の指針ともいうべき『*Desk Book on Style*』(村田聖明訳『ワシントンポスト記者ハンドブック』)があるが、そこに「The *WP* is pledged to disclose the source of all information when at all possible.」とある。

日本では、取材源を秘匿するため、ニュースソースは明示しないことがジャーナリズムの基本という考えが一般的に有るように思う。WP でも、Watergate の Deep throat のような例はもちろんあるが、それはむしろ例外。原則はあくまでも取材源明示だ。交通事故や刑事事件でも、警察の見解には、コメントした警察官の名前や状況を書くのが普通。「××県警と〇〇署の調べによると」などという表記はまず見あたらない。

第3は、op-ed page で論説や社外の原稿を採用するときの基準。Deputy Editorial Page Editor(論説副委員長)の Stephen Rosenfeld と長時間話し合った時、論説については「If I limited myself only to safe ideas, then I would not be doing my job. I want to bring things out better on the edge.」。Letters to the Editor を選ぶ基準は「We are especially looking for letters that reply to other things that have appeared in the newspaper.」。もし、社説のようなものがあるなら、なるべくそれとは違った意見、これまで報道されなかった視点や事実を載せていこうという姿勢である。

第4は、アメリカの若いジャーナリストが目指す一般的な目標は何かということ。日本ならデスク、部長といった社内の管理職だろう。日本では40代、50代の経験豊かな記者が第一線でバリバリ原稿を書くのは珍しいのではないだろうか。アメリカで、WP にせよ、NYT にせよ、一流紙の編集幹

部になりたいという夢を持ってジャーナリズムを志す若者など聞いたことがない。目標ははっきりしている。Columnist だ。Byline の延長といってもよいが、Columnist になると、多くの場合、見出しの上にゴシックの活字で名前が記される。

David Broder(アメリカ内政)、George Will(保守系論壇の大御所)、Richard Cohen(政治社会問題。リベラルだが型にはまらない)、Lou Cannon(人種問題など)、Jane Bryant Quinn(消費者の立場からの経済)……など、きら星のごとく並ぶ。*The Washington Post* Writers Group という Columnist によるグループもある。収入の点でも第1級待遇を受けるし、社会的なインパクトから言えば、Columnist の方が、社の編集局幹部より上といってよい。

第5は、社内の gender や人種の多様性だ。News Conference の出席者のうち、3分の1から半数は女性だ。Editorial Page Editor(論説委員長)の Meg Greenfield、National Desk では AME の Karen DeYoung、White House 担当(93～94年当時は2人とも)の Ann Devroy と Ruth Marcus、Editor では、Style の Mary Hadar と Outlook の Jodie Allen らがいる。

男女平等という点について言えば、東京へ赴任したアメリカ人記者達の家庭は、文字どおり、夫と妻の平等な協力によって運営されていた。二代にわたり、夫妻の記者が支局長として派遣されているが、その肩書きも co-bureau chief(共同支局長)である。

Minority では affirmative action の要請する quota 制は当然満たしているが、まだ、トップレベルに充分に人材が活用されていないという反省がある。長く Foreign Desk の Editor や AME を務めた Michael Getler がこの問題を担当する Deputy Managing Editor(副編集局長)に任命されていた(94年初め)。

アジア系では個人的にお世話になった3人の名前をあげておきたい。Book World の Assistant Editor and Art Director を務める Kunio Francis Tanabe は WP 本社に長期勤務する唯一の日本人だ。Jaehoon Ahn は、News Research Center の Online Editor だが、母国とアメリカのジャーナリズムに身を置き、韓国朝鮮問題に常に目を光らせている。Financial の Assistant Editor で、QC 活動に関する拙稿を担当してくれたのが、中国系アメリカ人の John Yang だ(彼は、アメリカ政治映画の傑作「Dave」で、White House Press Corps の1人として、UPI の Helen Thomas と共に出演していた)。

最後に、取材方法について。個人を尊重するという価値観は、アメリカ的な意味での家庭生活尊重につながる。アメリカ人に、日本の記者の特徴、夜討ち朝駆けのことを話すと、まず信じられないという顔をする。忙しい生活でも、家族と時間を過ごすことに最大限の努力を払うアメリカ人にとって、仕事の終わった後の聖域・家庭に土足で踏み込むようなことをされば、その人間は完全につまはじきだ。面白かったのは、Night Cops Reporter の Santiago O'Donnell に日本の夜討ち朝駆けのことを話した時だ。「Oh, I'm doing the same kind of thing. You know what? I got to know a police officer well. I found which church he belongs to, and went there on Sunday morning to attend services, and that's how I got acquainted.」。

WP を統括しているのは、Graham 家である。Katharine Graham は The WP Company の Chairman of the Executive Committee。息子の Donald が新聞の Publisher 及び Company の Chairman of the Board and Chief Executive Officer。新聞制作に関し、News は Len Downie、Op-ed は Meg Greenfield、経営については President の Thomas H. Ferguson が Don に報告、包括的な指揮を受ける。

Don によると、Katharine の時代から現在に至るまで、Graham 家と社の幹部との関係は「No Surprises」がルールという。編集や経営を任せはするが、重要事項は事前に知らせるということだ。

ここで、WP の歴史を簡単に記す。例えば、96年4月14日の front page の題字の左下には「119th Year No. 131」という数字が書かれている。WP が最初に刷られた1877年12月6日を起点に「119年と131日」、新聞が発行されたことを示すものだ。

WP の創設者は、時折誤解されるように、Katharine Graham の父、Eugene Meyer ではない。Chalmers M. Roberts 著『In the Shadow of Power: The story of The Washington Post』などによると、Iowa や St. Loius で新聞経営に当たってきた民主党系の Stilson Hutchins である。当時の発行部数は1万部。タイプライターも使わず、取材は足か馬車でという時代だった。

Washington には朝夕刊併せて数紙から10紙近くという時代が続くなか、WP の経営は、政治家や実業家など3代4人の手を移り替わる。Cincinnati の新聞人だった John McLean は、第1次世界大戦開始という時代背景とも重なって、派手な紙面作りで営業的な成功をおさめるが、

その息子の時代になって放漫経営にたたられ、競売に付されるという事態に立ち至った。

この苦境を救ったのが、California の投資家として巨額の財をなした Eugene Meyer で、1993年に WP を買収。己の信念に基づき、新聞に公共的使命をしっかりとたたき込み、現在の WP の基礎を築いた中興の祖といってよいだろう。

Meyer の女婿となり、娘 Katharine と結婚した Harvard 出身の俊秀 Philip Graham によって、WP は大きく発展する。競争紙 *Times Herald* 紙買収(1954年)、*Newsweek* の買収(61年)、*Los Angeles Times = Washington Post* News Service の開始(62年)、テレビ事業への進出など全て彼の元で行われる。John F. Kennedy や Lindon Johnson とも親しかった Philip は、政治への夢と養子としての新聞人の狭間に揺れ、精神の均衡を失い、63年夏、悲劇的な生涯を自ら閉じる。

こうして、Katharine Graham が WP の経営に当たる日が来る。*Newsweek* より Ben Bradlee を招致し、彼とのコンビで Pentagon 機密文書事件(71年)と Watergate 事件の試練を乗り切り、WP は NYT と並ぶ、時にはそれを越えるアメリカの一流紙としての立場を確立していくのだ。

現在、発行部数は、首都を中心に、平日約85万部、日曜版117万部。従業員総数3,000人。ビジネス部門1,100人。新聞の配達、印刷など1,200人。ニュースや論説など紙面の送り手が700人。値段は、平日25セント、日曜版1ドル50セント。宅配は4週間分が、9ドル20セント。印刷は、3版に分かれ、早版から遠隔地へ配達される。

アメリカ政治の核心を報じ、国際ニュースに定評があるといっても、WP は、アメリカの多くの新聞と同じく、地元を極めて大切にしている。読者の4割は大学を出ていない状況下で、「It is very important for us to cover these local community because so many people in this area are depending on the news.」と Don Graham。アメリカ企業の代表的ボランティア活動 The United Way や、地元の高校への奨学金、運動競技会の開催やクリスマスのチャリティーなど、実に活発に行われている。そんな中で、こんな光景も見る機会があった。本社2階のカフェテリアは、30種を超えるサラダ・バーや本格的な日替わりメインディッシュ、各種のデザートで圧巻なのだが、夕刻は筆談のメッカとなる。印刷部門で働いている聴覚の不自由な人達が仕事の合間に集まっているのだ。WP には現在、約70人の聴覚の不自由な人達がいるが、その採用に当たっては、Katharine Graham 自身がおおいに力を尽くしたという。

会社だけではない。それぞれの記者が、様々な社会活動をしている。Washington D.C. 南部のある中学校で、ボランティアによる補習教室を訪れた時、WP の新聞が届きにくい地域のため、その週の重要ニュースや論説などを編集した週刊新聞 *National Weekly Edition*（12万5,000部となかなかの好調だ）の Editor、Lawrence Meyer が現れたのだ。自ら出来ることをすべきと思って、と言葉少なに気持ちを語ってくれたものだ。

新しい技術革新の波に乗って、WP もまたエレクトロニクスを活用した電子新聞に乗り出している。96年に実用化の始まった「Digital Ink」は、この5月からインターネットに参加、「washingtonpost.com website」で、全世界に届けられることになった。「What the Post will have to do is be quick, intelligent and adaptable. We will have to watch how people are getting news and we have to be there.」と Don Graham。

アメリカの新聞業界は、決して楽な状況ではない。広告収入の落ち込みが経営を圧迫し、伝統を誇る新聞の中にも、大量の編集陣のレイオフに踏み切る所も出てきた。WP の場合、そんな事態は起きてはいない。

ところで、WP 東京支局だが、1966年6月6日 Richard Halloran で（後に、NYT 東京支局長。夫人は、ハロラン芙美子）と丸田康子によって、東京銀座の現オフィスに開設された。以来、16人の支局長や特派員が派遣されている。

その東京支局に今、リストラのとんだ余波が及んでいる。

WP の郵送停止である。東京支局だけではない。郵送費を節約するため、95年4月から、London、Paris、Berlin、Moscow、Cairo、Nairobi、Buenos Aires、Mexico、New Delhi、Beijing、Hong Kong といった全世界に広がる WP の海外支局で、日曜版を除く新聞の郵送が停止されたのだ。いくら電子新聞が発達したとはいえ、内容からしてもあの WP と同じではない。本社の幹部がその後まもなく来日した時、「For us, having no WP is like a marine without a rifle, a battleship without a flag on the mast」と抗議したが、事態は改善されていない。

WP を、毎日、読みたいよ——。

How much I want to read the Post? Oh, every day!

Postface

The concept of this book was first put to me in autumn, 1995, by Kuniaki Ura, senior editor in the editorial department of Kodansha International.

Reporting concerning Japan in the United States was a theme that, quite apart from my being in the thick of it everyday, was one that I had already examined in *The Japan Problem: How it is Reported in the U.S.* which I co-authored with Kuse Atsushi in 1987. Here was an ideal chance, I felt, to pick up the thread again and trace the major changes in U.S.–Japan relations since then.

Particularly in its idea that the time was approaching when, as I wrote in the foreword, a bilingual means of expression would become necessary, the proposal was in complete agreement with my own views on the subject.

I received invaluable assistance with translations from Nakayama Toshihiro, Special Assistant to Foreign Ministry of Japan who stood in for me for seven months at the Tokyo bureau while I was away working in the U.S. at the Post's main office from autumn 1993 to spring 1994.

The gathering, classification and preliminary selection of articles was carried out by myself, and the final selection and decision on which passages to quote was done by Mr. Ura, Mr. Nakayama and myself in the course of reading them together—which provided the opportunity for a dozen or more stimulating discussions for which I am deeply grateful.

For *Washington Post* stories from Tokyo, I drew on those in my files; for those originating from Washington, I am indebted to Kitamura Fumio (now professor at Shukutoku University) and Suzuki Akira, both of the Foreign Press Center, and to the staff of the Center.

Alice Crite of *The Washington Post*'s excellent News Research Center was most helpful in responding to my frequent request of articles, confirmation of all kinds of information, and the like. Thank you, Alice, thank you!

I would also like to express my heartfelt gratitude to *Washing-*

後書き

　本書のコンセプトを最初に筆者に示されたのは、講談社インターナショナル編集局副部長の浦晋亮氏で、1995年秋のことだった。

　アメリカの対日報道は、日々その渦中にいることに加え、87年に久世篤氏との共著で上梓した『日本問題―アメリカではどう報道されているか』で追究したテーマでもあった。その流れをベースに、以後の日米間の大きな変化を追う絶好の機会とも思い、ありがたくお引き受けすることとした。

　とくに前書きにも書いたように、bilingual な表現がそろそろ必要な時期に来ているのではないかという点では、筆者の問題意識とも完全に合致した。

　対訳部分の翻訳については、先般、私がアメリカ本社勤務時（93年秋から94年春まで）に、7ヶ月間にわたり、東京支局でピンチヒッターを務めてくれた外務省国連代表部専門調査員の中山俊宏氏の助力を仰いだ。

　記事の収集と分類、おおまかな選択は筆者が行い、三人で、読み合わせをしながら、記事の最終選択、引用箇所の決定をするという、刺激に満ちた会合を十数回にわたって持つことが出来た。両氏に心からの感謝を捧げたい。

　東京発の原稿は、基本的に筆者の手元にあるものを使い、本社発の原稿収集については、The Foreign Press Center の北村文夫（現淑徳大学教授）、鈴木昭両氏や同センターのスタッフの方々のお世話になった。

　WP 本社よりの記事の入手、様々な確認などについては、優秀なる News Research Center の Alice Crite が、度重なる私の問い合わせに快く応じてくれた。Thank you, Alice, thank you!

　また、WP へ入社以来、様々なチャンスを与えてくれたキャサリ

ton Post publishers, Katharine Graham and her son and successor, Donald Graham, as well as executive editor, Benjamin Bradlee and his successor Leonard Downie Jr. for the many opportunities they have given me. Also, I am indebted to the eleven Post correspondents in the Tokyo bureau with whom I have worked, as well as many friends who gave me help and advice on this project.

I would like to make clear that I am entirely responsible for the comments and translations in this book.

It should also be made clear that the copyright on The Washington Post articles rests solely with The Washington Post.

ーン・グレアム会長、ドナルド・グレアム社主、ベン・ブラッドレーならびにレン・ダウニー編集主幹に深い感謝の念を捧げたい。さらにこれまで東京支局で共に働いた11人の特派員はじめ、様々な形で私を支え、本企画にも貴重な助言をいただいた多くの友人に心から御礼申し上げる。

　解説、翻訳の全責任は筆者にあり、WPとはまったく関係ないことを明記させていただく。

　また、WPの記事のcopyrightは、すべてWP属していることも明らかにしておく。

Byline Index　筆者別索引

- この index は Byliner と journalist を中心に若干名を加えて作成した。
- 特段の記載がない場合は WP 本社。Tokyo Bureau は WP 東京支局。その他は最小限の説明を加えた。
- 肩書は、本書に最も関係の深い時期を選んだ。

A

Abramowitz, Michael—Metro　120
Achenbach, Joel—Style　151
Adachi Kinnosuke—journalist in America　143, 144
Ahn, Jaehoon—News Research Online Editor　242
Allen, Jodie—Outlook, Editor　242
Ando Yuko—Japanese TV anchor　192
Auerbach, Stuart—Financial　113

B

Behr, Peter—Financial　38, 114
Benedict, Ruth—Japanologist　177
Bernstein, Carl—Metro　24
Blustein, Paul—Tokyo correspondent　30, 36, 38, 42, 44, 54, 55, 65, 76, 86, 96, 98, 99, 102, 103, 105, 106, 108, 113, 122, 132, 175, 219
Booth, William—National　150, 202
Bradlee, Ben—Executive Editor, VP　239, 240, 244, 248
Broder, David—Columnist, American politics　70, 242
Brown, Warren—Financial　122
Bumiller, Elisabeth—Tokyo correspondent, Style　158, 215, 218, 222, 230, 234
Burgess, John—Tokyo Bureau Chief　29, 41, 56, 66, 82, 112, 113, 115, 160, 167, 178, 190, 228

C

Cannon, Lou—Columnist　242
Chandler, Clay—Financial　38, 40, 114
Chapman, William—Tokyo Bureau Chief, National　56, 112, 126, 134, 161, 188, 218
Chung, Connie—American TV anchor　192
Cohen, Richard—Columnist　242
Cramer, James A.—American scholar and businessman　131
Crite, Alice—News Research　246

D

Dahlby, Tracy—Tokyo Bureau Chief　28, 80, 100, 112, 182, 188, 196, 218
Desfor, Max—photographer　24
Devroy, Ann—National　242
DeYoung, Karen—National, AME　242
Diehl, Jackson—Foreign, AME　64
Dobbs, Michael—Foreign　133
Doi Ayako—journalist in Washington D.C.　134
Downey, Kirstin—Financial　121
Downie, Jr., Leonard—Executive Editor　120, 239, 240, 243, 248
Duke, Lynne—National　116

E

Editorial 36, 44, 59, 76, 78, 86, 87, 89, 112, 148, 232

F

Fallows, James—Japanologist 148
Feiler, Bruce S.—American teacher 187
Ferguson, Thomas H.—President of WP 243
Finn, Peter—Metro 85
Forgey, Benjamin—Style 228

G

Gallup, George—statistician 145
Getler, Michael—Foreign, AME 242
Graham, Donald E.—Publisher and CEO of WP 238, 243, 244, 245, 248
Graham, Katharine—Chairman of the Executive Committee of WP 50, 70, 71, 243, 244, 248
Graham, Philip—Publisher of WP 244
Green, Bill—Ombudsman 240
Greenfield, Meg—Editorial Page Editor 242, 243
Gunther, John—historian 145

H

Hadar, Mary—Style, Editor 242
Hall, Charles W.—Metro 204
Halloran, Richard—Tokyo Bureau Chief 245
Harris, John F.—Metro 78
Harrison, Selig S.—Carnegie Endowment, Tokyo Bureau Chief, National 46
Harwood, Richard L.—Columnist 84
Hauser, Ernest O.—journalist 145
Hendrickson, Paul—Style 232
Hiatt, Fred—Tokyo co-Bureau Chief 26, 27, 42, 58, 65, 67, 86, 98, 101, 104, 113, 126, 138, 174, 176, 188, 215, 216, 219, 226
Hilzenrath, David S.—Financial 120
Hinson, Hal—Style 217
Hoagland, Jim—Columnist, Foreign 30, 104
Holoway, John B.—journalist 219
Hutchins, Stilson—founder of WP 243

I

Ignatius, David—Financial, AME 129
Ishizawa Yasuharu—Tokyo Bureau, reporter 103

J

Jameson, Sam—LAT, Tokyo Bureau Chief 24, 160
Johnson, Chalmers—Japanologist 61
Johnson, Haynes—Columnist, National 70
Jordan, Mary—Tokyo co-Bureau Chief 32, 39, 44, 57, 59, 62, 164, 178, 185, 187, 188, 191, 193, 194, 198, 213, 215

K

Kaiser, Robert G.—Managing Editor 239, 240
Kashiwagi Akiko—Tokyo Bureau, reporter 107
Kastor, Elizabeth—Style 218
Kawakami K. K.—journalist in America 143, 144
Kemply, Rita—Style 217
Kenworthy, Tom—National 210
Kissinger, Henry—American politician 56
Kondo Seiichi—Japanese diplomat 48
Knight, Athelia—Investigative 240
Krauthammer, Charles—Columnist 48

Krisher, Bernard—*Newsweek,* Tokyo Bureau Chief 147

Kristof, Nicholas D.—NYT, Tokyo Bureau Chief 89, 163, 173

Kume Hiroshi—Japanese TV anchor 202

Kuniya Hiroko—Japanese TV anchor 192

Kurtenbach, Elaine—AP, journalist 42

Kuse Atsushi—Japanese writer and consultant 246

L

Lewis, Jo Ann—Style 218

M

Marcosson, Isaac F.—*The Saturday Evening Post* 143

Marcus, Ruth—National 242

Maruta Yasuko—Tokyo Bureau Manager 172, 245

Maske, Mark—Sports 219

Matsuyama Yukio—Japanese journalist 104

Meyor, Eugene—Publisher of WP 243, 244

McCombs, Phil—Style 208

McLean, John—Publisher of WP 243

Meyer, Lawrence—National Weekly Editor 245

Morgan, Dan—National 52

Mufson, Steven—Beijing Bureau Chief 87

Murata Kiyoaki—Japanese journalist 241

N

Nakayama Toshihiro—Tokyo Bureau, reporter 214, 246

Nonaka Tomoyo—Japanese TV anchor 192

Nye, Jr., Joseph Samuel—professor, Harvard Univ. 60

NYT Editorial—39, 89

O

Oberdorfer, Don—Tokyo Bureau Chief, Columnist 20, 24, 116, 130

O'Donnell Santiago—Metro 243

P

Parrott, Lindesay—NYT, Tokyo Bureau Chief 146

Q

Quinn, Jane Bryant—Columnist 242

Quinn, Sally—Style 148

R

Radcliffe, Donnie—Style 150

Rather, Dan—American TV anchor 192

Reid, T. R. (Tom)—Tokyo Bureau Chief 34, 36, 38, 53, 54, 64, 65, 66, 69, 74, 75, 76, 78, 79, 84, 87, 88, 92, 96, 99, 100, 101, 113, 118, 134, 150, 152, 154, 156, 158, 160, 161, 163, 164, 166, 167, 168, 170, 172, 175, 178, 180, 182, 184, 185, 187, 192, 194, 196, 198, 200, 202, 212, 214, 215, 216, 217, 221, 224, 230

Richards, Evelyn—Tokyo correspondent 176

Richburg, Keith B.—National, Hong Kong Bureau Chief 133, 186

Ringle, Ken—Style 80

Riper, Frank Van—photographer 166

Roberts, Chalmers M.—journalist 243

Roberts, Roxanne—Style 150

Rosenfeld, Stephen S.—Deputy Editorial Page Editor 130, 241

Rowan, Carl T.—Columnist 207

Rowen, Hobart—Columnist, Financial 128

S

Saar, John—Tokyo Bureau Chief 68, 80, 219
Sakurai Yoshiko—Japanese TV anchor 192
Samuelson, Robert J.—Columnist 52, 53, 130
Sanger, David—NYT, Tokyo Bureau Chief 37, 50, 74
Shapiro, Margaret—Tokyo co-Bureau Chief 30, 56, 88, 100, 101, 104, 158, 162, 172, 174, 176, 188, 190, 196, 199, 208, 213, 215, 219
Shimomura Mitsuko—Japanese journalist 191
Shimoyama Susumu—Japanese journalist 240
Sloan, Allan—Columnist 44
Smith, C. Douglas—Toyota in America 125
Streitfeld, David—Style 226
Sugawara, Sandra—Tokyo correspondent 45, 106, 108, 133, 184
Sullivan, Kevin—Tokyo co-Bureau Chief 31, 32, 33, 39, 44, 62, 164, 174, 176, 185, 193, 197, 198, 215, 220, 234, 241
Sun, Lena H.—Beijing Bureau Chief 87, 196

T

Tamaru Misuzu—Japanese TV anchor 192
Tanabe Kunio Francis—Book World, Art Director 242
Thomas, Helen—UPI 242
Togo Shigehiko—"Here I am!" 72, 126, 156, 180, 204, 210, 220
Tolischus, Otto D.—NYT, Tokyo Bureau Chief 144

V

Vogel, Ezra F.—Japanologist, professor of Harvard Univ. 59, 96

W

Weinraub, Judith—Style 220
Weymouth, Lally—Columnist 50
Will, George—Columnist 242
Willenson, Kim—journalist in Washington D.C. 134
Williams, Daniel—National 60
Woodward, Bob—Investigative, AME 24, 240
WuDunn, Sheryl—NYT, Tokyo correspondent 44, 191

Y

Yamamoto Hiroshi—Japanese journalist 27
Yang, John—Financial 242
Yoder, Jr., Edwin M.—Columnist 83
Yoshihara, Nancy—LAT 116
Yoshinaga Haruko—Japanese journalist 80
Young, John E.—Financial 118

From WP with love.

「Japan」クリッピング ワシントン・ポストが書いた日本
Views of Japan from The Washington Post Newsroom

1996年6月20日　第1刷発行

著　者　　東郷茂彦

発行者　　野間佐和子

発行所　　講談社インターナショナル株式会社
　　　　　〒112　東京都文京区音羽　1-17-14
　　　　　電話：03-3944-6493（編集）
　　　　　　　　03-3944-6492（営業）

印刷所　　大日本印刷株式会社

製本所　　株式会社　堅省堂

落丁本、乱丁本は、講談社インターナショナル営業部宛にお送りください。送料小社負担にてお取替えいたします。なお、この本についてのお問い合わせは、編集局第4出版部宛にお願いいたします。本書の無断複写（コピー）は著作権法上での例外を除き、禁じられています。

定価はカバーに表示してあります。

Copyright ©1996 by Kodansha International Ltd.
ISBN4-7700-2023-6